James Relly

Salvation Compleated and Secured in Christ as the Covenant of the

People

Considered in a discourse on that subject

James Relly

Salvation Compleated and Secured in Christ as the Covenant of the People
Considered in a discourse on that subject

ISBN/EAN: 9783337298203

Printed in Europe, USA, Canada, Australia, Japan

Cover: Foto ©Lupo / pixelio.de

More available books at **www.hansebooks.com**

Salvation Compleated:

And SECURED in

CHRIST,

AS THE

COVENANT of the PEOPLE.

Confidered in

A Difcourfe on that Subject.

By JAMES RELLY.

Wrote in the Year 1753.

LONDON:
Printed by J. DAVIS, BLEWETT's-BUILDINGS, FETTER-LANE, MDCCLXXIX.

Salvation Compleated:

And give thee for a Covenant of the People, &c. Isaiah xlii. 9.

GOD, and *Man*, who by reason of Sin, appeared to be at an infinite distance from each other, are brought together by Covenant relation in *Christ Jesus*.

This *covenant*, or *agreement*, is that; wherein they mutually undertake, to perform punctually the condition required on the part of each, that their contract might be legally valid, and without exception.

The person, given for a covenant of the People, is *Jesus Christ:* the parties, agreeing, or covenanting in him, are *God*, and *man:* whose covenant, consists in the unity of two natures, but one person, in our mysterious *Emmanuel* or *God with us:* where the offended, and offending natures, meeting together in covenant, make but one *Christ*, who is upon *that account* with propriety, called the Covenant of the People.

God, in all the fulness of his perfections, in the person of the Word, or divine nature of *Jesus*; and the people in all the fulness of their number, misery and imperfection in the man who is God's fellow, or the *human* nature of *Christ*; (thro' the alone love and good will of God towards men) peacefully met together in the God-man; who, hath taken into himself, the fulness of both natures, in the unity of one person thus becoming the covenant of the people.

The conditions, required of each party to be performed, for the validity of this covenant, and that it might be unexceptionable, are fulfilled in the same; as it consists in the personal oneness of both natures; there, God has made his demand of perfect obedience, according to the tenor of the law, without which he could not in justice justify man. And there, Man, as the party to whom the law was given, has perfectly answered its demands, that the gift of salvation, might not be injurious to the law. In this covenant, God, as a just judge, hath actually executed, what he threatened upon the breach of his law: which was *death*, appointed as the wages of sin. It was here, the soul that sinned died: for as *Jesus* when passing by the Angels that fell, took upon him the seed of *Abraham*, the mystical constitution of his humanity, was fallen man: who are therefore considered as members of his

his Body, of his flesh, and of his bone: in this sense, the soul that sinned was punished in his suffering nature; when he was made sin for us, by taking hold of our fallen nature, his collected, mystical body the Church, and also, by taking into that nature, the fulness of our guilt, sin, and curse: that he, being numbered among transgressors, might become for his children, the one public sinner: when he was speechless under the accusation of our crimes, and bare the chastisement of our peace, and was made a curse for us. Thus did he purge our sin, by his own blood and sacrifice, when he took the fulness of it into himself, until he had healed us by his stripes: we being in his Body through the whole of his doing and suffering, as members thereof.

And, as the *human* nature through obedience and suffering, in this covenant; has perfectly performed the conditions required on its part; it will also appear, that God has performed *his*, according to his promise: where he says, *I will hold thy hand, and will keep thee, and will give thee, for a covenant of the people,* &c. He, was to capacitate the humanity, or suffering nature of Jesus, to make atonement for sin, and to seal the covenant by his blood: and this was done where that humanity through the whole of his obedience to death, had its subsistance in the Deity. The human nature of *Christ* hath no personal subsistance

sistance in itself, considered a-part, or distinct from the deity; as all his *creatures* hath, but the personal subsistance, of the Holy *Jesus*, being in his Godhead, and not in his Humanity, all his words, and works, are cloathed with infinitude: all his obedience, temptations, poverty, afflictions, all the agonies, unknown sorrows, bruises, wounds, and bloody death of his suffering nature, was in that personal subsistance, which he had in his Godhead: therefore, was he, as truly God, as man, through all his humbled steps. Hence it is, that there is no part of his obedience, suffering, or death, but what is pregnant with the inconceivable merit, of his eternal power and Godhead. His bloodshedding, was in the merit, impassibility, and eternity of his Godhead. Therefore it is true that God has *purchased the church with his own blood*. The death of his suffering nature, was in the life, love, and immortality of his Godhead: Therefore it is true that God has *laid down his life for us*. The despised, shameful, bloody form in which he was exposed, was in the ineffable beauties and glory of his Godhead. Therefore, was it the *Lord of Glory* who was crucified. All his weakness, was in the strength, and power of his Godhead, therefore is it called the *weakness of God*. All the foolishness of his cross, was in the infinite, and unsearchable wisdom of his Godhead: Therefore, is it *that the foolishness of God, is wiser than men*,

Thus.

Thus, his every stripe, and pain, and rack, and torment, or falling clod of blood, or pearly sweat, has all the riches, value, power and merit of his Godhead in it: whilst the conditions required on either part are, fulfilled in the covenant: and all the mercies of it made sure to *David,* and his seed. It is in the faithful view of this Gospel, we can justify the most impartial justice, in acquitting the prisoner, and bringing him out of the pit, by the blood of the covenant. This deep contrivance loudly speaks the wisdom of God, *who has kmown his mind, or who hath been his councellor?* but where was the obligation or what necessity was the eternal mind under, to give this gift to man, this covenant to sinful people? Lo! here we see eternal *mercy* stoop, with condescention, to save a ruin'd race. Unmerited, unthought of, undeserved, it comes to us. Oh! *mercy* darling theme, in heaven, and favourite anthem of the just. *Mercy,* triumphant attribute; built up through time, and to eternity. *Mercy,* O 'tis of thee, that we are not consumed: thou art, the helpless sinners daily plea, and shalt be mine, till with my latest breath, my soul wafts to eternity.

David said, the Lord had made with him an *everlasting covenant, ordered in all things and sure:* this corresponds with the foregoing description of the covenant: for when

through

through faith we understand our memberſhip, in the body of the Lord, we know that God hath made a covenant with us in *Chriſt Jeſus:* in *general*, as a body compoſed of many members, and in *particular*, as diſtinct members of the ſame body: the perpetuity of which covenant is ſecured in that indiſſolvable union, between two natures, God and Man, in one Lord *Chriſt:* and every believer, having faith for himſelf in this Goſpel, can ſay with *David*, the Lord hath made with me an everlaſting covenant, ordered in all things and ſure, which is all my hope, and all my ſalvation.

In this covenant, our nature laid waſte by ſin, and once a barren wilderneſs, is now become a fruitful field. Once a pricking thorn, but now the true vine: of which we are the branches. Whilſt the eternal Father is the great huſbandman; who has in this covenant union, cultivated this once barren wilderneſs, our ſpoiled nature: when the plowers, plowed *Meſſiah's* back, making long and bloody furrows. It is in this covenant, our nature, which was the veſſel marred between the potter's hands, is now made another, and a nobler veſſel. In our firſt original, we were a little lower than the angels, yea, the loweſt of the intelligent beings; but to *us*, when ſinking, has God reached out the hand of love and power, and paſſing by more glorious natures, has taken *us* on himſelf: raiſing us to such an eminence, that *when he brought in his first begotten son into the world, he commanded all the Angels of God to worship him.*

In this covenant, our nature is raised from the dunghill to a glorious throne: Angels admiring, adoring, and willingly flying to execute his commands: whilst we, who were without strength, possess omnipotence, in our exalted Head; who now, having all power in heaven and earth, committed to his hand; and the government of providence, and grace, laid upon his shoulders; with stedfastness holds the reins thereof, over every world: and in infinite wisdom, and love, unspeakable to man; moves all the wheels from the greatest, to the most minute dispensation thereof.

In this covenant, the *spirit* is given, and infused, to all the seed: where the holy anointing, in its unmeasurable fulness, was poured upon our honourable and holy Head, *Jesus*; which comes down to the skirts of his cloathing, even to the weakest, and meanest member of his body. *The spirit of the Lord God being upon him, anointing him, to preach good tydings to the meek, to bind up the broken hearted, to proclaim liberty to the captives, and the opening of the prison to them that are bound*; and all this he has perfectly wrought, thro' the salvation of our nature in himself: where, he has given us *beauty for ashes, the oil of joy for mourning, the garment of praise for the spirit of heaviness, making us trees of righteousness, the plants of the Lord, that he might be glorified.*

In this covenant, we overcome the accuser of the brethren, and know the communion of saints, in the unity of the body. This testimony, mixed with faith to them that hear, proves that prophecy, which moves the dry bones, bringing bone to its bone, until the hope of the house of *Israel* is revived. And is that word, which is spirit and life, to all the holy seed: who are naturally dead in trespasses and sin. Nor is this mystery hidden from the followers of the lamb, *the secret of the Lord is with such that fear him, and he will shew them his covenant.*

Having shewn, that *Jesus* is this covenant, I proceed, in discoursing of the fulness of grace, and glory, laid up in him, as our inheritance.

First, In *Christ* our covenant, we have life: this is valuable, all that a man hath will he give for his life. We are represented, as being dead in trespasses and sin, by nature: without hope, and without God in the world. But, the scriptures assure us, that in *Jesus* we have life, *God hath given us eternal life, and this life is in his son.* Hence is it, the saviour saith,

because

because I live, you shall live also. The head and the body have but one life. It is now the alone concern of a christian man, to know that *Jesus* lives. It is also, that sufficiency of comfort, and support, which he affords to his saints, in the greatest distress: *I am he that was dead, but am alive, and lives for ever.* It is that assurance which a christian hath, that he can never be lost. For, *if when sinners, we were reconciled to God, by the death of his son, much more now, being reconciled; we shall be saved by his life.* When *Jesus* arose from the dead on the third morning, and shewed himself alive to many witnesses; there appeared to the spiritual eye, his beloved Bride, in the perfection of beauty: even, all his mystical members, *quickened together with him.* This the holy scriptures sufficiently teach, *and you hath he quickened, together with Christ,* saith the Apostle: of this also, the Prophet spake, when he said, *thy dead men shall live, together with my dead body, shall they arise.* The life of *Jesus* is the believer's life, not only as he lives *for* him, as mediator of the new covenant; nor only as he lives *in* him, by the revelation of his spirit; but as he lives in *himself* an unchangeable life, and that which hath no end: in this life of his, we live, according to the Apostle: *ye are dead, and your life is hid with Christ in God*: with his humanity, in all the fulness of the perfection of his Godhead; which, being all

engaged

engaged for the final preservation of our life, proves the *fountain* and *security* of it, to all who are members of his Body, of his Flesh, and of his Bones. That, indissolvable union between God and man, in the person of *Christ*, being the sure, and certain pledge, of this our security, whilst all who know their membership in the body of *Christ*, know what it is to live in his life. As the first *Adam* was made a living soul, and by his sin brought death upon *his* posterity, so the second *Adam* was made a quickening spirit, in whom all *his* seed are quickened and live, as they died in the former: The Church, being mystically quickened, in the resurrection of the body of *Christ*, which was sown a natural body, but raised a spiritual body; he *having died for us, that whether we sleep, or wake, we might live together with him.* To this purpose, most excellent are the words, in the communion office of the church of England: the body of our Lord *Jesus Christ*, which was given for thee, preserve thy body and soul, unto everlasting life. That once crucified, but now ever-living Body, of God our Saviour, preserves and secures our eternal life in its own: as the branch in the vine, or the exterior parts of the natural body are preserved, as living members, and live in the fountain life of the body: so all his children, as members of his body, live in the life, and unity of the same. Hence is

it

it, with propriety, he is called *our life:* and this character he bears as a living saviour; in whose life we live. This word mixed with faith, is the revelation of the son of God in our hearts, and proves through the operation of his spirit, that quickening power which raises us in our minds, from the ruins of sin and death, to that lively hope of immortality, and eternal life which is brought to light in the gospel. This is *Christ in us the hope of glory:* this is *Christ* dwelling in our hearts by faith: where the life and conquest of *his* humanity, is become the living food of every believer, in *his* flesh and blood, which is meat indeed, and drink indeed; and this feeding is in the heart by faith, where we discern, and feel such a relation to his flesh and blood, that his sacrifice, death, life, victories, triumphs, honour, and glory are all our own: and we rejoice in it, and are enriched in it, with the fulness of grace, and glory, and eternal life; and thus is it, we eat his flesh and drink his blood: the faith and meditation of it, being of the same nourishment to our mind and spirit, as meat and drink to the natural body. He having taken part of our flesh and blood, is not ashamed to call us brethren: and here we follow the Apostle's direction, reckoning ourselves *indeed dead unto sin, but alive unto God through Jesus Christ our Lord:* thus having eternal life in *Christ* our covenant.

This

This life is the gift of God, who hath given us his own son; *he that hath the son hath life*; such as hath not been produced, merited, nor deserved by us; neither does it depend upon any condition to be performed by us, for the continuation of it, but rests alone upon the life of *Jesus*. That peace, comfort and satisfaction, which this doctrine affords, flows from a stedfast belief in the heart, without fear or doubting, that the man *Jesus*, who was crucified without the gates of *Jerusalem*, died upon a cross, and was buried, is risen again; and now lives. This, is enough for us to know, since it is in *his* life, *we* live: accepted, in *his* acceptance; pure and free, in *his* purity, and freedom; exalted in *his* righteousness, and in *his* glory glorified. I speak not this to that meer traditional or historical assent, which is given in the world, to the death and resurrection of the holy *Jesus*; but I testify of this peace and joy in believing, to the faith of the operation of God, which is his gift to them that believe: and to them, again would I say, that as the perpetuity of this life in its fountain, is not dependant upon any condition performed by them, but upon the triumphant life of the lamb of God alone: to this life of his are we at all times to look, for strength, for acceptance with God, and for certainty of eternal salvation; and not to look for these things, to any measure of

know-

knowledge, or enjoyment, which we might have of it in the stream; as in *ourselves* nor to any habit, or worth, wrought *in us*, or *by us*, through such an enjoyment. Therefore, let the eye be stedfastly fixed upon *the* life of *Jesus*, and the heart be intirely satisfied *in it*, as our own; in all its glory, and unchangeableness: then shall we have a sufficiency of support: under all our trials, and afflictions, whilst here; and shall set to our seals that he is true, where he hath said, *because I live you shall live also.* Let all know, that this life is unchangeable: because *Jesus Christ* is *the same yesterday, to day, and for ever.* It is also eternal: for in that he died once, he dieth no more: but being alive, liveth for-ever. Of this, we cannot be deprived: because Jesus liveth. This is the life that can never fail, whilst he is alive. This life, is hidden from the face of the enemy: hidden in the glory of God; where his faithfulness, justice, love, and power, is engaged to support it, and to secure it from every invader, yea from all that seek its ruin: In this, let us therefore be glad and rejoice, with exceeding great joy. This life, has no infirmity attending it: nor, shall length of days, no, nor eternal ages, ever impair its health, or cause us to loath it. But, in its full bloom, and youthful vigour, shall it remain, when sun, moon, and stars shall fail, and pass away. Nor, can its unchanging duration

be

be meafured, but, by endlefs days, by the eternity of God himfelf. And our God affures us, that a moment of it, fhall not pafs, without a fulnefs of joy, and pleafure, for-ever more. Glory be to God on high, *when Chrift, who is our life fhall appear, we fhall alfo appear with him in glory.*

Secondly, We have righteoufnefs in this covenant. The holy fcriptures, experience, and common obfervation, jointly teftify, that man is far gone from original righteoufnefs: or, that we have loft the divine rectitude of nature, in which we were created. That, our nature once was pure is apparent, from the Fountain of purity himfelf: when, viewing the work of his hands, he pronounced it very good. And, that it is now unrighteous, and impure, is as evident; from the fame lip of truth who hath declared the imaginations of man's heart, to be evil continually: *all having finned, and come fhort of the glory of God.* Nature alfo teaches, that mankind is contrary, in habit, and action, to what it conceives of God: this found is gone to the ends of the earth, but more diftinctly, and with greater certainty, are they taught the truth of this matter, who in God's light, fee light. This want of righteoufnefs, renders mankind obnoxious to the wrath of God, guilty in themfelves, ftript of all lawful claim to eternal life, unworthy of the love and

favour

favour of God: nor can he, whose eyes are purer than to behold iniquity, have any delight in them, as thus confidered: It being inconfiftent with his moral character, as a God infinite in purity, and holinefs, to love, or delight, in what is unclean or finful. And as out of an unclean and finful nature, none can bring the thing that is clean; it is impoffible, that man, by any power whatever, fhould raife from *thence* a clean, and acceptable righteoufnefs, whereby he might be juft before God. Therefore is it, that *all our righteoufneſſes are as filthy rags,* and as a *menſtruous cloth,* and that *by the deeds of the law, no fleſh can be juſtified.* Withal, fuch is the miferable ftate of man by nature, that he cannot deliver himfelf: fince his utmoft efforts to do it by his own power and merit, would prove his great and final deftruction; had not God of his infinite goodnefs and mercy, provided better things for us: where he *gave us grace in Chriſt Jeſus, before the world began,* and declared him to be the Lord our righteoufnefs; therefore, now we believe, and confefs to the glory of God, that *in the Lord we have righteouſneſs and ſtrength.* Nor, is this righteoufnefs, meerly the merit of his obedience, or fufferings, reckoned or imputed to us, as fomething diftinct from his perfon, but as he is in *himſelf,* he is our righteoufnefs: this we poffefs in him, as the

D   members

members of his body, there being but one, and the same righteousness upon him and us: where we became *his* sin, he became *our* righteousness; *he being made sin for us, that we might be made the righteousness of God in him,* thus with propriety are we called *the righteousness of God.* Not as we are in *ourselves,* but as we are in *him:* having our mystical or spiritual being and existence in his humanity, and with him in God. Hence is it that the same name is named upon him and us: both the Saviour, and his Church, are named the *Lord our righteousness.* This is the righteousness wherein we are exalted; it is this, which has raised our nature to an eternal sonship; and seated it upon the throne of his glory: this is that matter of intercession for us, upon the right hand of the majesty on high; where *if any man sin, we have an advocate with the Father, Jesus Christ the righteous:* this is our righteousness in heaven; before the face, and throne of God for evermore; and always well accepted of him. The righteousness, shining in the face of the anointed without intermission, presents us ever in its own brightness, before the eyes of his glory, without blemish, spot, or wrinkle, or any such thing. Hence is it, that the manifold sin, and infirmity of our flesh, destroys us not, nor once deprives us of the love and favour of our God. Our Saviour is perfect righteousness, therefore,

are

are we compleat in him: even in the perfection of *Jesus* himself. To *this* there can be no addition made, nor can it ever sustain loss. He once took into his own body, the fulness of our curse and shame, and having by himself, through his unknown sorrows, purged our sin away, he sat down as our righteousness on the right hand of the eternal Majesty: where he is our everlasting righteousness. *Jesus* lives for ever, therefore it waxeth not old, it is durable riches and righteousness, it is that righteousness which sin can never spot nor stain. In this righteousness, let us wrap ourselves, and evermore appear before the king of saints. Nor, let our manifold imperfections hinder us at any time, to appear before him with boldness in *this* righteousness: for as much as our acceptance with him, is as that of *Christ* himself. Let our boasting be of *this* all the day long, and trampling all other righteousness under our feet, let our joy, and rejoicing, be in the Lord as our righteousness and strength. —Let us learn with chearfulness, to yield more hearty and constant submission to this divine righteousness. Never let us go about to oppose it, by endeavouring to establish one of our own. But be content for the honour and exaltation of the righteousness of God, to abide the crucifixion of the flesh however painful, to the utter ruin and death of our own righteousness; until every thought shall

shall be brought in subjection to the obedience of *Christ:* and, we never draw one moments satisfaction from the thought of any righteousness, but that which *Christ* is made unto us in this covenant. With *this* let us be satisfied, as our heavenly Father is satisfied with us therein. Never let us be looking forward in expectation of any other righteousness, or to be found in any other form before God, than what we are found in, as we are in *Christ* our righteousness.—Let this faith abide lively upon our hearts, least *this* righteousness becomes less valuable to us, for this will be the case where self-sufficiency, and self-righteousness creeps in: or where we are led, to think of any other way of coming to God than as those vile sinners, whose only and perfect righteousness is their Lord and Saviour.—Let us learn daily, thro' the knowledge of ourselves, and of this glorious righteousness, to be more deeply delighted with it: whilst our wonder, joy, and peace increasing, we pour contempt on all other righteousness: and anathematize, and follow with a hue and cry, to the death of the cross, every thought or suggestion, which would once propose in our mind, an expectation *of,* or search *after*, any other righteousness than our Lord; who is our covenant righteousness. Let the suitableness of *this* righteousness be more sensibly upon our minds, from the deeper experience we have

have of the neceffity of it, as alfo from the inexplicable bleffednefs of our being found in it. O! let it with inconceivable pleafure and fweetnefs, be fuitable to us: as raiment to the naked, food to the hungry, drink to the thirfty. Yea heaven itfelf, to fuch who were borderers on hell. Let us recommend this righteoufnefs to all poor finners: and that, not only with the calves of the lips; but more effectually, by the *work of it*, which is peace: and by the *effect of it*, which is quietnefs, and affurance for ever. Let that peace, calmnefs, and full affurance, which we have in our minds; of our acceptance with God, teftify to all, the divinity of this righteoufnefs: and prove matter of encouragement to all miferable finners, to fly hither for fhelter; where they alfo fhall fet to their feal that God is righteous in juftifying the ungodly.

And now, my brethren, as the neceffity, nature, and benefit of this righteoufnefs, is revealed from faith to faith, let us be attentive to the voice and teaching of that Spirit, whofe office it is to glorify *Jefus* in the revelation of this righteoufnefs: and this it does, through the deeper conviction, and certainty, it works on our hearts: of the enmity and perverfenefs of the carnal mind, which is not fubject to the law of God, neither indeed can be. This will be always to us a sure proof of the necessity of this righteousness. This spirit also discovers the lamb of God, our glorious righteousness; in all his divine heights, depths, breadths and lengths, until we have that inexpressible satisfaction in him as our righteousness, which is heaven itself. Our minds being thus staid upon him, the peace of God which passeth all understanding, as a flowing river is extended towards us: whilst the assurance and reality of the religion of *Jesus*, and of his being *the Lord our righteousness*, is rooted and grounded upon our hearts with such confidence, that all the powers of nature, sin and satan combined, shall strive in vain to shake our stedfastness, or drag us down to misery. Our joy shall be always alone in the Saviour, making mention of his righteousness, and of *his* only.

Thirdly. In this covenant we have holiness. Righteousness is that privation of guilt, and of every charge against us, through the attoning blood of *Jesus*, which leaves us no more conscience for sin: but gives us boldness to enter the holiest, and to lay claim to eternal life. Whilst holiness is that aptness, disposition, or meetness, for the enjoyment of God in the purity and perfection of his nature, without which no man can see the Lord: nor could heaven be heaven, if this was wanting: Therefore, is *Christ* made of God,
unto

unto us sanctification. And as he is our covenant we have a perfection of purity in him. We were indeed the vessel which was marr'd between the potter's hands, but yet he thought meet not to cast us away, but made us another vessel: this was brought to light at *Bethelem*, where that holy thing born of the virgin, was called the Son of God. It was there, our spoiled nature was born and created a-new. And all the curse, and misery of our birth, was destroyed in this holy nativity. Here, were we created a-new in *Christ Jesus*, that holy child, being the beginning of this new creation of God. It is here, that we are in him new creatures: old things being passed away, and all things become new. *In him*, are we made partakers of the divine nature: where each believer, as a part of his humanity, as a member of his body, partakes of that new created, pure and holy nature. Yea, in that humanity, are they filled with all the fulness of God: which dwells bodily in him. Therefore, have *they* in this holy nature of *his*, the same meetness for the enjoyment of God and glory, which *that man* has who is risen, ascended, and seated on the throne of his glory. In him has the Lord given us what he promised, a *new heart*, and a *new spirit*, having taken the stony from our heart, and given us a heart of flesh; even the holy, broken, pierced heart, of the crucified *Jesus*.

That

That one pure heart of *his* shall suffice for all the thousands of Israel: every member of his body, having a full possession of it, as his own. *Both he that sanctifieth, and they who are sanctified, are all of one:* therefore, that once suffering nature of *his*, which *as ours*, was purged and purified from all *our* offences, and impurity, is now *our* perfection of holiness: being made of God unto us sanctification. The holiness, and purity of his human nature, and all its meetness, for union and communion with God, is the portion of the people. In which he hath made them meet, for an inheritance amongst the saints in light. This our holiness is perfect, delighting in the Lord, and delighted in of him. This holiness is not only imputed, or reckoned of God to believers, as mystical parts, or members of the sacred humanity of Jesus; but it is richly and comfortably possessed by them through faith in the belief of this gospel: wherein they understand, and feel their membership in the body of the Lord *Jesus*: *he in them*, and *they in him*, enjoying the perfection of holiness; and that in such sort, as to bring divine satisfaction to their minds, concerning actual meetness, preparedness for God and glory: this is our true perfect holiness, or sanctification.

There

There is, what sundry call sanctification beside: *viz.* a change in manners and spirit, supposed to be always attendant on the belief of the truth. It is also proposed, that this is continually increasing in proportion to faith, or the knowledge of *Christ*. We have indeed in those propositions a very pleasant picture exhibited; but threatned by the prophet with the *day of the Lord, Isaiah* ii. 16. And that this is not our sanctification is evident from its imperfection: for notwithstanding such who preach for doctrines, the commandments and traditions of men, would impose upon us, with a sanctification in part: the divine law, which is evermore to be considered as the touchstone and standard of true holiness; will not by any means admit of it: but constantly declares the offender in one point, *guilty of the whole*.

As it appears, that sanctification, and perfection, are in the scripture terms synonymous; and that man in himself is not perfect, as knowing but in part, seeing but in part, not daring to say he hath no sin in him, where there is the least regard to truth: with safety and ease we conclude, that any partial change in man, however useful and necessary in common life, cannot be his sanctification; nor dare we give flattering titles to men nor things, by calling that pure, which the law, holy, just and good, will not acknowledge such.

Again,

Again, that this is not our sanctification, is farther plain from the Apostle, who tells us, that *Christ* is made of God unto us, *righteousness and sanctification*; what God hath joined together, let no man put asunder. *Christ* is here preached, as strictly in his own person, our holiness, as he is our righteousness; as perfectly and as fully the one as the other; and as instantaneously received, and felt in all its fruits and effects. Again, the change in man cannot be his sanctification, from the nature of true holiness, which always tends to the annihilation of self, and the alone exaltation of God our Saviour, emptying the creature of all his own wisdom, righteousness, goodness, and purity, that *Jesus* might be his whole Saviour. And this is only produced through the knowledge of *Jesus*, and our belief and trust in him, as our only and perfect holiness, But that holiness which a man supposes he hath in himself, tends only to lift him up in the pride and arrogance of his own mind; and being ignorant of the nature of true holiness, he exalts in a pharisaic impudence before God; pleading his own purity he takes part with Satan, and turns the accuser of the brethren, as though all were vile and impure beside himself. This holiness at best is but a picking, whispering, uncharitable, back-biting, evil-speaking, envying, malicious holiness. Hence is it we see many who are advocates for this holiness, hating their
fellow-

fellow-creatures with a perfect hatred, and that becaufe they think them not as good and virtuous as themfelves. Others will contend from this principle, with fuch earneftnefs for holinefs, that they run themfelves into all manner of ungodly tempers, until they are filled with all the fruits of unrighteoufnefs. Others are fo immerged in it, that they think it not enough to withdraw their company, fo as to have no dealings or correfpondence with the unholy people, but they ufe all diligence in back-biting, evilfpeaking, cenfuring, and condemning the finners; raifing them as many enemies as may be, daily feeking their ruin, rejoicing in their mifery, and would, if poffible, not only rob them of their life and being here, but alfo fentence them to eternal death. Thefe are the fruits of man's holinefs. Now I can be fooner perfuaded that I have not a being, than that this mifchievous fpirit can be the fprit of God's holinefs, fince I fee it bear fuch accurfed fruit. For us once to entertain a thought of our being holy in ourfelves, is an abomination before God, and a fhrewd fign that we are not yet wafhed from our filthinefs. When we once begin to pleafe ourfelves with the thought of our being better than we have been, or better than our neighbour, or draw the leaft comfort or fatisfaction from any holinefs we think we have in ourfelves, we difcover our enmity againft God, and are blinded with the pride of our nature. Pride and

and prefumption being the only eyes by which a man thinks he can fee at any time any holinefs out of *Chrift*. For, if the moft upright among the fons of men were to be carefully weighed in the balance of the fanctuary the fpiritual mind would difcern, not only imperfection attending fome particulars of their life, but the whole of it. Every thought, and word, and work unholy. I think it impoffible for man whilft here, to *do*, or *fuffer* any thing for God *fenfibly*, without that pride and vanity attending it, which is enmity againft God. He cannot fpeak a word for him boldly and affectionately, but he muft feel this tickling evil of pride if he knows himfelf. Nor has he in fecret one pious thought rifing in his bofom, if noticeable to him, but what he has this fecret pride and vanity attending it. I am fenfible this will not be very acceptable to many, becaufe it is taking away their Gods, and then what have they more? Befides, that which I call pride and vanity attending doing, or fuffering for God, is rather efteemed of by many as that only divine comfort and fatisfaction which is found in religion : the removal of which would leave them in a miferable fituation : However, as I fpeak not to pleafe men I fhall not be difcouraged. If any one fhould anfwer that the holinefs of man appears, in the *fight* that he has of this pride and legality of his nature, and in the *hatred* that he bears to it :

it: I would only afk fuch if they do not find pride rife again from the fight and hatred of their former pride? And from the fight of this rifing evil they may find it rifing again, and fo on to infinitenefs; where every difcovery of the nature and evil thereof ferves to exalt it and raife it higher; it ftrengthens itfelf from every meafure of hatred we feel in our hearts to it, ftill gaining a furer foundation. And thus it works, until he that feels this, is as fure as he is of his own exiftence, that there is no holinefs in man, and cries out with the prophet, *the heart is defperately wicked and deceitful above all things, who can know it?* This is a doctrine of mifery to the children of felf-righteoufnefs; but not fo to fuch who can deny themfelves, and make choice of *Jefus* as the better part, the one thing needful: they haftily retire from themfelves to God our Saviour, as their perfection of righteoufnefs and holinefs, being deeply fenfible that they are faved by grace, and that what man has in himfelf is not his fanctification, but only as he hath *Chrift* revealed in him, the hope of glory: and to fuch it appears, that *Chrift* only is their holinefs, as their nature is pure and fpotlefs in him. I am pofitive, that whilft a believer lives in the faith of this gofpel, continuing to believe in *Chrift*, as his perfection of holinefs, he will find the end of fanctification, or true holinefs anfwered in his fpirit, through that

peace

peace, satisfaction, actual readiness, and sensible meetness for the enjoyment of God in glory. Nor can his froward flesh hinder this by all its obstinacy, pride, and enmity. His meetness for glory and happiness is not founded upon any conformity which is supposed to be in the flesh, to the law and purity of God; but it is founded alone upon that conformity to it which he feels, as he has his spiritual being and existence in the holy glorified humanity of his God and Saviour: which being or existence is without enmity towards God, it having been destroyed in his body on the cross. And whilst he lives in the faith and understanding of his membership in that body, he shall without interruption feelingly possess the grace and glory of which I now speak.—Whilst we abide in this faith it is true, there is a gradual conquest of nature in its opposing powers, which are exercised in the tempers and passions of the mind; there is a casting down of every high thought and imagination, and a bringing of it into subjection to the obedience of *Christ*. This is that following of *Jesus,* under his influence, as our fountain of holiness, which he recommends when he says, *take my yoke upon you, and learn of me;* whereby the spirit and behaviour of the christian man becomes more like unto his Lord, in meekness, lowliness, love, joy, humility, self-denial, and heavenly mindedness.

And

And if any would ask, why might not this be called our holiness or sanctification? To this I answer, that if we take it to be what it is *not*, it will immediately cease to be what it *is*. At present we consider it as the effects of righteousness, where we believe *Jesus* to be our whole salvation, and live in him as such. But when we once would look upon this fruit or change as any part of righteousness, and would set it up in *Christ's* place, or endeavour to satisfy ourselves in it, as our holiness or sanctification, it becomes our shame, our own righteousness, our filthy rags and menstruous cloth. Besides, true holiness consists in a constant privation of itself, as it refers to any knowledge or conception which man has of it, as being in himself. It cannot be imagined, that our Lord calls upon us to speak a lie, when he would have us after we have done all, to acknowledge ourselves *unprofitable servants*; if this was not truth the lesson which the apostle teaches us would be impracticable in reality, where he exhorts each man *to esteem of others as better than himself*. Again, these fruits cannot be our sanctification, because they increase not to perfection; and this it does not, because the increase of it depends upon the life and constancy of that faith by which we as sinners rest in *Christ* for salvation, and as our perfect holiness. Therefore it neither increases, nor remains to be what it is in its

evangelick

evangelick nature, any longer than we thus believe. Not only the fight, but the expectation of perfection in ourselves, cannot but admit of such conceptions, which leads us from that true poverty of spirit wherein the fruits of holiness consist, into those thoughts which are highly affronting and derogatory to the honour of God's wisdom, love, and purity, which has produced that great and complete salvation in *Christ*, wherein he only is well pleased, and evermore delights in us. If we had perfection in ourselves from the fruits of faith, the effect would destroy the cause; the cause of this change or fruit is allowed to be that faith and trust, which we as sinners in ourselves have in *Christ Jesus*; but if we had perfection in ourselves, we should have this faith no longer; and therefore the cause being destroyed, the effect must of necessity cease, and is no longer produced. Therefore to expect perfection in ourselves is to turn from that we have in *Jesus*, or to withdraw that satisfaction we have therein; so that by looking to this for perfection we turn it into sin and folly. Let us therefore learn to be content *with*, and fully satisfied *in* that perfection of holiness which we have in *Christ* our covenant; let our glorying be alone in that. Let us not endure the temptation to turn from a certainty to an uncertainty; yea, rather from a certain truth to a certain falshood. And out of a foolish complaisance to what is called orthodoxy, to call that holiness which God and our own consciences tell us is unholiness, yea, enmity against the Lord. But let us honestly bear witness, that there is *none good but God ; and that all the imaginations of man's heart are evil continually,* and that *Christ* only is our holiness. And this let us do by a constant renouncing of all our own good, neither seeking nor expecting any thing in ourselves, whereof we might boast before God or man ; but faithfully abiding in our Saviour, as our alone purity and perfection ; depending, trusting, and believing in him with all our hearts ; and there shall we feel a constant readiness and meetness for glory and immortality, and shall want no other preparations than what we have in him, and by us possessed in him through believing. Our peace, love, joy, fellowship, and communion with God shall then abide ; nor shall the manifold corruptions, with which we are beset in the flesh, hinder us to wait with delight for the *coming of the great God, and our Saviour Jesus Christ.*

Fourthly, In this covenant we have peace and reconciliation. *In me you have peace,* saith the Saviour : *he is our peace,* saith the apostle : out of him all mankind comes under the denomination of wicked men : *because all have sinned, and have come short of the glory of God.* Nor is there any *peace unto the wicked, faith my God.* Therefore was it that he bare the chaftifement of our peace, and by his ftripes our breach of peace was healed, infomuch that *Jefus* is our peace, nor have we any befide him: and that not only as he has purchafed, or procured peace for us, nor only as the gofpel of his blood is to us the tydings of peace, but as he is in himfelf he is our peace, as having two natures in one perfon, being always *Emmanuel,* or God with us. When we look to *Chrift* on this account, we inherit and feel that peace to be our own, which he *himfelf* hath, with no other difference, than that he is the *prince,* and we are the *fubjects* thereof. All that fulnefs of peace, which always fubfifts and abounds in his perfon as God-man, is ours; for it is in that union our nature is in peace with God; and according to the meafure of our faith and underftanding, is our fenfible poffeffion of this matter. This is that peace on earth, and good-will towards men, which was mentioned in the angel's fong on the morning of the redeemer's birth. God and man, heaven and earth, have made peace in his perfon, and this peace remaineth without interruption. To have one's heart abiding here, is to have peace extended to one as a river; he has promifed to keep that mind in perfect peace, which is ftaid upon him. This peace in the fountain as our covenant,

venant, can never fail; a true believer's peace springs not from any matter of goodness, which he hath done or thought of; neither from any change, or quality, which he feels as wrought in him; but it ariseth alone from that harmony in righteousness and true holiness, which he perceives between God and man in the person of *Christ*; of whose body he being a member, or part, is therein put in possession of all that fulness of peace which the human nature of *Jesus* possesseth as in perpetual union with God. Thus have we everlasting and perpetual peace in our glorious covenant. Now this peace is in reality feelingly, and with unspeakable joy in our hearts, whilst we live in the faith of *Christ*'s being our peace; but when we depart from this faith, and begin to seek peace elsewhere, as in our repentance, hatred to sin, holy conversation, and the like; we err from the Lord, as those who have not known the way of peace, and either bring ourselves into misery and desperation, as those to whom there is no peace, or else, which is as bad, or worse, we rest in a false peace, and glory before God in own shame.

Let us **therefore** be fixed upon God our Saviour for **everlasting** peace. Let us carefully avoid, **treat** with disdain, and pour contempt upon **all** the offers of peace, which are made **unto us by** the flesh, upon what condition

dition foever, whether it be for repentance, for hatred to fin, for love to God, or for holinefs of life. Let all fuch offers of peace be flighted by us, trampled under foot, and eternally rejected; and let it be our fole contentment, fatisfaction, and exceeding great joy, that *Chrift* alone, as he is in himfelf, is in our peace. Let us at all times with chearfulnefs, readinefs, and infinite pleafure, accept of that peace, which his wounds, blood, and facrifice, tenders unto us, as having deftroyed the enmity which once fubfifted, and now makes over to us, as our own, that unfpeakable peace, which that once crucified, but now exalted man; has, as feated on the right hand of the majefty on high, and fatisfied with the travel of his foul. This is that covenant of peace, which fhall not be removed, faith the Lord.

If, at any time, through the darknefs and blindnefs of our mind, the malice or cunning of the enemy, we lofe fight of this covenant of peace, after we have believed; and are therefore involved in fin and fear, let us not think it enough that we are broken hearted for our paft tranfgreffions, that we weep and mourn for our offences, and refolve not to err from his paths for the future; I fay, let us not from the confideration and fenfe of this difpofition, fpeak peace to our fouls, and be at reft: for this is dangerous,

falfe

false, and deceitful; and speaking peace where there is no peace. Rather than accept of peace upon these terms, let us chuse sorrow, and refuse to be comforted, until we return as at the first to the joy of his salvation: to view the saviour, as our perfect peace, in whom God and man are in perfect amity, *the counsel of peace being between them both.* In this view let us constantly abide; that the peace of God, which passeth all understanding, may keep our hearts and minds in the knowledge and love of God our Saviour.

God was in Christ (our covenant) *reconciling the world to himself: not imputing their trespasses unto them.* The offended, and offending natures are here brought together in one Lord *Jesus Christ*: where they are reconciled, yea married to each other, in the unity of one person: which union is durable as the days of eternity. And this is our glory, as it secures our peace and reconciliation. To know this for ourselves with certainty, is to believe God: and no longer to go about to make him a liar: yea, indeed it is to be reconciled to him, and that in all the perfections of his nature; so as not to be affrighted at the discovery of any one of his perfections, but to rejoice in the infiniteness, eternity, and fullness of God. In this faithful view, we are reconciled to all his dealings

with

with us: being perfuaded that God is love, and in him there is no fury at all. It is here *our Maker is our hufband, the Lord of hofts is his name.* Here it is that he has betrothed us unto himfelf forever: yea, he has betrothed us in *righteoufnefs,* and in *judgment,* and in *loving kindnefs,* and *mercies,* and in *faithfulnefs,* and therefore we know the Lord. *He hath reconciled us, in the body of his flefh through death;* in that body we are brought very near to God; and whilft we abide in the living faith and experience, of our memberfhip in this body, we fhall feel the heights and depths of this reconciliation in our hearts; through much inward peace, and love of God, much nearnefs to him, and familiarity with him. We fhall not then fay, who fhall go to heaven to bring him down, or to the deep to fetch him up, for, by the blood of this covenant in *Chrift Jefus,* we are made nigh to God, the fupreme fountain of all love and bleffednefs. In this covenant God is familiar with us; nor ftandeth he at any time, afar off from us. He is familiar with us as a father, hufband, and friend: he opens, and difclofes his fecrets to us, nor does he ever wear a frown upon his face towards us, let us therefore beware of entertaining any thought of him, as a dreadful, or terrible Being: for this is to live and think of him, in the carnal mind: which is enmity againft him. Let

us

us be watchful againſt every ſound that repreſents him as an enemy to mankind: or, that with ſeeming ſolemnity and frightful devotion, goes about to hedge him round with the inconceivable terrors of his majeſty: ſo that the children of men dare not draw near, but ſmitten with horror and amazement, they endeavour to fly from the face of the Lord. Theſe thunders, and terrible appearances of God, are reſerved for the torment of devils, and is the portion of ſuch unhappy ſpirits, who refuſed to kiſs the ſon. But when our God appears for the deliverance of *Jacob*, and to ſave ſinners from the wrath to come, he covers himſelf with a veil of fleſh, and appears *in faſhion as a man*, not to affright us, but to baniſh our fears, and to cure all our woes: where he ſays, *Be not afraid, it is I*; racks and tortures, theſe inſtruments of cruelty may extort confeſſions, as they put the miſerable object to moſt exquiſite pain, but they never were intended to convey the power of love; nor is it expected they ſhould ever influence the mind with that divine and ſofter paſſion. Nor can the threats of damnation, the terrors of hell, and an angry God repreſented to the ſenſes; ever be of any uſe to bring ſouls to the knowledge and love of *Jeſus*, nor is God manifeſted thereby as a God of love; ſo that none are converted thereby to the religion of *Chriſt*. Let our ears be ſhut therefore

therefore to all these sounds, and only open to the voice of that blood, which speaketh better things than the blood of *Abel*. Under this sacred sound, let us always approach our God, believing in him as reconciled in this covenant, nor ever think any otherwise of him. It is in this covenant we cry unto him, *my father, my God, the rock of my salvation:* and he answers us, *that he has loved us with an everlasting love:* and that *he will not remove the covenant of his peace from us.* Here has he gathered us with everlasting kindness, and hath solemnly and peacefully sworn that he will *not be angry with us, nor rebuke us for ever.* In this let us evermore rejoice and abide with satisfaction, then shall we be saved from every devouring care and all disquietude of mind, and shall be without murmuring under every dispensation of his grace, and providence, however the desires and inclination of the flesh might be crossed and disappointed thereby. And, though his ways are in the great deep, and as the heavens are above the earth, so are his thoughts above ours, yet shall our joy and rejoicing be in his will. And ceasing from all anxiety of mind, we shall constantly know and feel, that *all things work together for the good of them that love God, and are the called, according to his purpose;* this is that true peace and reconciliation which we have in *Christ Jesus* our holy covenant.

Fifthly,

Fifthly, We have in this covenant strength and victory; strength for the war, and victory over the enemy. Our state here is compared to a warfare, from the trials we are exposed to, and the manifold enemies we have to encounter with; and how unable we are to maintain such a state, and to persevere therein, appears from the word of the Lord, which speaks of us as without strength; yea, our Saviour has declared, that *without him we can do nothing.* Our trials are numerous, I know of none that human nature is subject to, that a christian can be said to be exempted from; but with a difference truly, since *all things work together for good, to them that love God.* The enemies of our salvation are indeed powerful, politick, vigilant, implacable; the fulness of this consideration laid in the scale against our weakness, so abundantly outweighs the hope of man from himself, that it is not without surprise and wonder, we see one child of man persevere to the end in the way of the Lord; yea, we should look upon it as an utter impossibility, had we no other wisdom for our guide than our own, or no other arm for our defence; but *in the Lord have we righteousness and strength. Unto him shall men come, and all that are incensed against him shall be ashamed.* This affords us infinite matter of support under all our trials, that the captain of our salvation was made perfect through sufferings;

perfect in that power, which as our kinsman, and Saviour, is given into his hand; this he has received as a reward of his tormenting, bloody sufferings, and shameful death. He has also received it on our behalf, always to be employed for our protection and safety. He was made perfect also in the deep experience of all human miseries; not a trial awaits us, nor enemy for us to encounter with, but what he hath met with already, and conquered through his unknown sorrows. He is also perfect in simpathy, and fellow-feeling with us under all our infirmities, so that he is able to save to the uttermost, and also to have compassion on the ignorant, and on them that are out of the way. *Such an high priest becomes us.* He, by bearing all our sicknesses, sin, and sorrow, hath sanctified the whole state of trial to us; so that we cannot now tread in any afflictive path, but we behold the footsteps of God our Saviour before us; this keeps us fearless, and supports us in the lonesome tract; and by degrees learns us in whatever state we are therein to be content: this is our fortitude and passive strength in the time of trial. *When the enemy comes in like a flood, the spirit of the Lord lifts up a standard against him. This man shall be the peace when the Assyrian comes into the land.* That power and strength which we employ against the oppressor, that he might not make inroads upon our peace,

or

or lay waste the heritage of the Lord, is the strength and omnipotence of *Jesus* of *Nazareth*; this he hath taught us where he hath told us, that *all power in heaven and earth is given into his hand*; this strength is given to every one of us in him, but chiefly entrusted in his hand, as one to whom it is more natural to care for us, then it was for him to live: and being chosen to be the *captain of our salvation*, he hath strength, council and skill for the war. All the fulness of the Godhead dwells bodily in the man *Jesus*, and is the portion and possession of his human nature; in which nature of his we being made sons, are *heirs of God, and joint heirs with Christ*, in whom all that is called God, and that is to be worshipped, is our strength and support; hence it is we *can do all things through Christ strengthening us*. In him, as our covenant, have we strength for the war.

Take hold of my strength, saith the Lord, and be at peace with me. Let us not dishonour our God and Saviour, and that by our groundless fears, or blasphemous suggestions, as though sin and Satan had more strength and power to destroy us, than our Lord hath to heal and deliver us. Nor let us think that Satan is more watchful for our ruin than our God is for our welfare; or, that Satan hath more policy and wisdom to ensnare us, than what our Saviour has to prevent our misery.

misery. Let us not be afraid of our enemies, whilft our God is ftronger than they. Let us always oppofe his ftrength to theirs, then fhall we know the eternal God to be our refuge, and his everlafting arm our defence.

His ftrength is perfected in our weaknefs, when we ceafe to have any expectations from our own power or ftrength againft the face of the enemy, but wholly rely upon *Chrift* our ftrength, and by the fpirit of faith employ him as fuch, then will it appear, that he is the ftone cut out of the mountain without hands, which fmites the image of felf-fufficiency, until there is no place found for it, whilft this ftone becomes a great mountain, and fills all the earth, then are we ftrong in the Lord, and in the power of his might. The ftrength which preferves us fons of God, is that which maintains the fonfhip of *Jefus*; and this is the everlafting ftrength of the Lord *Jehovah*; in this we are impregnable, and look with defiance and contempt upon all the enemies of our falvation and peace, and have our glorying only in the Lord our God. All this fulnefs of ftrength, which is in *Chrift* our covenant, is to be poffeffed and made ufe of by us, and to be turned in every time of need againft the face of the adverfary. And this we do when we abide in the faith of our relation to him,

him, as one flesh and spirit with him, then we find that every lifted hand and moving tongue which is against us is against him, and that we are unconquerable whilst he is so. We use his strength when we cease from ourselves, and have not the least dependance or expectation, in any strength or resolution of our own, to overcome the least, or most despised of our enemies: but when our heart and eye is fixed, with all confidence, immoveably, and with full certainty upon God our Saviour as our strength, we go forth conquering and to conquer. This is our patience and fortitude in the hour of adversity, and a self-denying mind in the day of prosperity.

In this covenant, victory has declared for us against all our adversaries; yea, we are more than conquerors, for our enemies are made to serve us. The world, the flesh, and the devil, our three potent enemies, are destroyed in this covenant, as our Saviour assures us, when he bids us *be of good cheer*, because he hath *overcome the world*; also *that he hath crucified the flesh, when for sin, he condemned sin in the flesh*; and that he also hath *destroyed him that had the power of death, even the devil*; over all those principalities and powers our God and Saviour openly triumphed, and we in him. His victories and triumphs are all our own; therefore is it that *our warfare*

fare is accomplished, that our iniquity is pardoned. He hath not only conquered for himself, to get him an everlasting name, but he has conquered in our feeble flesh, and in our name; so that all his victories are truly our own; all the spoil and benefit thereof is ours. It is his will that his dominion and power should be our victory, strength, and joy, yea our heaven; therefore was it that he said, *I will that they may be with me where I am, that they may behold my glory.* Glory be to thee, O Lord. Our God and Saviour would have us be glad and rejoice in his victories as our own; therefore has he consigned them over to us, as the lawful matter of our triumph and comfort: where he says, *be of good cheer, I have overcome the world.* And here it is, and here only, that we overcome and inherit all things. This is the victory that overcometh the world, even your faith; that faith which persuades us that our Lord hath gotten himself the victory; that faith which informs us of the manner of this victory's being obtained in our name and nature; that faith which appropriates this victory, and lays claim to it, to all the benefit and joys of it as our own; that faith which rejoices and triumphs in it, and satisfies the soul in it, under all its tribulations; this is the victory by which we overcome the world; a greater victory than ever *Alexander* or *Cæsar* won; and yet it hath not cost us in our own

identical

identical perfons one blow, nor one moment's ftudy; but the coft was all our Saviour's, *who trod the wine prefs alone,* and conquered by his blood and death, by which blood we overcome through this word of our teftimony.

Thus have we ftrength and victory in *Chrift* our covenant. In the faith of this let us abide; then fhall we come to the fpirits of juft men made perfect, whofe life is a life of triumph. Here indeed fhall we triumph over the world, fin, death, and the devil, and rejoice with exceeding great joy; here fhall our joy be full. And if ever we are caught in the toils of fin and Satan, it is becaufe we abide not in this faith where we are always victorious; nor are thefe entanglements without the efpecial permiffion of the holy one, that we may know our own weaknefs, and not attempt by any power of our own to gain that victory, which is already won by *Chrift* our covenant, in whom we are *delivered from the hands of our enemies, and from all that hate us, that we might ferve him without fear, in holinefs and righteoufnefs all the days of our life.* Glory be to thee, O Lord.

Sixthly, In this covenant we have eternal reft. Victory leads us to reft, and this we have in *Jefus Chrift* our Lord. That prefent

fent ftate of things in which men live after fenfe and reafon is not their reft, it is polluted. But yet *there remaineth a reft for the children of God.* Mankind are defcribed by nature, as working, toiling. labouring, and like *Iſſachar* couching between two burdens, by which the reftlefs and unfettled ftate of the mind is plainly pointed out. The unbelieving ftate is as devoid of reft, as the Egyptian bondage was to the children of *Iſrael*, whofe increafing flavery kept them ftrangers to reft. Therefore is it *to him that worketh not, but believeth on him that juſtifies the ungodly*, that our God giveth reft, even all that fulnefs of reft which is in *Chriſt* our covenant. And this is the reft that *Jeſus* himfelf is entered into, by virtue of that one facrifice of his own body, blood, and foul, through the eternal Spirit unto God, as a lamb without fpot or blemifh. The compleatnefs and fulnefs of this one facrifice, hath adminiftered an abundant entrance for him, and we in him into eternal reft. This reft is fecured to us in the perfection of that facrifice, and in that infinite pleafure and fatisfaction that God has therein. It is in this facrifice that God refts in his love towards us, and it is in this we reft alfo in our confidence towards him. In the fufficiency of this facrifice we have perpetual reft, becaufe this man, after he had offered one facrifice for fin, for ever fat down on the right hand of God. And

as

as he laid the foundation of his reſt in ſuffering, blood-ſhedding, and death; ſo now is he entered upon it in all its glory, and that for eternity. With *him* are *we* entered into reſt, as we are *riſen with him, and ſeated with him in heavenly places in Chriſt Jeſus;* and thus have we entered with him as that ſpiritual ſeed, who had their being and exiſtence in him as his myſtical body; the compleatneſs and ſalvation of which depended upon the perfection and ſalvation of that real body of his fleſh. This body of his fleſh preſerved without a broken bone, infallibly preſerves the myſtical body in its own perfection, without the loſs or ruin of one member thereof. The body of his fleſh raiſed and ſaved from ſin and death; from all farther ſuffering, fatigue, and toil, and now ſeated where the wicked ceaſe from troubling, and where the weary are at reſt, has perfected the myſtical body in the ſame bleſſedneſs. The one being always contained in the other, without any poſſibility of a ſeparation. This body conſiſts of many members, yea the fulneſs of it is the church, conſiſting of the many thouſands of *Iſrael*, waſhed in the blood of the lamb. This body, as thus exiſting in him, entered in with him, to all that fulneſs of reſt, and glory, which he is entered into and abides *with* him, and *in* him there for ever. Thus have we reſt in the covenant, his reſt being truly ours; but though

H

this

this grace was given us in *Christ Jesus*, and this glorious rest reserved for us in him, yet having our foolish minds darkened through unbelief and vanity, and being strangers to the grace given us in *Christ*, we are by nature a miserable people in ourselves, and like the dove can find no rest for the sole of our foot. However, our ignorance shall not frustrate the grace of God, nor hinder us to enjoy this rest which we have in *Christ* our covenant. And therefore when the Holy Ghost sent down from heaven, receives of the things of *Christ*, and shews them to us, taking of the eye-salve of his blood and merits, and anointing our eyes that we might see his glory, then we perceive that we are already entered into that rest in our Saviour, which we had so long sought in vain. We then immediately begin to take possession of it in our hearts; and through believing to enter more fully into the glory of it. This is to know, and possess for *ourselves* according to our measure, that perfect rest which we have in *Jesus*, as members of his body, and as having our spiritual being in him. And as our fulness of understanding and light into this matter is, and according to that measure of influence it has upon our hearts, so is that assurance, quietness and rest, which we actually have in our own souls. This is to have rest in the covenant.

He

He that is entered into rest hath ceased from his own works, as God also ceased from his. This is that true sabbath of rest, into which the *Jews* could not enter, because of unbelief. God rested not until he had finished the works of his creation, and pronounced them very good. Neither doth the believer rest, until he see the second creation finished as the first, and also pronounced very good. And this creation he perceives is finished in *Christ*, where we are created a-new; and immediately upon sight of this we enter into a new state, and possess a new heaven, and a new earth, where we have a perpetual sabbath. When God rested on the seventh day, it was from all his works, and in this covenant rest, the believer ceases from all *his* works. He had been long before now striving possibly to be a creator, and would not hear of rest, until he had created some good habits, frames, or qualities in himself, from whence he might reasonably expect rest, and for a season tormented himself in vain, to makes ropes of sand. And here he had remained, had not the day-spring from on high visited him, and led him to the true rest. There all his aspirings drop down to the dust, his sabbath begins, and his toil is over, and ceasing from all his own works, he rests for ever in the new creation of God.

Their rest shall be glorious, saith the Lord. He that enters this rest, ceaseth from all his cares: the finished salvation is before his face for ever. He hath done plotting, contriving, and laying schemes to obtain happiness, or to secure what he has obtained: Such is the compleatness and sufficiency of that one sacrifice of the Lord Jesus, that it has at once obtained and secured his salvation. This delivers him from all fear, the bond-woman's tormenting son is cast out, so as not to be heir with the son of the free-woman. This rest is a divine satisfaction in the mind, as fully satisfied and contented with that redemption, which is in the blood of Jesus, even the forgiveness of sins. Nor are we any longer troubled, and careful about many things, but are content with our Saviour, as the one thing needful, the better part, which shall not be taken away from us: and so sure are we of his sufficiency, that we rest from all desire after any other matter to make us happy. And if at any time, through the legality and over busyness of our corrupt heart, our mind should be darkned, and we get into fearing, toiling, and caring again, let us remember from whence we are fallen, and cry out before our Saviour, return to thy rest, O my soul. Let us also be careful to avoid the taskmasters, since we are slaves no longer; and also to let our old tutors and governors know

that

that the Father's appointed time is come, when we should no longer be under their rule. Let not the censure of the Pharisee, nor the snarling of such who are holy in their own eyes, and wise in their own conceit, affright thee from thy rest. And if they should complain, that thou hast left them to serve alone, yea, if they should accuse thee to thy Lord, be not affrighted, and driven from thy rest, as though somewhat yet remained to be done, ere thou couldst be happy; remember thy strength is to sit still, and constantly believe, with all thy heart, that *Christ* and thee are one: that thou art free, as he is free, and all his rest is thine.

Having very briefly considered the nature of this covenant; and given a few hints of what grace and glory is secured therein for the heart that believeth; I shall conclude, with a few words more, by way of farther recommending this covenant.

This covenant is indeed given for the people, for the people of *Adam*'s race; nor has the Lord pointed out any particular people, by any especial qualities, which they might be supposed to have above others, as the persons for whom this covenant is given: but he has told us, that it is given for the people; for the lost and sinful people,

that

that none amongſt the people, however vile and hell-deſerving they may feel themſelves, may have any ground for this objection, that the covenant was not given for them: neverthelefs, the unbelieving mind will raiſe many objections, why they ſhould not believe, that this covenant, with all its fulneſs of grace, is given for them. And firſt, they judge themſelves unqualified for the reception of this goſpel, but, indeed, this is a miſtake, for I dare venture to affirm, that you are qualified for it; ſin and Satan has qualified you, whether you know it or not; for *the ſcripture has concluded all under ſin,* by which you are qualified for this ſalvation by grace. Are you ſinners, contemners of God's word and commandment, haters of God, and your minds enmity againſt him? Have you fleſhly luſts, which war againſt your ſoul? Have you a hard heart, wandering affections, pride, ignorance, unbelief, anger, deceit? And withal, are you thoſe, who although you feel theſe things, yet cannot mourn or be grieved for it? then are you a ſinner, and yet but a ſinner, therefore you are qualified for the belief of the truth, even of that redemption, which is in the blood of the lamb, the forgiveneſs of ſins; ſince it is for ſinners, and only ſinners, the Saviour died, and for them was given a covenant of grace. Again, you will ſay, that you are unworthy of the glory and riches of this covenant:

venant: that is true, in regard of any merit of our own, we are eternally unworthy, but in his love, who gave this covenant, you are worthy of eternal life; and if you are content, as a worthless sinner, to shelter you in this covenant, I bid you welcome in the name of the Lord. Here you shall feel all your wants supplied. May my God and Saviour shew you this covenant. Here is righteousness for you that are unrighteous; holiness for the impure in heart; life for the dead; peace and reconciliation for you whose minds are as a troubled sea; strength and victory for the weak and fearful, and rest for you that are weary: yea, here is perfect, finished, eternal salvation for you, and all secured in the power and glory of God. When you feel the deadness, unrighteousness, impurity, anxiety, weakness, and evil of your sinful nature, be not discouraged, but let your heart and mind be fixed upon *Christ* your covenant, and your eye be open to behold your compleatness in him, in whom you are just and holy, and blessed and saved, with an everlasting salvation. Let this knowledge be real in your heart, then you will be satisfied with *Jesus Christ* our Lord, and then there shall be no more complaining in your streets, nor leading into captivity; and as the corruption and enmity of your own hearts cannot make you afraid, neither will any pretended goodness or sanctity of man stumble you,

you, as though they had whereof they might boaſt; for in the knowledge of yourſelves, you will know human nature with that certainty, that it will be in vain they put the vizard on, and you will be as ſure, as you are, that your God and Father has created you, that *Jeſus* only is holy, that he only is the Lord: then it will matter nothing with you what any man pretends to be, for you ſhall gather every day with greater certainty from yourſelves and all mankind, that there is *none good but God*; and that *Jeſus* is the whole of your righteouſneſs, ſtrength, and purity, and he ſhall be your glory: and whilſt you are here, let me remind you of that word of God our Saviour: *bleſſed is he whoſoever ſhall not be offended in me.* When we come to reſt with ſatisfaction in this covenant, there are ſeveral offences ariſe, as the ſcandal of his blood. Whoſo is coming off from all to *Jeſus, the devil throws him down, and tears him.* There is then fiercer aſſaults from him, becauſe the agreement with death is broken, and the covenant with hell is diſannulled; the mind is at ſuch a ſeaſon more ſtrangely beſet; but bleſſed is he who takes no offence from hence at the covenant of peace. At this time alſo is ſinful nature more abundantly exaſperated, and a man's foes are them of his own houſhold, with a witneſs. This covenant condemns the carnal mind to torment, that *Dives,* once ſo rich in righteouſneſs,

ousness, goodness, and self-sufficiency is stript and crucified, and condemned to hell, by this revelation of the Son of God, and a gulph fixed to keep it there, whilst not a dram of comfort is afforded it from the riches of the covenant: therefore is it enraged, and, like a lion in a chain, roused up and provoked, it roars, and fiercely strives to devour, but happy is he that is not affrighted at it; yea, blessed is he who takes no occasion from thence, as perceiving it in himself, or others, to be offended at *Jesus*, or his free salvation. Again, there are those who watch for the reproach and dishonour of *Jesus*, and take pleasure in it, through the infirmities of his children. They cannot think how a man that is a sinner can be happy. They think the truth and power of the gospel stands in the goodness of man, and therefore they despise the treasure, when they find it in an earthen vessel. They either object against the gospel as a licentious doctrine, because they that believe it are men, and are subject to infirmities, as those who are yet in the body; or else they take occasion to wound and dishonour it, by grosly representing to mankind the sin and imperfections of them that believe: thus hardening the hearts of men against it, they are offended at *Christ* in his members, because they are tempted or afflicted, or because they have been found sinners. But, O my brethren, to you

you I speak, who know this covenant: remember the words of your Lord; *blessed is he whosoever shall not be offended in me.* O be not offended at *Jesus,* if those souls who are a coming to him are thrown down, and torn by the enemy: he is yet a God of love I can assure you; indeed he is. Let not this discourage you, or cause you to think that he regards not the peace of his children. O be not offended with *Christ* your covenant, when you see the struggles of nature in them that believe, or when you feel them in yourselves. Do not then say I am deceived by this covenant, because you feel yourselves no better, but rather worse, as to the corruptions of the mind, than what you were when you leaned upon your own righteousness. Let not this make you offended at the Saviour, or weary of him, nor angry with his gospel; for indeed he intends goodness and mercy towards you, and only means to drain you of your own righteousness and strength, that you may be compleatly happy in him, and that you may enter into the rest of the covenant.

O, be not offended with *Jesus,* from his childrens spots and infirmities; let his grace and love appear more free, rich and illustrious through their weaknesses, since where sin hath abounded, grace hath superabounded. You wonder, perhaps, why so many infirmities

infirmities attend them that believe, and profess to be happy in *Jesus*; but wait patiently, and our Lord will let you know the reason, and that there was a needs-be for them all, according to the order of his dealings, in his providence and grace with man. They have no pleasure in what is contrary to *Christ*, though possibly they have been seemingly more overtaken, and caught in the toils of sin and shame than any. They can tell you that sin is hell, and they find it so, and with strong cries and bitter tears, they have often besought their God, that they might never dishonour him, through the messenger of Satan buffetting them, when he has only answered them that his grace was sufficient for them. Our Lord designs to teach them, and others, by all their imperfections, the inexplicable riches of his blood and death. Our Saviour is satisfied with them, as the travail of his soul; and though they are black in themselves, yet are they comely in *Christ* their covenant, where all the fulness of his righteousness, grace, and mercy is theirs; and there are they without blemish, spot, or wrinkle, or any such thing; view them always there, behold them there, then will you never take offence at the faithful lover of souls, at our gracious, holy, compassionate God and Saviour; nor will you then, with the Pharisees, object against him, with saying, *this man receiveth sinners, and eateth with them.*

O, my brethren, beware of being offended at the myfteries of the grace of God, nothing is more common than for perfons to fet down that for foolifhnefs, yea, for a falfhood, which they themfelves underftand not, and for no other reafon, than becaufe they underftand it not. I doubt not, but this covenant will be treated thus by many, but if I might give my advice, it fhould be, not to pafs rafh cenfures upon any thing you read or hear, but learn to fufpend your judgement, until you have honeftly weighed it, in that thought and confideration, which is fubordinate to the teaching of the word and fpirit of the bleffed *Jefus*. Learn, with the difciples, to afk the meaning of fuch things that are too high for you, and he will give you to know the myfteries of the kingdom of God. As I would warn you to beware of being fo much prejudiced in favour of any man, to receive and fwallow from their hand, without any examination, that which might terminate in your hurt, and the difhonour of your Lord; fo would I alfo warn you of being prejudiced againft any child of man, fo as to reject the teftimony of the Lord upon that account. Is there not caufe to fear, that many fink into a dangerous fituation here, and that they reject, flight, and fpeak evil, either with anger or ridicule, of what they know to be the truth, and as coming from their own mouths could die for

it)

it) and that only, because it is professed, and born witness of, by such whom they, upon some account or other, are prejudiced against? Such is their hatred to their fellow-creatures, that they will spitefully and obstinately, and that contrary to their own consciences, trample on, and endeavour to suppress the glory of *Jesus*, rather than the object of their hatred should be thought to be in the right. And yet this is very consistent with the holiness and goodness of man, and such is the zeal of human nature for this; that when the man has once drawn his sword against his adversary, rather than he will put it up in peace, he will revengefully wound him, though it should be through the heart of the lamb of God. But, O my brethren, fly from this, let not your hatred to your fellow-creature be greater than your love to your God; nor slight the covenant because a sinful man bears witness of it. If you understand it not, spread it before the great prophet of his church, as what you want him to teach you, and he will guide you, and lead you into all truth.

And you that are entered into the rest of the covenant, let it appear that this rest is fruitful, and that it does not consist, as the carnal mind would suggest, in spiritual slothfulness. But that it rather produces an active mind for the glory of your God and Saviour.

There

There are none of the children of men, can serve God with that chearfulness which you serve him with. To you his service is perfect freedom; to you his ways are ways of pleasantness, and all his paths are peace. You can set to your seal that his yoke is easy, and his burden light. Your body, soul, and spirit are his, as bought with the price of his blood, and therefore would you glorify him in the one and the other. Nor let any thing be painful to you to exercise yourselves in, where *Jesus* may be glorified, and man benefited, and yet you may rest from your labours. You may rest from all your devouring care, you have a sufficiency in the covenant. There is your righteousness, purity, peace, strength, rest, and life eternal, and all for ever with the Lord, and well secured in all the power and strength of his eternal Godhead. Let your eye and heart be always fixed upon this fulness, that you may be without care. Let this fulness content you, under every apprehension you may have of distress and scarcity in the things which concern your present life. Be always satisfied with the riches of this covenant.

You may rest from all your fear, for greater is he that is for you, then they that are against you. In this covenant all your enemies are put under your feet, nor does there now remain any cause of fear. Here may

may you learn the heart of *Jesus*, by looking to him as your compleat salvation, and by beholding him in this glory, you shall sink into his spirit, whilst all his sacred tempers shall abound in you, if any have been injurious, you shall feel a heart to forgive them, and give glory to God. If you have enemies, as you must of necessity have, if you are in this covenant: you shall feel a heart to love them, yea all mankind, glorifying our Saviour. If you have trials in common life, you shall possess your soul in patience, trusting in *Jesus*. If you have provocations, you shall consider the meek and lowly heart of the crucified Lamb. If you are tempted, you shall endure with fortitude, looking to the author and finisher of your faith. If you are reviled, you shall not revile again, but render good for evil; blessing for cursing, and kindness for bitterness. The rage of your persecutor's spirits, and the sharpness of their tongues, shall not terrify you, you shall be as though you heard them not, with a bowing of the heart before our Saviour, and offering thanksgiving before his pierced feet, for this honour conferred upon you. Nor shall you be discouraged when they accuse you of sin and imperfection, because you are no deceiver, for you never pretended to be any thing in yourself, but a sinner. Learn to abide in the view of the covenant, where your conscience will be always void of offence towards

wards God and man. Let not the poverty, weakness, and shameful bloody form of your Saviour's death, ever make you ashamed, because he is your Lord and God. Nor all the slander, reproach, contempt, and scandal that may be cast upon you for his sake, offend you, where you may be represented as lovers and promoters of sin, because you only will have that man to reign over you. And when you have done and suffered all for the Saviour, with an eye to his spirit and temper in all your conduct and behaviour, remember you are a sinner, retire from it all to his sacred wounds, leave your glory in the dust, and let your glorying be in this, that he has loved you, and given himself for you, and have washed you from his sins in his own blood, Then shall this language be rooted upon your heart: *the Lord has made with me an everlasting covenant, ordered in all things and sure, which is all my hope, and all my salvation.*

F I N I S.

The Trial of Spirits.

OR, A

TREATISE

UPON THE

NATURE, OFFICE,

AND

OPERATIONS

OF THE

Spirit of Truth.

By JAMES RELLY.

The SECOND EDITION.

He that speaketh of himself, seeketh his own Glory: but he that seeketh His Glory that sent him, the same is true, and no Unrighteousness is in him, JOHN vii. 18.

LONDON:

Printed by M. LEWIS, in Paternoster-Row. 1763.

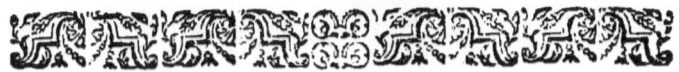

THE
PREFACE
TO THE
Christian Reader.

HAVING very minutely and impartially examined my motives in writing the following discourse: the testimony of my conscience is, that my sole aim was the honour and glory of Jesus Christ. Therefore, can I, with calmness and confidence, commit what I have written; unto His protection and blessing.

My endeavour, through the whole, hath been to shew, that all the works of God, and all His ways with man conspire to glorify Jesus Christ; and that by this we are to determine of the true and false spirits.

In the prosecution of this, I hope I have not seemed as one assuming oracular authority, nor given myself any majesterial airs, or positive beyond demonstration; forasmuch as I would carefully avoid this in all things, as that which my soul abhors. How fully I have escaped it, and how closely adhered to the scriptures for proof of what I have written, and that not according to forced explications, but according to their literal import, and what may rationally be drawn thence, I shall leave the reader to determine.

And as I would not darken counsel by words without knowledge, I have aimed at rendering my ideas intelligible, and that with as much plainness of speech as my capacity would admit of; hence I may have used more words and repetitions than will appear needful

needful to sundry of my readers; but I hope the intention will atone for the defect in this particular.

If it shall be thought, I have spoken a little too freely of mankind, where (attempting to discover the imposture they put upon themselves and others through pretensions to extraordinary holiness) I describe their fruits; I here declare, it proceeded not from a cynical principle, or spirit, towards them in general, nor from any personal pique to particulars; but, from candid and impartial observations, with self-evident experience, I was assured of the truth thereof; and thought it necessary for staining the pride of all flesh, and for the honour and glory of Jesus Christ our only Lord and Saviour, to speak as I have done, with earnestness and sincerity.

Whoever is dissatisfied therewith, and fain would prove me a false witness;

ness; I here tell them plainly, there is but one way to do it; and that is, by shunning all the evils I have mentioned, and by bringing forth with a constancy the contrary fruit.

And when they do this in truth and sincerity, Jesus will be glorified, and I will acknowledge my self a false witness: but until then, mere speculative argument and disputes, will not prove me such: but, with all their bitter invectives against me, it will plainly demonstrate the truth of what I affirm.

I am very well aware, that, where I have spoken slightly of the supposed holiness of man; their learning, wisdom and popularity, as tending to deceive, and through a false spirit, entice souls from Christ; from beholding their righteousness and strength in Him: it will be objected, that my own deficiency, makes me speak thus contemptuously of the opposite character: But

But let me here affirm, I envy no man the character of being holy, wise, learned, or popular; nor have I for years past desired it. I am very sensible that men of this character are set in slippery places, and too commonly rival Jesus Christ in the heart and affections of the children of men. And withal, being very well apprised of the pride and vanity of human nature, and how well men like to have it so: I look upon it as a really dangerous situation, and very derogatory to the honour and glory of Jesus, who saith unto all what he says to one, *My son, give me thy heart.* But forasmuch as this withholds the heart from Him, and makes men swallow, without trial, whatsoever is imposed upon them; I would set myself against it, and speak of it as I think it deserves, when it comes in competition with the Saviour of the body. And, if I am of the contrary character, I have the less to fear from this quarter, as not being likely to adulterate

terate the affections of the spouse of Christ, or to proselyte the souls of men to my person or excellencies, to which I have an utter, yea an irreconcilable aversion, and am persuaded my behaviour testifies it, as hating affectation, grimace, and fawning.

Having endeavoured, in this discourse, to prove the scriptures the rule for the trial of spirits, by the same rule I desire my doctrine may be tried, and not by the traditions, confessions of faith, and creeds of men (for by these, I doubt not, I shall be condemned.) I am persuaded the scriptures will acquit me, therefore to them I appeal; and where they will not justify me, I am content to acknowledge that I err, as not knowing the scriptures: but this I know, I am at peace with them all, and have not, in this treatise, wilfully injured one of them. Let me therefore earnestly beseech the reader to compare me with them, and to try
the

the spirit speaking in me by them, and if they declare themselves in its favour, is there, who calls himself christian, that will reject it, because it may be deemed contrary to the received maxims and traditions of men? are such protestants? what ever their profession is, are they christians? do not they prefer man to Jesus Christ, yea, make the witness of man to be greater than the witness of God? and is not this monstrous impiety? and O how shocking the thought, the masters in Israel will not attempt to undeceive them: whatever *gain* they may have from this quarter it is certain there is no real *godliness* in it.

I expect, when this book shall fall into the hands of *some* persons, they will immediately look into the title-page for the author's name; it being usual with them, if prejudiced in favour of an author, to read him with care, respecting many things therein as
very

very great, though probably far from meriting the admiration of any one. But, if the author appear to be one of whom they have before received an ill opinion, they will either throw it by and not look into it at all, or, if they read, prejudice and ill-nature makes them unreasonable criticks, they gather what they judge faulty therein, and treasure it up with joy; that by blazing it abroad, they may bring, if possible, the whole into disrepute. And, as to what they find therein truly great, they will endeavour to think it error: but if the truth thereof is too manifest for them to think so, then will they insinuate that it is only speculation, because they will not have the writer to be an experienced christian, or to be directed by the Spirit of Truth in what he writes, and therefore, that there ought not to be any regard paid to his writings. How ungenerous, tyrannical, and cruel this way of acting is, every man's reason

son will teach him, if he calmly attend unto it! therefore, unto reason I appeal: And how contrary it is to Christ and the Spirit of his gospel, the scriptures will testify: where all such partial and uncharitable proceedings are continually reproved and censured as a false and antichristian spirit, yea such a spirit, that none who truly walk with Jesus, can possibly be led by.

Therefore reader, if as a man thou wouldst behave humane, generous, and reasonable, and as a christian, impartial, charitable and faithful; I recommend this tract unto thee; give it a fair reading, nor do thou despise the treasure: because in an earthen vessel; but learn to distinguish the treasure from the vessel. And think not with thyself, that where there is a fine vessel there must certainly be precious treasures; but remember the word of the Lord, how that he hath

chosen

chosen the foolish to confound the wise, and the weak to confound the mighty, and the base, and the despised hath God chosen; and things which are not, to bring to nothing things which are.

This I leave with thee as my best advice, and pray our good Lord to seal instruction upon thee by what thou readest.

THE
Trial of Spirits.

1 JOHN iv. 1.

Beloved, believe not every Spirit, but try the Spirits, whether they be of God.

THIS scripture briefly contains the divine caution and advice of an apostle unto the Church of Christ. *Beloved*, a proof he cautioned not from contracted bowels, an ill-natured, or uncharitable principle—*believe not every spirit*; a plain indication that the false spirits require our belief; yea, truly they have their signs and lying wonders—*but try the spirits*. This supposeth man liable to err in this particular, but withal that we have a rule whereby to determine, to which we do well to give heed as unto a light shining in a dark place. *Whether they be of God*; an intimation, that there

there are spirits which bear his name, and work an appearance of piety, whom he acknowledgeth not; and when tried, to be rejected by us.

The Words naturally afford this doctrine: there is a rule given for the trial of spirits, whereby, if we impartially determine, we may know whether they be of God, or not.

In treating of this, I shall

First, Point out the rule, or standard, fixed for the trial of spirits.

Secondly, Shew the manner of trying the spirits by this rule. And

Thirdly, Attempt some suitable use and improvement of the whole.

Either there is a rule for the trial of spirits, or there is not; if not, all have the same force of argument in asserting their being of God, however different and contrary to each other in nature, work, or testimony; to grant which, would be at once to conclude God the author of confusion, and to father, not only all the corrupt sallies of the human mind, but all the lies and inconsistencies of the wicked one upon Him: to banish all order and unanimity out of the society of man, to open a gap for doubtfulness, uncertainty, yea, infidelity, with all

all its train of arrogance and horrors, to break in like a deluge upon us.—As this muſt be obvious to every ſeeing eye, the neceſſity of a rule to try the ſpirits by, will abundantly appear. If objected, that this is to ſuppoſe the ſpirit inferior to the rule, and that his teſtimony without this is fallible and uncertain.—I anſwer, the ſign is not greater than the thing ſignified: it is the ſpirit of truth himſelf who hath given us the rule as a tranſcript of his own nature, office, and operations, whereby we are to determine with certainty of him, as diſtinguiſhed from every falſe ſpirit. And with reſpect to the witneſs of the true ſpirit; the rule for the trial of ſpirits is ſo far from denying its infallibility, as rather with conſtancy to aſſert it, being a ſecond witneſs of the ſame thing, as deſcriptive of what is the matter of the ſpirit's teſtimony.— To this end hath the ſpirit himſelf given it us; and that we might oppoſe it to every ſpirit which anſwers not to the deſcription. Beſides, it will be always true in this world, that the heir, whilſt a child, differeth nothing from a ſervant, though lord of all. And this being the caſe, they know not what manner of ſpirit they are of: ſuch was the condition of thoſe whom our Saviour reproved on that account; and all of like character may need the trial of ſpirits for their reproof. Withal, the trial of ſpirits by the rule appointed for that purpoſe, as it will give the deſcriptive character of the ſpirit of truth, may be of uſe for edification to ſuch who,

who, though they are in a meafure under his influence, have not attained, with certainty, to know his voice. True it is, thofe who have received the perfect witnefs need no trial thereof for their own fatisfaction, becaufe they know His voice; as he, with unerring evidence, bears His witnefs to their heart: however, it is pleafing and delightful to them, when they confider the trial of fpirits; that the fpirit of truth is pointed out and defcribed, in his nature, office, and operations, as they have conceived and known of him in the heart. Moreover, if they would demonftrate to others, that they are led and fpeak by the true fpirit, they muft do it by this rule, as that which is appointed of God; otherwife, they ought not to cenfure, where their teftimony is rejected.—And this, I think, the apoftle's advice chiefly tends to, where he bids us try the fpirits whether they be of God; hence we have authority to deny that fpirit's being of God which doth not fpeak and act according to this rule and ftandard.

The rule or ftandard, which infinite wifdom hath fixed for the trial of fpirits is the holy fcriptures, containing the writings of the prophets and apoftles. *To the law and to the teftimony: If they fpeak not according to this word, it is becaufe there is no light in them,* Ifa. viii. 20.

As to the divinity of this rule we have proof fufficient from reafon and revelation. From reafon, where the prophecies fpeaking of the deftrucdestruction and revolutions of kingdoms, &c. describing the persons, yea pointing them out by name who should execute it, with other particular circumstances, and that some hundred years before hand, or ever the persons spoken of were born, hath yet notwithstanding been literally fulfilled in all particulars, according to the testimony of the Heathen writers themselves. What ever definitions of true virtue have been given, by the most famous theorists of any age, are but so many faint imitations of the scripture perfection. The most refined philosopher, drinking at this fountain, will find his ideas enlarged, enlightened, and quickened, and be able thereby to improve upon the most rational and sublime ethic that ever the wit or reason of man produced. Nor hath the evil and deformity of vice been ever painted with like perfection as in the holy writings, nor are there any motives so powerfully persuasive and exciting to virtue as here are found; yea, many things here are incontestibly proved evil, which borrowed the name of virtue among the wisest Heathens: virtue and vice, with them, was, as the stream or Nile among the Egyptians, abundantly obvious as present with them, whilst the spring or fountain-head remained a secret. But in the scripture, the rise and cause of each is assigned and opened to our view. Who is that divine Being, whom the Heathen acknowledge and ignorantly worship, but that God who hath revealed himself to man in the

scriptures? What is the cause of the apparent evil bias and depravity of human nature universally acknowledged and confessed in the world? there is nothing so truly and rationaly points it out as the scriptures, in the offence of our first parents. What are the sacrifices which all nations under heaven use, or have used, in their various religions, but an acknowledging the necessity of sacrifice to reconcile God and man? though what this sacrifice was, they neither knew nor were agreed upon: the scriptures only can shew this, in their testimony of the suffering Jesus. What are those faint acknowledgments of nature, but that sound which, the scripture says, is gone to the ends of the earth? All the predictions of the prophets concerning the promised Messiah have been exactly fulfilled in Jesus Christ, the author of the New Testament: yea, all the whole system of the Jewish religion, however fabulous and trivial many parts thereof might seem to the eye of reason, hath its witness in the person, life, death, and resurrection of the holy Jesus, as the antitype and substance of the whole. Beside, it might be urged for the divinity of the scripture, that never book was wrote like it: with so much honesty, self-denial, and disinterestedness in the writers. All such, who go about to deceive their fellow-creatures and impose upon them in matters of religion, do it under a profession of extraordinary sanctity: they conceal their own faults, and as much as
lieth

lieth in them the faults of all who are of their party, left the goodness of their cause should be suspected. What man is there who, when he publishes his life to the world, will publish his faults and miscarriages? while he is picking out all the flowers thereof to oblige the world with a nosegay, will he present them with his stinking weeds also? nay, he is cautious of that; and therefore whilst he speaks of his good works and dispositions, he says nothing of his evil ones, except in general terms, that he is a worthless creature, or the like; but this confession is designed to evidence his goodness by his humility; or, probably he will acknowledge some abominations in particular which he has been guilty of, but then it was in the days of ignorance, and the like, before his conversion. This confession is designed still as a foil to set him off to admiration, as though he had not sinned, had not been guilty of faults since he commenced a christian. But this was not the case with those who wrote the scriptures; they confessed themselves men of like passions with others; they published their own faults, and the faults of such who with them were the heroes of the cause; and did not, in general terms *only*, acknowledge their worthlessness. Furthermore, they published their faults not only as committed in times of ignorance, but after they were eminent for religion, the knowledge and worship of the true God, and truly their faults were none of the least.

Now, had it been their design to impose upon mankind by their writings, or to aggrandize themselves in any shape, it would have been the greatest madness and folly in them, to set themselves upon a level as they did, with the meanest of the people: to publish their own faults, and such that were so heinous, committed by them even while they were prophets and apostles: they could not have taken a more unreasonable and unlikely method, had they sought themselves, and their own glory: nor can it be objected that it proceeded from their foolishness, for their writings evidence they wanted not understanding: it is therefore sufficiently apparent, that those writings were wholly dictated by the Spirit of God; and, that the writers thereof wrote as they were moved by the Holy Ghost: and not as they were moved by interest, vain glory, or self-seeking in any respect. The holy scriptures are writings that do not favour of the things of men, but of the things which are of God, as may rationaly be gathered from the foregoing hints. This, and much more, I might offer as reasonable proof of the scriptures divine original: but, as all who believe the Bible, are not called upon to consider these things as the ground of their faith therein, there is yet to them more certain proof by revelation; where the Spirit of Truth opens the scriptures, and bears witness to their conscience of their divinity; upon the simple credit of which witness, the mind is fully persuaded,

suaded, and is not suffered to call the truth in question, else what shall they do, who being illiterate and incapable of argument, are ignorant of reasonable proof respecting this matter? reason and divinity forbids our thinking as those superstitious bigots, who denounced anathema's on all such that knew not their law; nay, notwithstanding their ignorance, they are capable, by the grace of God, of knowing and believing whatever is requisite for their salvation and comfort.

The holy scriptures thus known, are always to be considered as the rule given us for the trial of spirits: Search the scriptures, said He, in whom is hid all the treasures of wisdom and knowledge, for they testify of me. And the Holy Ghost commends it in the Bereans as a noble act, that they tried the spirit, speaking in the apostles themselves, by the scriptures, Acts xvii. 11.

Having thus pointed out the rule whereby we are to try the spirits, I shall proceed to treat of the method thereof. As it would be endless to bring every false spirit seperately to its trial, and would render my writing on the subject too voluminous; I shall by this rule attempt a description of the Spirit of Truth in His nature, office, and operations: by which means every false spirit will be at once searched out and detected.

Whilst treating of the nature of the Spirit of Truth, I shall not presume to propose it meta-

physi-

physicaly of his being and essence, for, besides my incapacity for such an arduous task, He Himself assures us, that none, by searching, can find him out to perfection, Job xi. 7; shall therefore rather confine myself to the consideration of Him according to His properties and dispositions, as revealed in the scriptures.

As a tree is known by its fruit, so also is the Spirit of Truth—*and the fruit of the spirit is love, joy, peace, long-suffering, gentleness, goodness, faith, meekness, temperance,* Gal. v. 22. *For the fruit of the spirit is in all goodness, and righteousness, and truth,* Eph. v. 9.

Hence we discern somewhat of the native properties and dispositions of the Spirit of Truth; it is love, free, pure, unchangeable, everlasting, *which suffereth long, is kind, envieth not, vaunteth not itself, is not puffed up, behaveth not itself unseemly, seeketh not its own, is not easily provoked, thinketh no evil, rejoiceth not in iniquity, but rejoiceth in the truth: beareth all things, believeth all things, hopeth all things, endureth all things, never faileth. Whatsoever things are venerable, whatsoever things are just, whatsoever things are pure, whatsoever things are lovely, think on these things,* Phil. iv. 8. For this is the fruit of the Spirit, and a specimen of his divine nature. The Spirit is described as the life and quickening of mankind to everlasting happiness; therefore called, *The Spirit of Life,* Rom. viii. 2. Again, it is said, *the Spirit giveth Life,* 2 Cor. iii. 6.

and

and that the *Spirit of Life entered* into the flain witneffes, Rev. xi. 11. *It is the Spirit that quickeneth,* John vi. 63. From whence it appears the property of the Spirit to give life.

Again. The Spirit is faid to *enlighten the eyes of our underftanding,* Eph. i. 18. *In him was life, and this life was the light of men,* John i. 14. it being the property of the Spirit to enlighten.

Furthermore, the Spirit is compared to water—*with joy fhall ye draw water out of the wells of falvation,* Ifa. xii. 3. *For, in the wildernefs fhall waters break out and ftreams in the defert,* Ifa. xxxv. 6. *Jefus ftood and cried, if any man thirft, let him come unto me and drink; he that believeth on me, as the fcriptures hath faid, out of his belly fhall flow rivers of living water: but this fpake He of the Spirit,* &c. John vii. 37, 38, 39. *I will pour water upon him that is thirfty, and floods upon the dry ground: I will pour my Spirit upon thy feed, and my bleffing upon thy offspring,* Ifa. xliv. 3. *Then will I fprinkle clean water upon you, and you fhall be clean,* Ezek. xxxvi. 25. *That he might fanctify and cleanfe it with the wafhing of water by the word,* Eph. v. 26. Hence we learn the nature and property of the Spirit is to cleanfe from all filthinefs, as water; and by his comfortable influence to allay the thirft of panting fouls.

Moreover, the Spirit is likened to fire—*He fhall baptize you with the Holy Ghoft, and with fire,* Matt. iii. 11. *There appeared cloven tongues like as of fire, and they were all filled with the Holy Ghoft,* Acts ii. 3. *The fire fhall try every man's work, of what sort it is*, 1 Cor. iii. 13. the nature and property of the Spirit, as fire, is to purify from all drofs, to burn up and confume every falfe work.

Again, the Spirit is compared to wind—*awake O north wind, and come thou fouth, blow upon my garden, that the fpices thereof may flow out*, Cant. iv. 16. *The wind bloweth where it lifteth, and thou heareft the found thereof, but canft not tell whence it cometh and whither it goeth: fo is every one that is born of the Spirit*, John iii. 8. Thus, as wind, the nature of the Spirit is to refrefh by his gracious influences.

Having briefly confidered the nature, and properties of the Spirit of Truth according to the fcriptures, I haften to treat of His office, in that relation wherein it concerns mankind.

When our Saviour was about to leave the world, left his difciples fhould be overcharged with forrow, he promifed them another Comforter, whom he called the Spirit of Truth; and left they fhould be fearful of this promifed Comforter, that he would promote an intereft contrary to what they had already engaged in, he affures them, that when this Spirit came, he would not fpeak of himfelf—*when the Spirit of Truth is come he will guide you into all Truth, for he fhall not fpeak of himfelf; but whatfoever he fhall hear, fhall he fpeak: and he will fhew you things to come. He fhall glorify me, for he fhall receive of mine, and fhall fhew it unto you*, John xvi. 13, 14. *He that fpeaketh of himfelf, himself, seeketh his own glory; but he that seeketh his glory that sent him, the same is true, and no unrighteousness is in him,* John vii. 18. From hence it appears, that the proper office of the Spirit of Truth, is to glorify Jesus: and this He doth by speaking of Him, and shewing us the things which are His; and not by speaking of himself.

For our better understanding in this important matter, I shall endeavour

First, To shew what is intended by a spirit speaking of himself. And

Secondly, What by the Spirit of Truth shewing us the things of Christ, and speaking of him only, which according to the word is his proper office.

For a spirit to speak of himself by man, is when he makes it his business to take of the learning, wisdom, eloquence, honour, or piety of man, and shew it to the world, thereby seeking his own glory: and this he doth when from this principle men labour to be admired, and aim at ensnaring their fellow creatures on these accounts.

Again. The spirit speaks of himself in man; and consequently seeks his own glory; when he leads us to eye his impulse, operation, or work, as the object of our faith, and

and foundation of our hope: when the spirit by which we are govern'd in matters of religion, in order to witness his being of God, leads us to consider his impulse on the mind; from whence, through the working of the passions, flow sudden transports of joy, sorrow, love, desire, &c. and would thence persuade us of our being possest of the Spirit of Truth; this spirit evidently speaks of himself, and seeks his own glory, and not the glory of Christ.

Again, When the spirit which is in man, would lead him to any change, as wrought within him; consisting in habit and principle; or to any reformation of life and manners, taking an occasion thence to speak peace to his mind, as unto one who is under the work and government of the spirit; I say, when this is the case, it is manifestly a spirit which speaks of himself.

That spirit who insinuates that he is injured by the preaching of Christ *only*; (as where the testimony of free and compleat salvation in Jesus Christ, is accused of denying, or slighting the work of the Spirit) may be said to speak of himself, and seek his own glory; it is evident he is in a seperate interest from the Lord Jesus, and therefore cannot be the Spirit of Truth.

Above all, that spirit which denieth that Jesus is come in the flesh, is of antichrist; by which, as I think, we are not to understand, a denial of his incarnation only, or his having a body of flesh, but a denial of his having answered

ed the end of his coming in the flesh; which was to evidence the love of God to mankind, to take away their sin, and to save them with an everlasting salvation: this is in effect to deny that Jesus is come in flesh.

I shall not particularly consider that spirit, who not only professes equal infallibility with him who dictated the holy scriptures; but a right to contradict them, where they clash with its suggestions: as mistaken, and untrue; or else as containing a lower dispensation of matters; and therefore that his light, and affirmations, are preferable to what is taught in the Bible. This spirit refuses to stand trial by the Scriptures; therefore, I have nothing to do but to warn all against this spirit: because there is no end of the evil and danger he will lead men into: a mischievous, lying spirit, pretending authority for all his evil works.

I am persuaded that as many as believe the scriptures; where they tell us, that when the Spirit of Truth is come, he will not speak of himself, nor seek his own glory; but the glory of Christ; by receiving the things which are his, and shewing them unto us; will acknowledge, that in all the instances I have mentioned, the spirit speaketh of himself, and seeketh his own glory, and therefore is not the Spirit of Truth.

The Spirit of Truth, when He is come, will glorify Christ, by receiving of the things which are His, and shewing them unto us: He leads not the sons of God to view any impulse, operation, or work wrought in them, nor any thing wrought by them, thro' His power, as the foundation of their faith, or matter of their comfort; nor, will he suffer them to gather the least confidence thence; but it is His nature and office to speak only of Him that sent him. It is to *Jesus* He leads; and points Him out perpetually, as made of God unto us, whatever we want or stand in need of. Whatever influence we feel; whatever change, or reformation is produced in us by the Spirit's testimony of Jesus; or whatever we are enabled thereby to do, or suffer for Him; the Spirit of Truth is so far from speaking of it to us, or from once presenting it to our view, that he faithfully leads us off from all apprehension or trust therein, and is constantly employed in shewing us the things of Jesus and glorifying Him.

By the things of Christ, I would understand the mystery of His Person, birth, life, sufferings, death and resurrection; with all the grace and glory abounding in Him: yea, all those things which tend to manifest Him to mankind, as lovely, valuable, precious, and glorious; under every consideration endearing him unto the souls of men.

By the Spirit receiving of those things, I conceive, is intended the ministry of the Holy Ghost, in this particular: all the glory of what our Saviour was, and did, in the flesh, the Spirit of Truth is now commissioned and sent to reveal unto the children of men.

In

In the day of his humiliation, his judgment was taken away; and there were none to declare his generation. His own disciples were offended because of him; they stumbled at his unknown sorrows, his shameful and bloody death: nor could they bear the many things which he had to say to them; neither understood they when he spake to them of the *mystery of God, and of the Father, and of Christ.* Though all these things were then done and spoken by our Saviour, yet the explication of all was reserved for the administration of the Spirit—*But the Comforter, the Holy Ghost, whom the Father will send in my Name, he shall teach you all things, and bring all things to your remembrance, whatever I have said unto you,* John xiv. 26.

Thus hath the Spirit of Truth received in trust, the fulness of the mystery of Jesus, to manifest unto mankind; therefore it is said, he shall receive of the things which are mine, and shall shew them unto you. I am aware of this objection, the Spirit is said to convince, regenerate, &c. and that this is appointed him as part of his office, as well as that of shewing us the things of Christ: I answer, whatsoever may properly be called a work of the Spirit, is wrought by his glorifying Jesus, and shewing us the things that are his. And where ever any work of the Spirit can be distinguished from this, we must be excused when we deny that spirit and his work, as one who speaketh of himself; and therefore false, as the scriptures are true.

Indeed

Indeed the Comforter, the Spirit of truth, when he is come, will reprove or convince the world of sin, righteousness, and judgment. The scripture expressly says, *He reproves of sin*; what sin? Unbelief, says Jesus—*of sin, because they believe not in me.* It is not the office of the law, as naturally in us, nor as revealed from Sinai, to convince of the sin of unbelief; this is the work and office of the Spirit of Truth. Unbelief lurks and gathers its strength under the shadow of the law: unbelief joins itself in affinity with the law principle in our nature, yea agrees with it in numbering the manifold imperfections thereof, taking occasion from a consciousness of sin to strengthen itself, and to fill its mouth with arguments against the grace of God, whilst its own nature and sinfulness is still unknown: but when the Spirit of Truth comes, manifesting Jesus in the fulness of his grace and glory, unbelief is detected, and the evil nature thereof declared as making God a liar, believing not the record which he hath given of his Son, how that he *hath given to us eternal life, and this life is in his Son,* 1 John v. 10, 11. in this the Spirit speaketh not of himself, but of Christ: shewing that the sin of unbelief consists in a rejection of him; nor can the world be convinced of it until the Spirit of Truth reveal it, by shewing them the things of Christ, manifesting, in the fulness of his grace and glory, that Jesus whom they had rejected.

The

The Spirit also reproves of righteousness and judgment—of *righteousness*, said the Saviour, *because I go to the Father*; intimating that he could not have been accepted of the Father, had he not fulfilled the law, atoned for sin, and brought in everlasting righteousness. But forasmuch as he is gone to the Father, the Spirit of Truth will shew from thence that he hath fulfilled all righteousness; and is therefore accepted and received into glory. Hence man is convinced of the insufficiency of his own righteousness and the all-sufficiency of Christ's —*of judgment, because the prince of this world is judged.* This judgment to condemnation passed upon him in the death of Jesus, where mankind were delivered out of his toils, and he judged and condemned as their deceiver. All this doth the Spirit of Truth teach us by shewing us the things of Christ, and glorifying him.

The regeneration, or renewing in the spirit of our mind, ascribed to the Holy Ghost as his work and office, is wrought also by the revelation of the Son of God; that is, by discovering to us the redemption which is in his blood, the forgiveness of sins; we are delivered from the guilt and slavery of sin, and brought into a new state, where *old things are done away, and all things are become new*, 2 Cor. v. 17. For as our nature was regenerated and born anew in Christ Jesus, through whose sufferings and blood it was *purged* from all sin, Heb. i. 3.

reconciled unto God, Col. i. 21, 22. and fully conformed to his Image, Rom. viii. 29. the Spirit of Truth receives of this and shews it unto us; withall witnessing our interest therein, as those whom Christ personated in all that he did and suffered: by this means, *being dead unto the law,* we *are married unto another, even to him who is risen from the dead,* that we might *bring forth fruit unto God,* Rom. vii. 4. Hence we have *the answer of a good conscience towards God, by the Resurrection of Jesus Christ,* 1 Pet. iii. 21. As the Spirit of Truth shews us this, he, by teaching and enabling us to resolve our all into Jesus, authorizes the conscience to appropriate his condition, his righteousness, holiness, yea all his gracious qualities and full conformity to God, until we come to the language of the apostle, who says, *as he is, so are we in this present world,* 1 John iv. 17. Thus doth the things of Jesus which are shewn us by the Holy Ghost attract and draw the soul until we wholly leave ourselves, and *are found in Him,* Phil. iii. 9. In him we are put in possession of a new and clean heart, new desires, new will, new affections, a new consciousness of ourselves, which is not after the old Adam, but after him who is risen from the dead. By this new and spiritual birth we pass out of darkness into light, yea *translated from the power of darkness into the kingdom of God's dear Son,* Col. i. 13. where *being born of God* we *cannot sin,* because the *immortal* remaining *seed* is pure, 1 John iii. 9.

iii. 9. In all this the Spirit of Truth glorifies Jesus, as him in whom we are regenerated, born anew and changed, being *God's workmanship, created anew in Christ Jesus unto good works, which he hath before ordained, that we should walk in them*, Eph. ii. 10. According to this grace, the Spirit of Truth reveals Christ in the heart through a gradual manifestation, and as we discern him from faith to faith; he teaches us to put him on, Rom. xiii. 14. until we come *unto a perfect man, unto the measure of the stature of the fulness of Christ*, Eph. iv. 13. This is a wonderful and great change, and is thus described in the scriptures: *We all, with once face, beholding, as in a glass, the glory of the Lord, are changed into the same image, from glory to glory, as by the Spirit of the Lord*, 2 Cor. iii. 18. Thus whatever the Spirit worketh for the salvation, and comfort of mankind, is all wrought by his shewing us the things of Christ, and testifying of him that he might be glorified. He shews us the mystery of the person of Jesus, as God-man, Rom. ix. 5. as *Emmanuel*, or *God with us*, Matt. i. 23. and how that we, as the church, are *the fulness of him that filleth all in all*, Eph. i. 23. *Members of his body, of his flesh, and of his bones*, Eph. v. 30. *Heirs of God, and joint-heirs of Christ*, Rom. viii. 17.

Being thus interested *in*, and related *to* the human nature of our Lord, we are together *in* and *with* that nature related unto God; the union of natures in him, being that marriage-union,

where

where our *Maker is* our *Husband*, Isa. liv. 5. that blessed and eternal life of ours, which *is hid with Christ in God*, Col. iii. 3.

Again, the Spirit is said to bear witness with our spirit that we are children of God, Rom. viii. 16. and in this also he glorifies Christ. The matter of this witness is, that God *hath given to us eternal life, and this life is in his Son*, 1 John v. 11. That he died for our sins, *and was raised again for our justification*, Rom. iv. 25. and hath *put away sin by the sacrifice of himself*, Heb. ix. 26. hath by *one offering perfected for ever, them that are sanctified, whereof the Holy Ghost also is a witness to us*, Heb. x. 14, 15. His argument is the faithfulness and truth of him who hath spoken it; and being infinite in wisdom, and in power omnipotent, he can overthrow the enemies of our peace, and persuade our hearts beyond all uncertainty and doubtfulness. Thus doth he witness our sonship, and withal, shew us the method of it as by one Lord Jesus. To bear which witness from any work of our own hands, from any reformation, or change wrought upon us, from any frame, or disposition within us, or from any light, knowledge, &c. would be to deny the Lord that bought us; to run counter to his religion, to walk by sight and not by faith; to make the spirit speak of himself, and not of him that sent him: but the witness of the Spirit of Truth is known by its agreement with the scriptures, which teach that we *have the adoption of sons by Jesus Christ*, Eph. i. 5. arguing the reality

reality and fecurity of this grace, from the truth, faithfulnefs, and unchangeablenefs of Him who gave it us. *I am the Lord, and I change not, therefore ye fons of Jacob are not confumed*, Mal. iii. 6. *Jefus Chrift the fame yefterday, to-day, and forever*, Heb. xiii. 8. and fuch is the perfuafive power and force of this witnefs, thro' illumination, influence and argument, that all our reafonings and unbelieving objections fall before him; and its tyranny ceafing, the confcience is brought into a ftate of purity and peace, not ftaggering through unbelief, but *believing in hope againft hope*, Rom. iv. 18. that is, whilft from a deep conviction of the defperate wickednefs and deceitfulnefs of the heart, Jer. xvii. 9. reafon and fenfe deny all ground of hope from ourfelves, yea would rather urge our defpair: The Spirit of Truth points out Jefus to us in all his fulnefs, and fuitablenefs to our neceffities, witneffing our intereft therein, and that with fuch almighty power, that we believe in hope of what the Spirit teftifies concerning Jefus, againft the hopelefs and defperate views we fhould have of ourfelves, were we to judge ourfelves by ourfelves, or to compare ourfelves with ourfelves: thus whilft in the world, and in ourfelves, we have tribulation, we have peace and joy in the beloved Jefus. From all which, the truth of this propofition ftill appears, it is the office of the Spirit of Truth to glorify Chrift.

I come now to the third thing propofed, the confideration of the Spirit of Truth in his operations; it is compared by our Saviour to the wind: *The wind bloweth where it lifteth, and thou hearest the sound thereof, but canst not tell whence it cometh, and whither it goeth; so is every one that is born of the Spirit,* John iii. 8. it bloweth where it lifteth, denoting the free agency of the Spirit in his operations, as not obligated thereto by any human power, nor to be resisted thereby when he will work.

As we are in no wise conducive to the winds blowing, neither are we to the Spirit's operations; we merit it not; nor is our wisdom, diligence, or faithfulness, any inducement thereto; to hasten, increase or strengthen it: for it bloweth where it lifteth, *when* it will, and on *whom* it will: sometimes on such *who seek him not,* Isa. lxv. 7. passing by many who were in search *after the law of righteousness,* Rom. ix. 31. Thus taking occasion to baffle the wisdom and abase the pride of all flesh, plainly evidencing, that human excellencies and abilities are of no advantage in this particular; declaring it impossible for man, by the best observations he is capable of making, to point out by an unexceptionable rule, the person qualified and prepared as a proper object of the Spirit's operations.

The operations of the Spirit are unlimited: sometimes by the word, as where he makes use of any portion of the scripture, thereby to reveal the things of Jesus to the heart. The application of the promise, by the Spirit, is a

customary

customary phrase amongst such who profess christianity, and to be feared, often used ignorantly: it is probable, that many who use it, understand nothing more by it, than that when some particular text of scripture coming to their remembrance stirs them up to sorrow, joy, gladness, &c. from the consideration of which influence, they persuade themselves of its being applied by the Spirit, and so rest thereon. I need not be at much expence of time, or argument, to shew that this is not the Spirit of Truth; because he neither reveals Jesus, nor *speaks* of him, but suffers the mind to rest in that influence it felt on the remembrance of the literal word.

Again, when the promise is conditional, and requires certain qualifications in such to whom it may be said to belong, there are sundry, who imagining they are possessed of the qualifications required, lay claim to the promise on that condition, but especially if the promise occur to the thought suddenly and unexpected, they think it must be the Spirit of Truth, that applies a word of promise so suitable to their state, and therefore take comfort and rest therein.

Now this is to be under the law and not under grace, forasmuch as the promise is here embraced and trusted in upon law terms: when we suppose ourselves to have that qualification, which the promise as conditional requires in us, and upon that condition lay claim to it, it is manifest judaism; a seeking salvation by the works of the law, and not the christian religion which directs all our trust and confidence to Jesus Christ. The Spirit of Truth teaches us that whatever specious appearances there may be, we have nothing in reality on condition of which we can claim the favour of God in the promise; for the scripture having concluded all under sin, Gal. iii. 22. affirms that *Abraham had not whereof he might glory before God*, Rom. iv. 2. Therefore that Spirit which lulls us in a false operation cannot be the Spirit of Truth, but of error and falshood; as it is apparent that this way of resting upon the promise is antichristianism, and in effect, a denial that Jesus Christ is come in the flesh.

Again, there are promises of an absolute sound; such as, *I will be their God, and they shall be my people*, Jer. xxxi. 33. *I will heal their backslidings and love them freely*, Hos. xiv. 4. and sundry others of like import. Now when those promises occur with energy to the remembrance, there is a resting on them as unconditional, in expectation of what is promised being fulfilled as an act of God's sovereign pleasure; nor is this the operation of the Spirit of Truth, for this would be to make *the promises of God against the law, which God forbid*, Gal. iii. 21. Forasmuch as the law would be against the absolute promise of salvation, as not respecting the demands of justice and holiness.

The

The manner of the Spirit of Truth's operating by the word, is to refresh and comfort from the views of Jesus thereby. Whatsoever we cannot read Christ in, is scarce worth our perusal; nor is that sweet that hath not the favour of his name. *All the promises of God are in Christ Jesus yea and amen, to the glory of God by all his witnesses,* 2 Cor. i. 20. And when ever the Spirit of Truth brings any part of scripture to our remembrance, he brings Jesus in it, without whom all is dead and killing letter: if the promise he brings is conditional, he comforts us from the views of the condition being fulfilled in Jesus, and the promised grace freely ours by union with him; or if the promise hath an absolute and unconditional sound, he shews us by what means it is so; even by the obedience to death of the blessed Jesus, in whom God is our God, and we his people, and that consistent with his strictest justice and purity. Thus the Spirit of Truth, in all his operations by the scriptures, glorifies Christ, opening the wells of salvation in him, whence we draw water with joy, Isa. xii. 3.

The law is not against the promises of God in Christ, though they give the waters of life freely, because of satisfaction rendered by his life and death, and *everlasting righteousness* brought *in*, Dan. ix. 24.

Sometimes the Spirit of Truth may be said to operate without the scriptures, though always agreeable to them; as where, thro' the
internal

internal discoveries of Jesus and of our redemption in his blood, he frees the mind from guilt and fear, proceeding to quicken, comfort and strengthen the heart in him; and this he often doth without the concurrence of any portion of the written word in the remembrance thereof, nor need any one fear being deceived in those views of Christ, and comfort in him, which may not have any particular text of scripture attending it upon their mind: the main question is, whether it is agreeable to the word or not? Is it from a view of what Christ is, of your relation to him, and redemption in his blood, that your consolations abound? then it is according to the law and to the testimony, be assured it is the operation of the Spirit of Truth, nor is there any deceit therein, tho' you may not have what is called, the application of a text of scripture therewith. There can be no error, according to the word of the Lord, where man is abased and Christ alone exalted—*the loftiness of man shall be bowed down, and the haughtiness of men shall be made low, and the Lord alone shall be exalted in that day*, Isa. ii. 17. in that day Abraham became *dust and ashes*, Gen. xviii. 27. the Psalmist *as a beast before God*, Psal. lxxiii. 22. Job abhors himself *in dust and ashes*, Job xlii. 6. Jeremiah's *Heart is desperately wicked, and deceitful above all things*, Jer. xvii. 9. Isaiah is *undone, a man of unclean lips*, Isa. vi. 5. Daniel's *comeliness was turned into corruption*, Dan. x. 8. Paul was the chief of sinners, 1 Tim. i. 15.

i. 15. and John *fell as dead at his feet*, Rev. i. 17. O how glorious the day when man is abased, his haughtiness brought low, and the Lord alone exalted! But concerning Jesus, he glorifies him, he exalts him above all heavens; declares him to be *the desire of nations*, Hag. ii. 7. *the strength of Israel*, 1 Sam. xv. 29. *the salvation of God unto the ends of the earth*, Acts xiii. 47. upon whom is hung *all the glory of his Father's house*, Isa. xxii. 24. whose *throne endureth for ever and ever, the scepter of whose kingdom* is eternal righteousness, Heb. i. 8. whose name is above every name, to which all things in heaven and earth bow, *and every tongue shall confess that Jesus is the Lord, to the glory of God the Father*, Phil. ii. 9, 10, 11.

Again, the operations of the Spirit of Truth are to be distinguished from the passions, for want of which distinction, many things have been fathered upon the Holy Ghost, which were manifestly the fruits of man's own corrupt passions. Where the passions are mistook for the Spirit's operations, people will not fail to assert, that they are led by the Spirit in this and the other thing, though it be manifest they be influenced in what they do, by pride, anger, envy, hatred, malice, &c. and because their zeal, in the execution thereof, is such; as to animate and invigorate them to that degree, that they can sustain any loss, suffer any reproach or extremity, even to death, for the cause they are engaged in, they think certainly they are

led

led by the Spirit of Truth, elſe they could not have ſuch fortitude and comfort in ſuffering, and doing what they have done. But alas! what is it that a perſon thus infatuated will not do, what is it they will not ſuffer to gratify the fleſh, either in pride, aiming at ſelf-righteouſneſs, applauſe, or praiſe of men, or to be revenged on ſuch who may be the object of their anger, envy or hatred? The truth of this doubtleſs occaſioned that memorable and ever bleſſed ſentence of the Holy Ghoſt: *Though I ſpeak with tongues, have the gift of propheſy, have all knowledge, have all faith, though I beſtow all my goods to feed the poor, and my body to be burned, and have not charity, it profiteth me nothing,* 1 Cor. xiii. 1, 2, 3. The paſſions, whilſt kept in ſubordination to the Spirit of Truth, are pleaſant in religion, and renders the exerciſe thereof delightful. But when miſtaken for the Spirit, and followed, they lead into ſo many enthuſiaſtic extravagancies, that whoſo looks coolly on, and tries the ſpirit, will eaſily perceive the deception; and indeed to judge of the operations of the Spirit by the paſſions, is to be always at a loſs. To raiſe the paſſions is an art, in a great meaſure depending upon geſture, ſound of voice, pronunciation, &c. but the operation of the Spirit is not dependent upon any human power or excellency, nay but chooſes rather to work without it. *Chooſing the fooliſh to confound the wiſe, and the weak to confound the mighty, and the baſe, the deſpiſed, and*

things

things which are not, hath God chosen to bring to nothing things that are, 1 Cor. i. 27, 28. And *I, brethren, when I came to you, came not with excellency of speech, or of wisdom, and my speech, and my preaching was not with enticing words of man's wisdom, but in demonstration of the Spirit and of power,* 1 Cor. ii. 1, 4. It was the saying of a certain orator, touching the effect his orations had upon the people, in raising the passions; that it did not so much matter *what* he said, as *how* he said it; however excusable this might be in Heathen policy, it is utterly unworthy a christian minister's imitation; yea to be had in abomination of all who would win souls to Jesus Christ. The Spirit of Truth operates according to judgment, and always comforts the heart from suitable discoveries of Jesus. A judicious christian will check, with disdain, his swelling passions, however pleasing, unless some chearing view or consideration of Jesus, his beloved Bridegroom, be at the bottom; as the rise and spring of all; and then he will be cautious, however pleasing they are, of following them too far, lest he forget or lose sight of his Beloved.

When we hear, read, or meditate of Jesus, of his despised life, his bitter suffering, his bloody and shameful death, we may be effected thereby, as the daughters of Jerusalem were when they saw him go forth, bearing his cross, and yet our sorrow and tears flow all from passion: where there is no faithful view of a suffering

fering Jesus, there is no operation of the Spirit of Truth. Such who know him thus, only after the flesh, mourn in the tumult of their passions, to think on the sufferings of such an innocent and good man; they hate the instruments of cruelty, are extremely angry at the Jews, the Roman soldiers, and all who were concerned in his death. In like sort the history of his resurrection fills them with joy and gladness: now where this is, without apprehending the end and design of his suffering, dying, and rising again, of their interest therein, and benefit thereby, it can be but the false flame and working of the passions, and not the operations of the Spirit of Truth; forasmuch as Jesus is not glorified, either in his personal dignity, or in his end and design in suffering and dying, which was to save his body the church, and to put a new song in her mouth, even *of mercy and judgment*, Psal. ci. 1.

The operations of the Spirit of Truth produceth the proper effects; whilst, as the light enlightening the mind, he shews us the wretchedness of our nature, and as life from the dead, quickens us to feel it; self-loathing, abasement, and an utter abhorrence of ourselves, naturally becomes the principle and temper of our souls. But from the revelation of the Son of God in the heart, we are inspired with joy and gladness. He glorifies him as *made of God unto us, wisdom, righteousness, sanctification, and redemption*, Cor. i. 30. and opening our understanding

standing to difcern this; he perfuades, encourages, and ftrengthens our hearts to the belief of the truth, and fills *us with joy and peace in believing*, Rom. xv. 13. and, as he enlightens and confirms us more fully in the faith, Jefus appears more valuable, more glorious and precious; and thus growing in grace and in the knowledge of our Lord and Saviour Jefus Chrift, 2 Pet. iii. 18. the righteoufnefs of God being revealed to us, from faith to faith, Rom. i. 17. we are led on by the fame fpirit *in the unity of the faith, and of the knowledge of the Son of God, unto a perfect man, unto the meafure of the ftature of the fulnefs of Chrift*, Eph. iv. 13. until we have fo fully ceafed from ourfelves, as to have no more expectation of what is good and acceptable from any work of our own hands, than we would have of grapes from thorns, or figs from thiftles; but all our prefent joy and happinefs, and expectation of future glory, is in Jefus the Lord that loved us, and bought us with his own blood. Thus all the operations of the Spirit of Truth confpire to abafe the creature, to ftain *his* glory, but to exalt the love and grace of the Creator, yea to fet on high the Man of God's right hand, the Son of Man whom he hath made ftrong for himfelf.

Having in fimplicity, and I truft agreeable to the fcriptures, confidered the matter according to my propofals; I would now attempt the natural and proper ufe of what I have already faid on this fubject.

If

If it be allowed that the scriptures are the rule for the trial of spirits, let us then faithfully make use of them to that purpose, and always beware of prefering the traditions of men to them: let not the wisdom, learning, holiness, or popularity of any man deceive us, so as to receive implicitly what they affirm; nay, if they were *apostles* let us try their spirit by the scriptures, whether they be of God or not. It is too common, where men are counted wise in their generation, learned, holy, and withal popular, to be blindly followed, and all that they say, however inconsistent and unscriptural, esteemed of as the oracles of God: thus, on the credit of their character, their doctrine and traditions are received. For a man to call in question the truth of what they affirm, after the trial of their spirit, would be deemed an unpardonable crime: such is the course of this world: nor may we expect they will undeceive the world in this particular, as that would be to deny themselves, which goes hard with men of their substance. *Mystery Babylon the great, the mother of harlots and abominations of the earth,* and the root of apostasy from Christ. Beloved, believe not every spirit, but try the spirits whether they be of God; bring them to the scriptures, let that indeed be the rule of your faith and practice, and, if it should be thought a deviation from the beaten track of man's traditions, be not terrified, neither be afraid of being singular for Christ, when you have

have the signature of the Spirit of Truth for what you do: this will preserve you from being tossed about with every wind of doctrine; nor will you then cry, Lo! here is Christ, or lo! there is Christ; but you will strictly abide by that rule, whereby you may know the Spirit which is of God.

Is it true, that the nature of the Spirit of Truth is known by his fruit? and is *the fruit of the Spirit, love, joy, peace, long-suffering, gentleness, goodness, faith, meekness, temperance?* Gal. v. 23. All who profess to believe the scriptures, acknowledge these as the fruits of the Spirit, though the greatest part are yet at a loss where to find them as really produced and brought forth. They read the fruit of the Spirit is love, but when they look to such who profess to *have* the Spirit; they perceive bitterness, envy, strife, uncharitableness, and all the reverse of love; or where there is an appearance of love, is it not contracted to the narrow limit of a party? is it not to such who wear our own complexion? or, if now and then it make an extraordinary advance towards such, who are not within those pales, is it not because they are popular? is it not because their persons are had in admiration? But when doth it extend to our enemy, and that in heart, and not in tongue only? when doth it satisfy his hungry soul with bread, and relieve his thirst with water? whose soul is that, which will always bless where it is cursed? and who is he, that will always do good
where

where evil is done unto him? shew me the man or the woman upon earth, and I will shew you one who brings forth the fruits of the Spirit of Truth: and yet this is the plain and positive doctrine of the Lord Jesus; *but I say unto you, love your enemies, do good to them which hate you, bless them that curse you, and pray for them which despitefully use you,* Luke vi. 27, 28. every proud boaster would do well to consider this, and ask his conscience calmly, in the presence of him who searcheth the heart and trieth the reins, am I the man? certain it is, the envious, the malicious, the uncharitable, the bigot, cannot be the person. And with what face, any man can boast of his bringing forth the fruits of the Spirit, or with what conscience he can please and sooth himself in the thought thereof, whilst he answers not in character to this doctrine, which our Saviour hath so plainly distinguished his religion by, in its influence and powerful effects, from all religions upon earth, I cannot understand: but sure I am it is unscriptural, and I think, utterly inconsistent; and indeed instead of loving our enemies, &c. is it not with us yet, rather, *an eye for an eye, a tooth for a tooth?* yea, is not this our wretched case, the more we boast of the Spirit, and profess to bear his fruit, the farther we are from it and the more contrary to his nature? is it not from the profession of bringing forth the fruits of the Spirit, which is love, &c. that men take an occasion to hate their brethren their

fellow

fellow-creatures? whence is that language of the heart, *stand by thyself, come not near to me, for I am holier than thou?* Isa. lxv. 5. Whence is it we think ourselves authorized to run counter to our profession (which is the love of God and man) in back-biting, evil-speaking, slandering, lying, uncharitably censuring, bearing false witness against our neighbour, but from a selfish and mistaken conceit of our being something, when we are nothing? All manner of persecution is inconsistent with christianity, yea expressly forbidden, where we are taught to love our enemies, and to *esteem of others better than ourselves*, Phil. ii. 3. But alas! how few are there (if any) who fully follow these blessed maxims; but on the contrary, are full of strife and hatred, living in open violence, or secret whisperings; and though, under the truly valuable government of these kingdoms, they are indeed restrained from an immediate dipping their hands in each other's blood; yet will they, thro' hatred and evil speech, murder without mercy, all such whose supposed errors in principle, or practice, have rendered them the objects of their hatred and contempt, and all under a profession of bringing forth the fruit of the Spirit, which is love.

    I am persuaded these things are too obvious and well known to require particulars in proof thereof, forasmuch as they are not confined to corners, but stalk in open day: and is this the method of doing *good unto all men?* Gal. vi. 10.

is this the method of *esteeming others better than ourselves?* Phil. ii. 3. is this the acknowledgment we make of our having *nothing but what we have received?* 1 Cor. iv. 7. are those the fruits of the Spirit of Truth? God forbid; every reasonable man must conclude, that if a spirit is known by his fruits, that spirit, from whom such fruits as these proceed, must be diabolical; else where is the love of the Spirit, which is free, impartial, unchangeable? where the *joy, peace, long-suffering, gentleness, goodness, faith, meekness, temperance?* &c. True, there are appearances of this amongst christians, and so there is in uncultivated nature, where nothing sways but reason and the natural disposition of the mind: will it be urged that it is in a greater measure among christians? it is granted it ought to be so from their profession: but whether it is so is a matter of dispute I think. Whether love and friendship amongst the Heathen, are not with more truth and constancy, than they are in the generality amongst those called christians? yea, the former would scorn such mean and pitiful behaviour, as such who are counted most eminent amongst the latter, make no conscience of. The spirit of the one is open, generous and free; they fail not to appear in their own colour; whilst the other, under a cloak of religion, a pretended zeal for holiness, the glory of God, and the good of souls, give the most pregnant proofs of their pride, hatred, malice, revenge and covetousness;

ness; as though the wrath of man, with the spirit of Satan, was to work the righteousness of God, and to bring forth the fruits of the Spirit of Truth. *But be not deceived, God is not mocked; for what a man soweth, that shall he reap,* Gal. vi. 7. O my brethren, how long shall we call light darkness, and darkness light.

As you profess to bear the fruits of the Spirit, only produce them, Jesus shall have the praise, and you the comfort. If the fruit of the Spirit is love, what is the object thereof? If it is self, I confess there is a plentiful produce of self-love in the world: but if it is God and your neighbour, bring it forth and it is well; loving the Lord your God with all your heart, love your neighbour as yourselves, yea better than yourselves; for this is the love of the Spirit; and then all hatred, evil speaking, whispering, and treachery will cease of course. Is the fruit of the Spirit joy? shew it by your rejoicing in the Lord alway, in every state and condition, and let the whole of your conduct, towards your fellow-creatures, be such as will increase their joy, and not their distress. Is the fruit of the Spirit peace? have not only peace yourselves, but seek it and ensue it; be always a maker and promoter, but never a breaker of peace: join not yourselves with the sons of bluster and violence, who jump upon the threshold and fill the house with strife. Is the fruit of the Spirit long-suffering? forbearing revenge, suffer all wrongs and injuries done you with patience, and rest in the will of God. Is the fruit of the Spirit gentleness? laying aside all haughtiness and austerity, be easily entreated and approached without fear. Is the fruit of the Spirit goodness? O how extensive is this! let your heart be heavenly, compassionate, affectionate, kind, tender, without guile, and all your actions be benevolent, just and refreshing towards man, self-denying and sincere towards God. Is the fruit of the Spirit faith? stagger not through unbelief, but be strong in the faith, giving glory to God; always believe him, always trust him, in every state, in every condition, be satisfied, be content; never murmuring nor repining. Is it meekness and temperance? let your spirit and practice shew it forth, that you may have both name and thing. It is not sufficient to say we have the appearance of those things, or that we have them in reality, whilst inconstant, imperfect.

All the fruits of the Spirit of Truth are perfect, else they would not be proof and evidence of his nature. If all the works and fruits of the Spirit of Truth are declarative of his nature, they must be perfectly holy. And if those works and fruits are wrought and produced in man, do they not, must they not answer this character? I confess, the common solution of this, perfection in part, but not in degree, is not intelligible to me; and I rather think it is too intricate and scholastic, for the plain and simple doctrine of christianity,

which,

which, in divine wifdom, is ordained for the edification, not only of the learned, but the unlearned, yea *the way-faring men, tho' fools fhall not err therein*, Ifa. xxxv. 8. Befide, it appears to me utterly inconfiftent with the main end and defign of the chriftian religion, which is the glory of God, and the good of mankind: becaufe, if it may be fuppofed that the fruits of the Spirit are in a man, who yet can be proud, malicious, angry, envious, hateful, uncharitable, &c. wherein is God glorified, or his fellow-creatures benefited by his fruit? but, fhould it be urged, although the fruit of the Spirit in man do not perfectly free him from fin, yet it keeps under the lufts, paffions, and corruptions of his heart, fo that they do not break out at any time to the difhonour of God, or the prejudice of his fellow-creature: fhould this be allowed, though I cannot fee how it may, (nor have I known amongft all my acquaintance one fingle inftance of it) it is ftill granted, that though they are delivered from the outward acts of fin, yet the feed and evil thereof remains. Who are they, that believing the fcripture, will deny that our Saviour expounds the inclination as an act of the heart before God? Matt. v. 28. Therefore, what a falfe foothing of the foul muft it be, when a perfon, under the power of his paffions and corruptions, reckons of himfelf to have the fruits of the Spirit, and confequently to be in a ftate of fafety, becaufe, at times he feels a contrary difpofition of mind, looks upon himfelf as having two principles in him, good and bad; reckoning of his condition towards God by the good principle, though his fpirit and conduct are manifeftly under the power of the bad; and here values himfelf on the account of inward holinefs, and takes occafion to be very bitter againft fuch whom he thinks deficient therein, though he himfelf brings few other fruits to light than what I have already mentioned.

I am perfuaded there are but few, if any, fo abandoned amongft the human race, but what their confcience, at times, accufes or excufes them; there is a principle in them which cannot but approve of true virtue and piety, and acknowledge the evil of vice: Why might not a perfon of this character conclude he hath the fruits of the Spirit, and therefore that all mankind have them? Becaufe if this propofition, perfection in parts, but not in degree, be true, then the leaft meafure thereof is perfect, and denominates the perfon fanctified, yea, one who hath the fruits of the Spirit. And, if it can be proved that all mankind have at times, good and pious motions, yea, habitually a witnefs for God in them, accufing or excufing them, as Rom. ii. 15. then, notwithftanding their meafure is fmall they are all fanctified, all filled with the fruits of the Spirit, which may not be granted. If it fhould be urged, that the pious motions and difpofitions which are in chriftians, are different in nature from thofe which

which are in mankind in the general, and that this difference is commonly defined as working *for* life and *from* life: that a chriſtian, knowing the grace of God, works *from* life; that is, rejoices, obeys, and performs all the exerciſes of religion as naturally as the ſun riſes, as we breathe, and the like; which is not the caſe with the unregenerate, who are driven by the threats of puniſhment, or drawn by promiſes of reward in all they do; if this is the caſe, why is it ſuggeſted that chriſtians cannot have comfort, nay cannot have life, except they work and obey? and if it is thus natural for them to obey, why then all the exhortations and motives made uſe of to excite them to it? what need of all this ſpurring, where is it ſo natural for them to run? beſides, who is there, knowing his own heart, that is not appriſed of this? He cannot *do*, *feel*, or *ſuffer* any thing for God, but what he muſt be ſenſible that his mind cleaves to it; and, more or leſs, takes comfort thence, and hath dependence thereon; nor can he, I believe; whilſt in the body, be wholly free from a legal temper.

Should it be granted, that mankind in the general, not underſtanding thoſe terms of diſtinction, working *from* life and *for* life, nor being converſant with the ſcriptures, have *greater* expectations from the work of their own hands; and may be ſaid more abundantly to work *for* life: but are there not times when they are, in meaſure, ſenſible of the inſuffisufficiency of of their own works to save them, and therefore appeal from themselves to the goodness and mercy of God? If it is supposed that there is the least spark of good, the doctrine of perfection in *parts*, but not in *degree*, cannot deny their being sanctified, nor their having the fruits of the Spirit, however small their measure. Probably it may by urged, that real christians are changed, are reformed from all vice, whereas the generality of mankind remain in their sins. This indeed would be a powerful argument, if the change, or reformation, was so effectual as to make men new creatures in themselves: True it is, there are many who are reformed from drunkenness, uncleanness, thefts, swearing, gaming and all outward crimes: but what are they reformed unto? is it not unto spiritual pride, with prayer? to anger, hatred, malice, with the use of sacraments? to all uncharitableness, with the reading of the scriptures? to back-biting, evil-speaking, lying and slandering, with a precise and pretended holy life? Now we will suppose a man living in drunkenness, whoredoms, thefts, gamings, &c. and another to be reformed from all this wickedness; and to pray often, to hear sermons, to frequent the Lord's table, to give alms, to fast, to keep the sabbath, to have been deeply afflicted for his sins, to have received comfort from his amendment of life, and trust in the grace of God through Christ, to have comfortable views from the

work

work of sanctification carried on in him, &c. and yet this person be spiritually proud, that is, good in his own eyes, better than what he has been, better than his neighbours; a whisperer, back-biter, evil-speaker, revengeful, yea, a murderer, (if to hate one's brother be murder, as the Holy Ghost says it is, John iii. 15.) now what says the scriptures of these two persons? what think you of them? the scriptures call the former, a dog, a swine, 2 Pet. ii. 22. and calls the latter, a serpent, a viper, Matt. xxiii. 33. When a man is apprized of his danger, he is more easily provided against the hurt he may receive from a dog, or swine; for they, though enemies, are more public and generous; but a serpent lies concealed in your paths, and biting your heel, gives you an unexpected wound: though the rending of a dog, or a swine, may often be very hurtful, yet the sting, or bite of a viper, is much more dangerous, and, by reason of its emited poison, often proves mortal. When a person, utterly unacquainted with the nature of those animals, beholds a foaming dog, or a swine bedaubed with mire, he will avoid them as dangerous and nauseous; but seeing a serpent of a beautiful colour basking in the sun, judging by the outward appearance, he concludes it harmless, as beautiful; and becoming familiar with it, gives it an opportunity of biting him; whilst the poor afflicted wretch, to excuse his credulity, cries out, Who could have thought it!

who would have expected it from a creature of so beautiful an appearance! A dog, a swine, however fierce and cruel, are not so much to be dreaded, because they are impoliticly rash, and run upon us with noise and clamour; but a viper, a serpent, is the most subtle of all the beasts of the field; we are hardly secure from their attacks; when we think least of it, and are walking in the greatest security, we are stung without warning. And, as I would avoid the fellowship and acquaintance of both, so would I much more that of the viper and serpent, as more dreadfully dangerous. And yet, persons who answer this character, are generally the greatest boasters of the Spirit's fruits, and most contentious for inward holiness and purity: but, have not this self-righteousness and holiness, been, in every age, the bane of Zion's peace and love? what bred the contentions in the church between the Arians and orthodox, in the first ages of christianity, on which account there was so much blood shed, and each party, as they had power, revenged themselves on the other? was it not, that the one thought themselves more orthodox, and consequently more righteous, more holy than the others? What was it occasioned the Popish persecutions, when such dreadful fires were kindled, in which, many of the noble army of martyrs rendered up their souls to God their Saviour, but the same cursed principle? What occasioned the persecution of the Protestant dissenters by the

hierar-

hierarchy, but the same principle? And when so many of *them* had fled to a strange land, on account of religion; what moved them, when they had power, to persecute, even to death, others of their fellow-creatures on religious accounts, but the same cursed principle? What makes one set of christians hate another, and persecute them with vile names, reproach and anathema's, when they have no farther power to punish, but the same principle still? What makes one christian persecute another with the sword of the tongue, wound his name, his character, yea, murder him according to the scriptures, and all probably without knowing the person they smite, or the truth of what they smite him for? is it not self-righteousness, self-holiness, that accursed, hellish thought? O! it is the fountain of enmity against God, and of all contentions, strife, hatred and confusion amongst men. From hence that unruly evil, the tongue, takes occasion to destroy where the hands are tied. And to explain this more fully, hear what James saith, when he spake of it as in the tongue: *The tongue is a fire, a world of iniquity; it defileth the whole body, and setteth on fire the course of nature, and is set on fire of hell. For every kind of beasts, and of birds, and of serpents, and of things in the sea, is tamed, and has been tamed of mankind: but the tongue can no man tame, an unruly evil, full of deadly poison; therewith bless we God, even the Father; and curse we men; who*

are

are made in the similitude of God, Jam. iii. 6, 7, 8, 9. When self-righteousness sets this unruly evil a going, there is no end to its slanders, bitter invectives and murders; therefore prays the Psalmist, *Thou shalt keep them secretly in a pavilion from the strife of tongues,* Psal. xxxi. 20. Can that, which is the cause of so much mischief, so much evil, be the fruits of the Spirit? God forbid; can that, which hath a tendency to puff up man, to make him wise, orthodox and holy in his own eyes, and from thence to bring forth the cursed fruits before-mentioned, be the fruits of the Spirit? God forbid: is it possible that man can be wise and holy in himself, in his own eyes, without being puffed up, and consequently bring forth such fruits? I think it impossible: and from thence conclude, that we cannot find the fruits of the Spirit, in truth and perfection, in man. But then some one will say, if they are not to be found in man, according to his spirit and behaviour in life, why have you mentioned them, as what we are to know the nature of the Spirit of Truth by? To this I answer, though we have sought for them amongst the many thousands of Israel here below, and cannot find them in their perfection and glory, yet is it in reality a glorious truth: that all these blessed fruits of the Spirit are brought forth and produced in man. And if you would know this wonder of a Man, this Person, so worthy of admiration, in whom all these fruits abound, and in perfect beauty

shine,

shine, give me leave to say tis JESUS! who only is holy, who only is the LORD. Come, see, wonder at, and admire the fruits of the Spirit in Him! In Him is love, without partiality, without bitterness, without wavering, without dissimulation: how infinite, how unspeakable his love to God, even the Father! he loved him with all his heart, and mind, and soul, and strength; he loved so, that it was his meat and his drink to do his will. How great his love to the sons of men! and without partiality, as extending to Jew and Gentile, to bond and free; to the most wretched of mankind, yea, whether they are fifty, or five hundred-pence sinners, with infinite frankness, his love extends without distinction to them all. Without bitterness, as admitting of no ingredient of wrath, no spark of anger, fury was not in him, but love was all his intention, desire, heart and nature towards man; without wavering, as stedfast, unshaken, having loved his own he loved them to the end: no consideration whatever, not that of the unknown sorrows and dreadful sufferings, which so sorely amazed his soul, could shake his love or cause a momentary wavering; not that of the enmity of man, yea, the base ingratitude of his own houshold, the thought of which, though it wrung sweat in bloody drops like rain from him, caused not the least shadow of turning in his love to man. Love! undissembled love led him through his unfathomed humiliation,

where

where his judgment was taken away, where dwelt the darkness of the shadow of death: and tho' death and hell put on their most dreadful forms, and, armed with all their terrors, sought to oppose his passage through to light and immortality, as the representative of man; yet singly armed with love, he would not, could not flee, but greatly swallowed up death, and the grave in victory, and destroyed him who had the power of death, that is the devil. O how fervent, how sincere his love, passing knowledge, stronger than death, enriching the children of men with grace, glory, and immortality! This indeed is love, the Spirit's fruit of love; such, that for the salvation of man, sinful man, endured the cross and despised the shame. The force of that ancient maxim, love your friend, and hate your enemy, was here repelled; and love, love without dissimulation, and that to the most inveterate enemies, proved to the greatest demonstration: feeding their hungry souls with bread, the bread of life; and quenching their thirst with the waters of life: Yea, not withholding his own flesh and blood, but freely giving it for the life of the world, making it meat indeed, and drink indeed, to his church. He blessed where he was cursed, and prayed for such who used him despitefully. Behold every fruit in its greatest perfection and ripeness abounding in him! The joy of the Lord was his strength; he rejoiced not in iniquity, but in the truth; in the glory of God and

and the falvation of man. He was the Prince of peace, the God of peace, the Son of peace, the peace between heaven and earth, between God and man, between Jew and Gentile, between every believer's confcience and God the judge of all men. His birth proclaimed God's intention of peace to the earth, his every action and fuffering in life promoted it, his bloody death and paffion hath for ever ratified it, and the gofpel of his blood is the tidings of this everlafting peace to mankind. He hath the fruit of long-fuffering, who endured the contradiction of finners againft himfelf; when reviled he reviled not again, but bare it with patience and long-fuffering: How amazingly hath he fhewn it in all the diftrefs and torments of his life and death! How infinite his forbearance and patience towards mankind, notwithftanding the manifold provocations wherewith they have provoked the eyes of his glory! He truly hath the gentlenefs of the dove, humane, kind, eafy of accefs, and as eafy to be entreated; no aufterity, fternnefs, fhynefs, fury, or paffion to be feen in him; but all is gentle, mild, fweet, calm, furpaffing the utmoft defire and conception of our mind. His goodnefs exceeds all defcription. Is it good to be compaffionate? he hath compaffion on the ignorant, and on fuch who are out of the way. And as a father pities his own children, fo he pities them that fear him. Is it good to be benevolent? as his ftores are immenfe, fo is his benevolence boundlefs. He hath healed

all

all our maladies, and fupplied all our wants, according to the riches of his grace. In brief, his goodnefs towards God and man is perfect. To do good, and to communicate is his nature and property.

Faithfulnefs is the girdle of his reins: faithful in things pertaining to God, and faithful to man: faithful in his word, in his offices, in his relations: faithful to every facred name he bears, and character which he affumes: faithful in his love, friendfhip, fympathy and kindnefs. O he is a friend who fticketh clofer than a brother, nor is there any unfaithfulnefs in him!

Meeknefs in perfection dwells in him: Mofes was meek, but not perfectly fo; witnefs his wrath when he brake the tables of the law; his fury and unadvifed fpeech at the waters of ftrife; and though he was more meek than any man upon earth, yet it was but a figure and fhadow of the meeknefs of Jefus; for in him it is without mixture or contrariety: his meek and lowly heart is always the fame; nor can he ever be provoked to fury and anger, or ever drop an unadvifed word.

Temperate in all things, as one who ftrove for the maftery over Satan, fin, and death; and therefore, when accufed of gluttony, winebibbing, fedition, &c. it was no farther true, than as, when made fin for us, *he* bare thofe offences of the people in his own body upon the crofs; and the character of finners falling
upon

upon him, He was numbered amongſt the tranſgreſſors. For in himſelf he was temperate; not ſo in profeſſion, or appearance only, that he might gain the praiſe of men: for he ſought not his reputation thereby, nor was his honour or kingdom of this world. His uſe of abſtinence, and faſting, was not that under the holy guiſe he might have an opportunity of devouring the widow's houſe, and amaſſing the preſent world: But his temperance was ſincere, without guile, yea, univerſal, in meats, drinks, apparel, ſleep, and bodily reſt, in his uſe of the world, its riches, honour, pleaſures, cares, the paſſions of the mind, or whatever the ſoul of man may be temperate in; and thus all the fruits of the Spirit of Truth abound in him.

Who is he that would learn the nature of the Spirit of Truth from his fruits? let him come and learn it here, in the perfect man, who, thus adorned, is fairer than the ſons of men, from whoſe lips drop grace and truth. When we look to man, to ourſelves, for theſe fruits; we find ſo many contrarieties and imperfections, as to imbitter our reflections, and makes us cry, O my leanneſs! ſo that we cannot learn the nature of the Spirit of Truth there, as already obſerved. And if we would diſtinguiſh between *man* and *himſelf*, according to different principles in him, ſo as not to judge of his *good* by his *bad*, but conſider his good in the abſtract, bringing it for tri-

E   al

al to the standard of all good, the divine nature, there is neither proportion nor comparison; so that man may not, considered after what he is in himself, be justly the object of his own or another's admiration: nay, the Father hath reserved this honour and glory for the beloved Son, who is the head of his body the church, *that in all things he might have the pre-eminence.*

We are called upon to consider him as the Apostle and High-priest of our profession: to rejoice in him, to admire him, to love him, to boast of him, to gaze upon him as *the beauty of holiness,* yea, the *perfection of beauty,* the *chief amongst ten thousand,* the *altogether lovely;* to esteem of him as precious above all.— *Whom have I in heaven but Thee? and there is none upon earth, that I desire besides Thee.* This is the christian's chief delight, his highest pleasure.

Whatever the holy scriptures define as the Spirit's fruit, that Jesus is in himself; insomuch that he is the true and glorious fruit of the Spirit of Truth; he is love, he is joy, he is peace, he is long-suffering, he is gentleness, goodness, faith, meekness, temperance, against whom there is no law. Let us admire him, adore him, and rejoice in his light.

Furthermore, having a little considered the state and condition of mankind, how poor, how vain a creature man is, notwithstanding his boasting of his fruits, his holiness, &c. and how

how that Jesus only is perfect, only is holy, the just admiration of all his people.

I would farther consider wherein his children are benefited by what he is in himself: *I am like a green firr-tree*, says he, *from me is thy fruit found*, Hos. xiv. 8. Again, *I am the vine, ye are the branches*, John xv. 5. Our Saviour, by comparing himself to a *firr-tree*, points out his everlasting verdure and fruitfulness; and, by telling the church that *her* fruit is found from *him*, he sheweth that *his* fruit is *hers*, that *she* hath a just claim to it, and that *she* cannot cease to be fruitful whilest *he* is fruitful. *I am the vine, ye are the branches*; whereby he sheweth, that as the vine and branches make one tree; so he, and his children, make one body: and as the branches were naturally in the vine before a sprout appeared; so were his children in him as beloved and chosen from everlasting: and as, in the fulness of time, the vine puts forth its branches, in order to bear fruit; so did *he* bring forth his children into existence, that *he* might bring forth fruit unto God: and as the vine, consisting of stock and branches, is dressed by the husbandman, in order to its fruitfulness; so was Jesus, consisting of head and members in one body, bruised, afflicted, and dealt with by the Father, the great Husbandman, for the destruction of sin, and the bringing forth of good fruit: and as the vine brings forth all its fruit upon the branches; (having no distinct fruit from the branches, nor any other way of bearing it,) so Jesus hath brought forth all the fruit of his obedience and sufferings, with every gracious quality that was manifest in him, upon his people; nor, according to the consideration of this union between him and them, has he any distinct fruit from them, or any other way of bearing fruit but upon them. Thus he bears *their* fruit, and, as he says, from *me* is *THY* fruit found. In this mystery of our fruitfulness in Christ, he alone is glorified and hath the pre-eminence; for here the branch doth not arrogantly assume the character of being fruitful in itself, considered as distinct from the tree; and independent thereof, else the husbandman, casting his eye upon it, seperate from the tree, might say, O thou blessed and fruitful *branch!* to the dishonour of the *tree;* but considered in the tree, and as fruitful only in that, the husbandman beholding it as having all the branches laden with fruit, says, O thou blessed and fruitful *tree,* my pleasure prospers in *thee!*

Thus hath Jesus the pre-eminence, glory and praise, where all our fruitfulness is in him: of this we attempt to rob him, when we, commencing proud boasters, talk and contend for *our* bearing fruit and doing wonders, forgetting him on whom our help is laid, and from whom all our fruit is found. *As the branch cannot bear fruit of itself except is abide in the vine, neither can ye except ye abide in me,* John xv. 4. hence it appears, that the christian only is fruitful as

he

he abides in Chrift. He is in him as a *member of his body, of his flesh, and of his bones*, Eph. v. 30. And according to this myftery he hath produced all the fruits of his life, death, and refurrection upon us; and when Chrift is revealed in us *the hope of glory*, Col. i. 27. the confcience cleaves, yea, is united and married unto him; infomuch, that all that he is, and all that he hath done, becomes ours, according to the affurance of the underftanding and teftimony of the mind. We, thus receiving him, have power given us to become the fons of God, John i. 12. and, according to the confcience, we do the works which he did, as he promifed, John xiv. 12. All his fruitfulnefs being upon us, we bear it, and bring it forth in Spirit unto God, being *married unto him who is rifen from the dead, that we might bring forth fruit unto God*, Rom. vii. 4.

But as in phyfiognomy, when we would guefs the nature and condition of a perfon, we look into the face, for what concerns the whole perfon; fo, as Jefus is the Head of his body the church, he is alfo her face; and whoever would guefs of her nature and condition in general, or that of any one member in particular, let them look into her face, and learn it there; there alone is the beauty and perfection of the king's daughter feen, cloathed with her garment of wrought needle-work. In this view every chriftian appears as led by the Spirit of Truth, as bearing all the precious fruits thereof, as having clean escaped the garment spotted by the flesh, no more fulfilling the lusts thereof; having this testimony, that they please God, yea, that they always do the things that please him, because of Jesus their Head and Forerunner.

If it is true, that the office of the Spirit of Truth, according to the scriptures, is to glorify Christ; then may we know whether the spirits which speak, or profess to preach the gospel, are of God, or not.

I have already shewn, according to the word of God, that where a Spirit is found speaking of himself, it cannot be the Spirit of Truth, and therefore not of God.

And if it is true, that by a spirit's speaking of himself, we may understand it's pointing out, and testifying of the impulse, operation, or influence of the mind as productive of joy, sorrow, love, desire, though centering in heavenly things; thence persuading mankind of their being possessed of the Spirit of Truth; there, nor only permitting, but encouraging them to found their hope: I say, if this is to speak of himself, and consequently to be a false spirit; let us not believe nor follow that spirit, but with all boldness, and the assurance of understanding, reject it as not of God. And in so doing, let us not be *afraid of man, who shall die, nor of the son of man, who is but as grass.* Neither let their high titles, learning, or wisdom be of any weight with us, when we are

led

led, in purfuit of the Truth, into fingular paths. We would difclaim all foolifh, affected fingularity, where the confcience is not concerned, as that which is vain and ridiculous. But when a man, fimply aiming at the glory of Chrift, without partiality, fearches the fcriptures, what his confcience clearly, and without doubtfulnefs, from thence fuggefts unto him, is the Truth, which he is to abide by, though all the world fhould teftify the contrary. And, however fuch an one might be charged with error and obftinacy, yet will he abide by the teftimony of his confcience, nor may he depart thence on any account whatever, unlefs he will pierce himfelf through with many forrows. If this is not true, then our determination, in cafes of confcience, and matters of faith, muft not be in our own bofoms, as evident in the fcriptures. But the church hath the keeping and power of this, fay they, who would have the clergy only to be the church; and others would perfuade us, that the expofitions on the fcriptures, and dead bodies of divinity, wrote by learned and holy men, and approved of by the multitude, have the power and keeping of it. If this is not true, then the martyrs of old fhed their blood and laid down their lives for trifles, yea, for nothing, when they died for the teftimony of a good confcience. But we have not fo learned Chrift, nor are we thus taught by the fcriptures, to

which

which we do well to give heed, as unto a light shining in a dark place.

If that spirit, which speaks of reformation and change wrought upon man, thence, persuading you of your safety, and glorifying himself in you as the author of this change; if this spirit may be deemed to speak of himself, and therefore antichristian; let us not blindly follow the multitude, whatever profession of piety and virtue, whatever plea of consolation the good man (so called) hath, from the contemplations of his own pious actions and habits, but faithfully confess ourselves christians, whose hope and rejoicing are in Christ Jesus, and not in ourselves; being well assured, that the Spirit of Truth will not speak of himself, will not lead us for salvation, nor consolation, to any change, or virtuous habit, which he, by revealing Jesus, hath wrought in us, but will always glorify Christ, as him alone in whom we are saved, without works of righteousness as wrought by us; as him, who in the fulness of his grace and glory, is the only comfort and joy of our heart.

If that spirit, who insinuates that he is injured by the preaching of Christ alone, is antichrist; let us be aware thereof, and constantly reject it, as not of God. I mean by this spirit, that which stirs up, and raises objections against gospel-faith and doctrine, insinuating that it destroys the work of the Spirit, by not making it a chief subject; but, that, by ascribing the whole

whole of our salvation to Christ, we exclude the work of the Spirit. This objection makes such a wide distinction between Christ and the Spirit, as to make their works and interests different.

That there is an inexplicable mystery in the Deity is certain, of which, it appears to me, the highest arrogance to attempt a definition; yet, that Jesus Christ and the Spirit of Truth have separate interests, the scripture denies; teaching us, that the whole Godhead is interested in the honour and glory of Jesus: as where it says, *He that honoureth not the Son, honoureth not the Father*, John v. 23. And concerning the Spirit of Truth; he says, *When he is come, he will not speak of himself, but will glorify me*. And, as all the fulness of the Godhead dwells bodily in him, (and he is *God manifested in the flesh*) we conceive, according to the scriptures, that God, Father, Word and Spirit, is to be believed on and trusted in, approached unto and worshipped in Him. And, as such who object to the divine honours given Jesus in the church, as derogatory to the Father, may not be said to have seen his day, nor digested the scriptures concerning him; so those who object to the faith and doctrine of Christ alone, as denying the work of the Spirit, or as deficient without our adding to it the work of the Spirit, as a distinct subject; may be said, either to *err, as not knowing the scriptures, nor the power of God* concerning this matter; or else, to speak, from a warm and inconsiderate zeal, what they have nothing to support, but
the

the doctrines and traditions of men. For, I think, I have proved by the scriptures, or at least given such hints that any unprejudiced and impartial enquirer may easily perceive, that the office and work of the Holy Ghost consists in glorifying Jesus, in testifying of him, shewing us what he is, what he has done, drawing us to him, persuading us of our salvation and glory in him, stirring us up to the acknowledgement and confession of his worthy praise. And the clearer this is, the more evidently the work of the Spirit of Truth appears. How dreadful the mistake then, when either thro' enmity to Christ, or zeal for the traditions of men, light is called darkness, and darkness light; and many object to the work of the Spirit of Truth itself, that it opposes the work of the Spirit, and thereby take part with a spirit of delusion and falshood against the truth itself: and this will be always the case, until we are content to see with our own eyes, hear with our own ears, and judge for ourselves, and no longer see and hear with other men's eyes and ears, nor judge by their determinations. Well might the apostle, in the words of the text, say, *Beloved, believe not every spirit, but try the spirits whether they be of God.*

 O my brethren, how long will it be e'er we shall think for ourselves? when shall we be delivered from the tyranny of tradition, and no longer enslaved thereby? let not the authority of any, though called great men (and on some accounts probably, truly accounted such) sway with

with us, when what concerns our eternal life and happiness comes under our confideration; but, let us *to the law, and to the teftimony*; there firſt let us ſacrifice all our favourite ſentiments, yea, every darling opinion that claſhes with the ſacred word; with this let us offer all in man, on the credit of which we would ſwallow their doctrines without examination by the word; whether it is learning, wiſdom, piety, or popularity; and abiding the deciſion of the ſcriptures be content to be judged thereby, and, by its ſimple authority to determine of what we hear.

My aim in ſpeaking thus, is to draw all, who profeſs chriſtianity, to the ſcriptures, as the rule of their faith and practice. By them would I be tried in all things, particularly in what I here write. Yea, to them I appeal, and that not according to any private interpretation, but according to what every generous and candid mind may diſcern in them.

The holy ſcriptures poſitively declare that ſpirit, which denieth that Jeſus is come in the fleſh, to be antichriſt; by which, if we may not only underſtand a denial of his incarnation, but, that of his having anſwered the end of his coming, which was to fulfil all righteouſneſs, to atone for ſin, and to ſave his people with an everlaſting ſalvation, let us then learn to avoid, firſt, that ſpirit which denies the incarnation of our Lord Jeſus Chriſt, or his coming in the fleſh, or that he, *who is God bleſſed for ever, amen*, according to the fleſh, came of the ſtock of Iſrael.

The

The apostle gives us such a plain description of antichrist in those words, that except we wilfully shut our eyes against the truth, we cannot fail discovering it; for as it is the office and work of the Spirit of Truth to glorify Christ; insomuch that *no man can say that Jesus is the Lord, but by the Holy Ghost*; so is it the true characteristick of antichrist to deny the eternal power and Godhead of the Lamb.

Let us then reject this false spirit as an enemy to our Saviour; and with this the spirit which denieth his having answered the end of his coming. For it is at best but a compliment paid to Jesus, where his Godhead is confest, but the all-sufficiency of his blood and sacrifice denied; truly to deny the latter, is to deny the former, whatever pretension there may be to the contrary, whatever pleas those false spirits may make for the denial of his Godhead as contrary to reason, or for the denial of his all-sufficient grace and merit for our salvation and happiness, without works of righteousness as done by us, as having a tendency to destroy holiness, and make people careless of good works. I say, notwithstanding those pleas, let us upon the authority of the scripture, reject every such spirit, as not of God. Do the scriptures say that Jesus Christ was *God manifest in the flesh?* 1 Tim. iii. 16. Do they say, that *He bare our sins, in his own body, on the cross*, 1 Pet. ii. 24. and *hath appeared to put sin away by the sacrifice of himself?* Heb. ix. 26. Then this is the language of the
Spirit

Spirit of Truth, and plainly teſtifies that the other is not of God.

What if our reaſon cannot attain the comprehenſion of all that God hath revealed, muſt we therefore doubt, and deny it? Wherein is he honoured and glorified in the credit we pay to him in his word, if we believe him no farther than it is demonſtrate to our reaſon and ſenſes? it may indeed be urged, that this is credit ſufficient to the teſtimony of man becauſe fallible, and therefore liable to err: but is it ſo to him who is infallible and cannot lie? I ſuppoſe it will not be affirmed. How inconſiſtent and falſe then is the ſpirit which denieth that Jeſus is come in the fleſh! Altogether as falſe, and much more inconſiſtent, is that ſpirit which, profeſſing the dignity of his perſon, denies the all-ſufficiency of his merit, as deſtructive to holineſs of life. Here may it be ſaid, *vain man would be wiſe though born a wild aſſes colt,* Job xi. 12. Vain man would be good, though *there is none good but God,* Luke xviii. 19. Vain man would do wonders, though *it is not in him that walketh to direct his ſteps,* Jer. x. 23.

The Phariſees of old accuſed our Saviour of deſtroying the law and the prophets by his doctrine, and of ungodlineſs in his practice, as breaking the ſabbath-day, &c. their brethren of this generation, though they will not immediately accuſe him, as the former Phariſees did, yet it is plain they ſuſpect him, yea, are very jealous of him; they are for ſoftening his words,

words, as though they were wifer than he; and for mixing his doctrine with cautions, and proper expofitions upon his phrafes, left it fhould hurt weak minds. And as for the faith of his gofpel, who can bear it? that is reckoned fo deftructive to holinefs of life, and in itfelf fo dangerous on many accounts, that whofoever will confefs it, muft partake of the afflictions thereof; deny himfelf, and take up his crofs, yea, lofe his life, for the fake of Chrift and his gofpel: forafmuch as it is impoffible that any man fhould live godly in Chrift Jefus, without fuffering perfecution, 2 Tim. iii. 12. As for the godlinefs which reafon plans, that is admired by all, yea even by fuch who are far from the practice of any, becaufe it makes a fair fhew in the flefh, makes trial of its purity by reafon, and not by the perfections of God, and is therefore looked on as real godlinefs: whereas, if it was to be tried by the perfection of God (of which his law is a tranfcript) all the pride, vain-glory, felf-feeking, &c. with which all that man is capable of doing abounds, would appear, and all his righteoufnefs become filthy rags. But the reafoning plan cannot difcover this, and therefore allows man to pride himfelf in his own works, under the notion of delight and pleafure in virtue, and that without any confideration of reward, yea, allows him a fecret pleafure and thankfulnefs of heart, that he is not as other men, nor as this or that publican; yea farther,

it

it will allow him, as that which is lawful, the praise and respect of his fellow-creatures, and that he should take pleasure therein, and esteem of it as a blessing attending the uprightness of his heart and the cleanness of his hands; yea, and that he should look on it as a particular mark of God's favour to him. Now this is the good man, for whom *some would even dare to die*, Rom. v. 7. But we will suppose this man brought over to believe the gospel, that is, to believe and confess that Jesus Christ, in the mystery of his person, by his obedience to death, hath eternally saved him, and perfected him in righteousness and true holiness to God, and that without works of righteousness done by him: from whence it appears so far from being lawful for him to pride himself in his own works, that he now rather denies them, and having done all things commanded, confesses himself an unprofitable servant, and acknowledges all that delight and pleasure which others profess to have in doing good, to be in *him* but pride, self-righteousness, and a lifting up of the heart against Christ: he can no longer thank God that he is better than other men, as he has known his heart *to be desperately wicked and deceitful above all things*, himself the chief of sinners, and hath therefore learned to *esteem of others better than himself*: he can no longer count it right, with Christ, for him to court the praise and respect of his fellow-creatures, nor ever think he has deserved it, or that it is any mark of God's favour;

because

becaufe he knows now, that the friendſhip of the world is death; and his maſter hath faid, *Wo unto you when all men ſhall ſpeak well of you, for ſo did their fathers to the falſe prophets,* Luke vi. 26. We will farther ſuppoſe, that this man, notwithſtanding the change which hath paſſed upon him, hath made no alteration with reſpect to his former exerciſe of piety, is yet as upright, as virtuous, as liberal, as truly religious, and of as tender a conſcience as before, yea, we will ſuppoſe him *more* abounding in all this, yet foraſmuch as the before-mentioned change has paſſed over him, and he with his whole heart and ſoul, declares all his righteouſneſs to be filthy rags, and as a menſtruous cloth, whilſt in the Lord alone he hath righteouſneſs and ſtrength: He ſhall now be ſuſpected, accuſed, condemned, laden with calumny and reproach: there are none who will die for him *now*; however great his character, and admired his conduct before, yet *now* is he looked on as a *peſt* amongſt men. This truly is the croſs of Chriſt, and happy is the man who can glory therein. For a *good* man ſuch as he was under his firſt character, ſome would even dare to die: but for a *righteous* man, ſuch as he is *now*, whoſe tranſgreſſion is forgiven and ſin covered, who worſhippeth *God in the ſpirit, rejoiceth in Chriſt Jeſus, and hath no confidence in the fleſh,* ſcarcely one will die. Hence have we a ſpecimen of the enmity of man's heart againſt Jeſus Chriſt and his goſpel; and hence we may in a meaſure account for the afflictions and perſecutions

tions which attend all who truly believe the gospel.

But let not this antichrist, who denieth that Christ is come in the flesh, that he hath by his coming fulfilled all righteousness, and finished the salvation of his people, ever fright us from the profession of our faith; let all his objections and reproaches be disregarded by us, as the fruits of his enmity against Jesus Christ our Lord. Let the all-sufficient merit and glory of his person and atonement be ever valuable, ever dear to us.

There is an everlasting fixed jealousy deep rooted in the christian mind, of every work, word, or thought, lest it would be a competitor to Jesus and his atoning blood, nor can his eye spare, or his heart pity, whenever he finds the traitor out, but would with the Psalmist pray, *Let burning coals fall upon them, let them be cast into the fire, into the deep pits that they rise not again,* Psal. cxl. 10.

Is it true, that the spirit of truth, whether he reprove the world of sin, regenerate to God, or witness to the spirit of the believer that he is born of God, doth *in* and *by* all glorify Christ; then will it appear that the Father, in all his counsel and purposes, intended the glory of his Son. He designed it in creation, as creating all things *by him*, making him the first acting cause of all things, and *for him*, that he might govern all, as his rightful inheritance. He glorified him in permitting the fall of man, that as fin abounded in them, he might exhibit him, as his much more abounding grace. He glorified him in their recovery, when he made him his falvation unto the ends of the earth. He glorifies him in all his dealings with man, as being now afcended above the higheft heavens and filling all things, filling all the works and ways of providence towards us; and not only fuch, which are more chearing and delightful, but the more gloomy and difmal alfo: whether it is loffes, the lofs of health, or friends, or goods; whether it is croffes, all our ends, aims and endeavours fruftrated; all the defire of our hearts denied us; tormented by bodily pains, wounded by evil tongues, hated and defpifed by all; adding to all this, the fharper trial ftill, the fufpenfion of all divine comfort from the foul, attended with the fierce affaults of the enemy through fiery temptations, and the horrid ferment of a corrupt heart. How dreadful and afflictive foever all this may be in its nature, yea, coming on us as the tempeft of a whirlwind upon a feather, yet may we fearlefs ftand, for he that rideth upon the wings of the wind, Jefus, our Lord and God, filleth all things, fo that we fhall not be moved. He fpeaks to us out of thick darknefs, he fpeaks to us out of the burning flame, he fpeaks to us out of the tumultous waves, and his conftant language is, *Be not afraid, it is I*; yea, though *clouds and darknefs are round about him, righteoufnefs and judgment are the habitations of his throne*. He fills every

ftate

state and every condition wherein we are, and where *he* is, there is the fulness of grace and love. To know this, is to be *content* in every state wherein we are; but if we know it not, he is the same, and changeth not. He girds us when we know him not. And if at any time, through frightful appearances, we are driven as men to our wit's end, even there Jesus meets us, saying, *Be not afraid, it is I.* Nor can all our fears and ignorance turn his heart away, or alter the property of his grace. He filleth all things, need we wonder then that all things should work together for our good? O glorious grace! O stupendous love! shall we not learn hence submission to the will of our heavenly Father, since he always wills our welfare, and hath made Jesus to be all in all unto us! Herein is the Saviour glorified. In the glorious face, and fulness of this divine Lamb, the Spirit of Truth points out the evil of sin: Can any thing speak its heinousness more fully than that amazed and sorrowful heart of Jesus, when beneath its pressure in the garden it sweated showers of ruddy drops? Can any words or device of man paint the abomination in a truer, stronger light, than that bruised and swoln face, that head so pierced with thorns, that back so rent with scourges, those hands and feet so bored and torn, those deep vented sighs, those cries, tears, groans, and breaking heart-strings? all evidencing soul-pangs, yet unheard of, by reason of their inexplicable

plicable height, depth, breadth, and length. From hence the Spirit of Truth reproves of sin and aggrandizes the offence, shews, from the all-sufficiency of his death and grace, the curse and evil of unbelief; and if this Spirit, in its reproof, influence and testimony, glorifies Jesus, let us beware of that spirit which would use arguments and means derogatory to the honour of Jesus, to convince, convert, or comfort man.

Is it true, that the Spirit of Truth, in all his operations, glorifies Christ? then all such operations as have a tendency to bury us in unbelief, either from a sense of our sinfulness and unprofitableness, or a doubtfulness of the all-sufficient merit of our Saviour's blood and death, cannot be the operations of the Spirit of Truth, because Jesus is not glorified. Whatever operations on the mind tend to puff up, to make us wise, righteous, holy, or powerful in our own esteem, cannot be of the Spirit of Truth, because it is a lifting up of the heel against Jesus, and a casting *off* our dependence on him. But whatever operating power and influence (upon our heart) tends to lead us to *him* for righteousness and strength, to *him* for wisdom and purity, to *him* for eternal salvation and comfort, shews us *his* glory, and endears him to the soul, yea, constantly leads us out of ourselves, to have all our hope and dependence on *him*; this is the Spirit of Truth, the Holy Ghost, the Comforter: O let us hear his voice and know it, submit to his teachings,

teachings, and then will he guide us into a.. truth. And let us not limit him to particular texts of scripture, nor sermons, nor sacraments, nor prayers, nor meditation, as respecting the means or method made use of by him to honour and reveal Christ in us the hope of glory. The great question is, whether is Christ Jesus, our dear and only Lord, glorified, or not,? let him do it *with* or *without* means as used by *us*, as it shall seem best in his sight. Let us not fail to distinguish between the operations of the Spirit and the passions, in *ourselves* and *others*; in *ourselves*, left when, having had our passions worked up, we conclude we are believers, such that know and enjoy much; but when we cool and find ourselves other men than we imagined, we deem God changeable, and the joys of his spirit fleeting; or else, as men awaked and recovered from drunkenness, we are ashamed of the raptures we seemed to be in, of all our swelling words, yea, of the whole of our behaviour; would fain hide us from ourselves, and from all before whom we had boasted of great matters; our faith and joys having left us to shame and confusion of face. Let us carefully make this distinction, lest, mistaking our passions for the operations of the Spirit of Truth, and being of a sanguine complexion, we go about to force things upon mankind which are contrary to the truth itself; or, if it happen to be the truth, the man of passions will assert either, as it comes on his mind,

mind, with all the abfolute pofitivenefs of infallibility, will tell you, he will pawn his foul for the truth thereof, or that it is as true as JEHOVAH liveth; if you afk for proof, it is that he hath experienced it, or hath had it revealed to him; whereas, probably, it will not be many days before he is found, not only denying this, but afferting, with equal pofitivenefs, what is diametrically its oppofite: this is odious and dangerous, and always to be avoided by every Chriftian. A fpirit which is pofitive, without proof, is a fpirit to be fufpected, as favouring more of paffion than of truth.

Let us learn alfo to make this diftinction in others, that, as we would not deceive ourfelves, we may not be deceived by them, either by converfing with them, or by hearing their report; enquire thus by the fpirit which is in you: are they, in their meafure, judicious? Do they fing of mercy and judgment, or, do all their joy and comfort fpring from fcriptural and faithful views of Jefus, and of what he is made of God unto man? Are they confiftent, not afferting with one breath, what they contradict with another? are they conftant, in fpeaking of Jefus, and profeffing him? for *Jefus Chrift, the Son of God, is not yea and nay, but in him is yea.* Do they aim more at fealing inftruction upon the mind by fcripture-proof and argument, than at raifing the paffions, by gefture, noife, change of voice into loud fpeaking, or unnatural tones? where

we

we can discern this, we have reason to conclude, that they are led by the Spirit of Truth, and not by their passions. But on the contrary, where we find them much in joy and transport, and but little in judgment, not having that scriptural and faithful idea of Jesus, from whence true comfort springs, not being able themselves to account for their joy, as to any view of divine love, from whence it should arise: where they are inconsistent and inconstant, *affirming* and *denying* the same thing, not abiding in one voice concerning Jesus: where the aim is more at the passions, than at instructing the mind, and building it up in the faith of the gospel; and that by artful gestures, unnatural sounds, much noise and vehemency of words: Where there is a profession of knowing by the Holy Ghost, and of being immediately directed by him (in things which come more particularly under the cognizance of reason) and that often contrary to common honesty: This, and the like, where we find it, speaks the passions of a corrupt mind more than the Spirit of Truth. Therefore it will be well, if we hold only *common* friendship and sociableness with persons of this character; holding ourselves in a readiness to do them good, when it shall please our Lord to make use of us to that purpose, but not to connect too close with such *who are given to change*, lest it should prove a trap and a snare unto us. For they think it right to be your *friend* to-day, and your *foe* to-morrow; to do you a *good* turn one day, and an *evil* one another day; *to-day* hosannah, *to-morrow* crucify; and yet pretend to be directed by the Spirit through all. If this spirit (viz. their passions) calls them to any thing, they *ardently* follow it, trampling all moral honesty and engagements beneath their feet; and will not submit to the scripture rule and decision of things.

But the Spirit of Truth teaches judiciously, consistently, faithfully; blessed are all they, who are no longer governed by their passions, but are led by that *true* and *peaceful* Spirit, which always glorifies Jesus in all his operations and teachings.

I have before noted, that the revelation of Jesus Christ, by the Spirit of Truth, produceth its proper effects in every one who believeth his holy gospel; and that *this* consists in a deep abasement and abhorrence of ourselves, working to an eternal, inexplicable veneration for the name and person of our ever adorable Jesus. But then let us remember, by the way, that, as it is not every one who compliments Jesus with calling him *Lord* that enters his kingdom; neither does every one who professes self-loathing and abasement, know any thing of it, as it will plainly appear. Self-abasement proves itself in a second fruit, which is very visible and intelligible to man, and doth not consist in profession, or word only. Self-loathing and abasement supposes a real conviction of the evil of sin, and withal a right sense

and

and underſtanding of the *root*, and various branches thereof, as *rooted* in the heart, and *ſprouting* in all our works, words and thoughts, as the Lord teſtifieth, *that every imagination of the thoughts of man's heart is only evil continually*, Gen. vi. 5. and *that the heart is deſperately wicked and deceitful above all things*, Jer. xvii. 9. until we know that we are *carnal and ſold under ſin*, Rom. vii. 14. *in* us, *that is in* our *fleſh, dwelleth no good thing*, Rom. vii. 18. That whilſt we ſerve the law of God with the mind, we ſerve the law of ſin with the fleſh, Rom. vii. 25. until we know that we are the chief of ſinners, 1 Tim. i. 15. and in ſelf-loathing and abaſement fall dead at his feet. And wherever this is, according to the ſpirit and power of the goſpel, it will produce this ſecond fruit, an eſteeming *of others better than ourſelves*. We can no more judge nor condemn our brother, becauſe we are very ſenſible we have nothing but what we have received. It is *here natural* to us to forgive the injuries done us. We are *here* preſerved from hopeleſs ſorrow and ſecret murmurs under the deepeſt calamities which befal us, or the moſt grievous ſlights put upon us. In ſhort, a perſon truly exerciſed in *this*, can never fall far below his expectations, nor be much deceived in the courſe of this world. Should we *now* uncharitably cenſure our fellow-creature, the quick and powerful word of God would ſeize us—*Why doſt thou judge thy brother, or why doſt thou ſet at nought thy brother?*

let

let him who is without sin cast the first stone at them.

Where there is true self-abasement the conscience will not admit of back-biting, evil-speaking, revenge, hatred, slander, and uncharitableness, because the true knowledge of our own hearts will *prevent* us therein; teaching us pity and compassion towards the most abandoned, yea, peace and fellow-feeling with all mankind. But where self-loathing and abasement is only in *word* and not in *power*, people can profess to know themselves, and yet hate their neighbour, backbite them, speak evil of them, slander them, uncharitably censure them, &c. as being worse than themselves; for, if they do not really think them worse than themselves, they sin grievously against the light, to judge and condemn them, where their conscience testifies their own worthlessness to such a degree, as not to admit of their being better than their neighbour; how like a two-edged and sharp sword doth God point his word against such as those! *Thou art inexcusable, O man, whosoever thou art, that judgest, for wherein thou judgest another thou condemnest thyself, for thou that judgest dost the same thing*, Rom. ii. 1. A person who professeth to know himself, and behaveth *thus* towards his neighbour, *turns judgment into gall, and the fruit of righteousness into hemlock*, Amos. vi. 12. *Turns judgment into gall;* when instead of judging righteous judgment consistent with truth, and according to the *love* and *spirit* of

the

the gofpel, they judge according to appearances, according to the gall, bitternefs, and rancour of a felf-righteous and prejudiced mind. And as for the fruit of righteoufnefs, which I have fhewn to be felf-loathing and abafement, and from *thence* peace, and love towards mankind; *that* they turn into *hemlock*, a noxious and poifonous plant, with which, having poifoned themfelves, their heart is lifted up, and being fwoln with pride and felf-fufficiency, and ignorant of their own true ftate, they fpit their venom with fuch zeal and fiercenefs, as if envy, malice, revenge, murder, and fury was the moft demonftrative proof of being a real chriftian: fuch fpirits as thofe, are not content with fmiting kindly, and reproving, unlefs *their precious oils* break your head. Can fuch as thofe know what felf-loathing and abafement is? if they do, what means this inconfiftent, hateful, hurtful practice? do they not thereby greatly injure their own confcience, condemn themfelves, and difhonour the Lord who bought them? truly this is fo far from proving felf-abafement, through the revelation of the Son of God, that it proves the *reverfe* rather; pride, arrogance, and felf-fufficiency, the natural and predominant qualities of a foul unacquainted with Jefus Chrift. How foolifhly they deceive themfelves by calling *light* darknefs, and *darknefs* light! But let not *us* be thus deceived; for in the day of the manifeftation of Jefus, the haughtinefs of man is brought low, his pride abafed, and the Lord
            alone

alone exalted. And if this is proved by a second fruit, as before-mentioned, let us remark, that true self-abasement excites to love, forgiveness, friendship, kindness, fellow-feeling and compassion amongst men, and as it is an everlasting stain upon the glory of all flesh, Jesus only remains to be adored, reverenced and esteemed of all his children. *Unto you therefore which believe he is precious,* 1 Pet. ii. 7. Precious in his name; *his name is as ointment poured forth, therefore do the virgins love him.* The name of Jesus is precious, not only in its sound, or as that by which we distinguish his beloved person from all other beings, but great is the *mystery* of his precious name; he is called Jesus, because he saves his people from their sins; his name is expressive of the condition of his person. If he rightly bears the name of Jesus, then *hath he saved* his people from their sins; and if he bears that name for ever, then hath he saved them with an *everlasting* salvation. This is the name that gives glory unto God on high, brought peace to the earth, and good-will towards man. All his sacred names, whether the *Woman's Seed,* the *Shiloh,* the *Wonderful,* the *Plant of Renown,* the *Desire of Nations,* the *Branch,* or *Emmanuel,* are gathered into this unctuous name *Jesus.* This name however compendious, contains not only all his former names, but all the grace and glory revealed and pointed out by them, is at once exhibited in this new and glorious name *Jesus.* It is a name a-
bove

bove every name; every knee shall bow to it in heaven, in earth, and under the earth; yea, *every tongue shall confess, that Jesus Christ is Lord, to the glory of God the Father*, Phil. ii. 11. All that is called God, and that is to be worshipped, is known in this name. Now is the day come, when *there shall be one Lord, and his name one*, Zech. xiv. 9. *This name is a strong tower, the righteous shall run into it and shall be safe*. How chearing, how balmy, how valuable this name is to a christian no tongue can ever tell! it is a full confession of his faith, and a perfect *answer* given to every one who asketh, a reason of the hope that is in us. Would they ask us of what religion? we answer, *Jesus*. Would they ask us what proof we give of christianity? we answer, *Jesus*. Would they ask what righteousness we have? we answer, *Jesus*. What holiness? *Jesus*. What wisdom? *Jesus*. What redemption from sin, hell, and death? *Jesus*. What hope of eternal glory? *Jesus*. This name is an answer of faith, given by the christian, to men or devils, who would reason with him. How dry and tastelefs is every book, sermon, and ordinance, which is not sweetned by this precious name! without this, the most admired oratory is but a meer croaking. How empty and flat the finest eloquence where this emphatic name of *Jesus* is not found! what is all the wisdom of words, and the enticements of speech, where *this* is not? what is all preaching, praying, reading, meditating on religious matters, where
this

this name is not the doctrine, the argument, the application, the petition, the converſation, yea, the anointing in all? I ſay, what is all, without this, but formality and dulneſs? Therefore is this name truly ſweet and precious to every chriſtian; the name of *Jeſus* is written upon his heart.

Jeſus is truly precious in his perſon to a believer, and that under two conſiderations, that of his *myſtery* and of our ſalvation in him, and that of his *beauty* and powerful attraction.

He is precious in his *myſtery* as *God-man*; wherein the Creator's marriage with the creature is exemplified: in which union, through his blood-ſhedding and death, we are made the righteouſneſs of God, holy, pure, and without ſin. He is precious as our durable riches and righteouſneſs, as him in whom are all our treaſures of grace and eternal glory.

He is precious, as beautiful, and of powerful attraction: Oh! he is *fairer than the ſons of men! He is white and ruddy, the ſtandard-bearer amongſt ten thouſand!* When we have but a glimpſe of that *perfection of beauty* which dwells in him; we wonder, we admire, we love, we adore, and loſe ſight of heaven and earth in him! He becoming *all and in all* unto us; forgetting all things, yea, for a ſeaſon forgetting our benefits and riches by him; we gaze upon *his* glory, and, through the views of *his* brightneſs, ſwallow large draughts of wonder, delight, love, deſire, and joy unſpeakable! we
forget

forget both our poverty and riches, and caught up into amazement at the beauties of his holiness, we are as those created on purpose to admire *him! his* glory, *his* beauty, *his* excellency, is all the language of our souls! without considering *our* knowledge, *our* faith, or salvation, we only now consider him, contemplate him, and cry, it is good for us to be here; wondering and silently admiring the untold beauties of that *dear Man* who died for us. Whilst the beamings of his beauty, warming and attracting the heart, at length burst our feeble souls with praise: Hail *Son of Mary,* hail, hail, all hail thou *Bridegroom* of the Church; hail thou *perfection of beauty,* who shineft out of Zion! Glory be to *Thee* thou beautiful Emmanuel! Glory be to *Thee* thou *altogether lovely* Lord Jesus! Glory and honour be to *Thee* my Beloved: *Thy head is as the most fine gold, thy locks are bushy, and black as a raven, thy eyes are as the eyes of doves by the rivers of waters, washed with milk, and fitly set; thy cheeks are as a bed of spices, as sweet flowers; thy lips like lillies, dropping sweet-smelling myrrh; thy hands as gold rings set with beryl; thy belly as bright ivory overlaid with sapphires; thy legs as pillars of marble set upon sockets of fine gold; thy countenance as Lebanon, excellent as the cedars; thy mouth is most sweet, yea thou art altogether lovely.* Glory, honour, and eternal thanksgiving, be to *Thee* thou lovely, beauteous *Son of man,* who art *in the midst of the gol-*
den

den *candlesticks, cloathed with a garment down to the foot, and girt about thy paps with a golden girdle; whose head and hairs are white like wool, as white as snow; and whose eyes are like a flame of fire; whose feet are like fine brass burning in a furnace; and whose voice is as the sound of many waters: who holdest in thy right hand seven stars, whilst out of thy mouth goeth a sharp two-edged sword; and thy countenance as the sun shining in its full strength.* Glory be to Thee O Lord. O how excellent the *Person!* how divine the *beauties* of our *Jesus!* In comparison of *him* all created glories are gross darkness, and the most refined beauty is deformity. *He* is indeed precious beyond description; and yet what we now see, is but *darkly, as through a glass*, but when we shall see him with open face, and without a cloud, what shall we see! what shall we feel! *that* our tongues dare not attempt to tell; nor is it possible that words should ever paint it, because it *doth not yet appear what we shall be*, but it is enough, *that we shall be like him, for we shall see him as he is;* until *then* we express all the desire of our souls in a few words: We *beseech thee shew* us *thy glory*, let thy presence go up with us, and let all thy goodness pass before us.

He is precious in his atoning blood and death; where he is to the *Jew a stumbling-block, and to the Greek foolishness,* he is to us, *the wisdom and power of God unto salvation.* How precious the form, where he looks like he had

had been slain! and that his *sufferings, blood* and *death* are precious to the christian; witness that sharp-sighted and burning jealousy in every true believer's bosom; of all things in heaven and earth, lest it should take place of his precious blood, or join itself with it in the matter of our redemption and salvation; and whatever we detect assuming these honours, whether they wear *earthly* or *heavenly* forms, we spare them not, but pursue them with anathema's to the lowest hell, as traitors to the King of glory. And *to* every sound and object, which would charm our hearts from this, let us shut our ears, our eyes, and resolutely abide by the fountain of his blood, and evidence how precious a crucified Jesus is to us; yea, and in comparison of *this*, let us, with Job, say, *If I was perfect, I would not know my soul, but would despise my life.* In this sense, sacrificing *all*, whether *light, love,* knowledge, faith, yea, all *our* goodness, to the honour of *His* most precious blood.

He is precious in his gospel; his gospel is his heart and nature transcribed to man. All who profess to preach the christian religion are in a measure sensible, that the gospel is the only valuable sound; and therefore whatever they preach, each calls what he preaches, the gospel. Is preaching upon state affairs the gospel? is the preaching of dry morals, or the rules of Seneca, the gospel? is the preaching against the divinity and atonement of the blessed Jesus, the gospel? or is it the gospel to make man a co-partner with Jesus Christ in the work of salvation? is the threatning mankind with hell and damnation for their sin, and promising them eternal life on the amendment of their ways, the gospel? or, is it the gospel to preach the necessity of *this*, and the *other thing*, as wrought *by us* as our own work, or *in us* as the work of the Spirit, for our salvation and eternal life? if the gospel is not only God's good word, or sayings, but as the angel declared, *tidings of great joy, which should be unto all people*, if it is to be distinguished from the *law given by Moses*, as that *grace and truth which came by Jesus Christ*, wherein does that, which I have mentioned, answer this character? The gospel is the revelation of the love of God unto mankind by Jesus Christ, in whom he hath destroyed our sins, and saved our souls, through his death and sacrifice; or, it is contained in these words, *God was in Christ, reconciling the world to himself, not imputing their trespasses unto them*, 1 Cor. v. 19. and as the gospel thus exalts Jesus as the *salvation of God unto the ends of the earth*, and abases the creature; it is precious to the christian; it is a *joyful sound*, it refreshes and chears the heart, and is a cordial to the fainting spirit: It is what a truly christian heart prizes above thousands of gold and silver: nor is there any famine they would so much dread as a famine of the chearing word. Until a person knows to distinguish it from every other sound, there will

will be no real satisfaction; they will be expecting it in the *whirl-wind*, in the *fire*, and in the *earthquake*; but when they have heard the *small still voice*, they cease from noise and clamour, and converse with Jesus in a calmer manner, in a more familiar way: the gospel, as the *wisdom and power of God*, recommends itself to their conscience, insomuch that they no longer look to the character of man, as learned, wise, or holy, to recommend the word unto them, and indeed here is the main difference between *such* who know the gospel in truth, and such who do not; the *former* being taught it of the *Holy Ghost*, the *latter* receiving it from *man*. *Whoso will lose his life for my sake, and the gospel*, saith our Saviour, *the same shall find it*. And, as all our power and excellencies are slain by the reception of the gospel; we have the most reason to expect it amongst the people who are most despised, against *whom* are vented the most bitter invectives, calumnies and reproaches, especially where they endure them patiently and joyfully; a true sign that they have lost their lives for Christ's sake and his gospel. Thus is it precious to the christian who counts himself no loser, though he hath lost all to win Christ and his gospel.

Jesus is precious in his people; therefore were they of *old accounted of*, as the *only excellent ones upon earth*. When we once learn the relation between *Jesus* and his people, expressed in these words, *Forasmuch as you did it unto them*,

G 2

them, you did unto me, Matt. xxv. 45. And when Saul, madly breathing out slaughters against his children, was asked this question by him, *Why persecutest thou me?* Acts ix. 4. *Then,* and not until *then,* are we able to conceive aright of the children of God, and to set a proper value upon them; as it will plainly appear unto us, that Christ and his people are so truly *one,* that there is no meddling with *one* without the *other.* All the deeds, whether good or bad, done unto them are set down by Jesus, and confirmed in heaven as done unto him. All the slights put upon *them,* are but so many slights put upon *him*; *their* joy is *his, their* sorrow *his, their* temptations *his, their* griefs *his, their* troubles and persecutions all *his.*

Read, and tremble, ye smoaking fire-brands, whom nothing will satisfy but the destruction of his people: Ye children of violence, who oppress them, and always study to work them distress and anguish: Ye venemous and subtle spirits, who lie in wait for their halting, and by evil speech, with sly serpentine insinuations endeavour as much as in you to ruin them. I say, tremble when you read, that whatsoever you do unto *them,* you do unto the *Lord* who created you, and redeemed you! O horrible to consider then how he is treated amongst men! yea, and amongst such who profess to be his friends! Would you have it thought that you are mad against *Jesus,* and earnestly desire *his* destruction? would you have it thought
that

that you study to load *him* with distress and anguish, and to lie in wait by evil speech and serpentine cunning to ruin *him*? God forbid, say you, that we should treat *him* so. But what will you do to acquit yourselves of it? the word of God finds you guilty, the Holy Ghost maintains the charge against you: Is Christ divided? or can you when you wound, distinguish the *head* from the *members*? doth not the harmony of the body teach us, that the *head* cannot be an idle spectator whilst the other *members* are a mangling, nor be insensible when they endure torment? The children and bride of Jesus are the most *tender* part of his body, they are the apple of his eye, Zech. ii. 8. which part is so quick and sensitive as not to admit of the smallest dust without intolerable torment; yea, when in the days of his flesh, he was buffeted, spit upon, and scourged, until his bones appeared through the bleeding furrows, yet he complained not, but endured it patiently, and unto the end prayed for his persecutors. But no sooner did the zealot Saul and his fellows begin to afflict his poor church, but as one awakened by the most exquisite torments, he cries out with the utmost fervour, *Saul, Saul, why persecutest thou me?* why didst thou keep the cloaths of the men who stoned *me* at Jerusalem, why wast thou consenting to *my* death, and with a merciless and unrelenting eye, beheldst *me* dashed in pieces by the ponderous stones thrown upon

my

my head, with all the furious rage of men, whose hearts were harder than the stones they threw? why didst thou drag *me* with spite and cruelty out of every house, and make havock of me? And is it not enough that thou hast treated *me* thus at *Jerusalem*, but that thou must pursue me to *Damascus* also, to bring me bound before the blood-thirsty priests? What have *I* done to thee? wherein have *I* offended thee, that thou puttest me to this *second* pain, by *far* more grievous than the *first*? constraining me thus to reason with thee, *Saul, Saul, why persecutest thou me? is it not hard for thee to kick against the pricks?* to fight against thy God, a potsherd of earth to strive with his maker? Learn hence, what a tender feeling Jesus hath of all the miseries and distress of his children. And O! would to God that every persecuting Saul, every envious, malicious, back-biting, slanderous, lying spirit against his people, could so effectually hear the Saviour's voice, crying to them, *Why persecutest thou me?* why art thou envious and malicious against *me?* why dost thou backbite and slander *me?* why dost thou so cruelly speak lies of *me?* But then some one will say, If we believed them children of God, we would not treat them so; but as we think they are not, they deserve such treatment. When a certain Jewish zealot, who thought that none but such of his own nation had any right to his love, hearing our Saviour enjoin us to love

our

our neighbour, impertinently afked him who was his neighbour: (thereby making an antichriftian diftinction, as if none were to be fo accounted of, but fuch of his own nation, church and fentiment) He was anfwered in a parable, where, under the fimilitude of the Samaritan, he was taught that his fellow-creature, of whatever nation, church, or fentiment, was his neighbour. Moreover, fhould it be granted that your diftinction is juft, as you do not always know who are the children of God, or who are not; you have no authority for your diftinction: and when you have once acknowledged them fuch, nothing is more common than for you to call back the verdict you once paffed in their favour, and to *condemn* whom you once *acquitted*, whenever you have received fome ill impreffions toward them; and, blinded with prejudice and paffion, you thus deal with them, tho' *contrary*, probably, to your own fentiment, and unto what you would have others think of you. But what then, you poor changing worms! do you think God is fuch a one as yourfelves, *juftify* and *condemn*, juft as you do? I am perfuaded, you would fain have him fo, but for your happinefs, and the happinefs of thofe whom you condemn, *Jefus* is the fame yefterday, to-day, and for ever. O *then* do not deceive yourfelves with foolifh quibbles, forafmuch as you have caufe to fear, you wound and injure *Jefus Chrift* in every *fon or daughter*

of

of Adam, whom you thus grieve and oppress. It is an eternal inconsistency for you to profess friendship to the *Head,* whilst you wound and vex the *members;* to profess love to the *Bridegroom,* whilst you hate the *bride,* and pour contempt upon *her* in any one individual of his children. To say, I abhor the thought of giving *Jesus* pain, and immediately pierce the *apple of his eye.* Consider these things, you that *eat up his people as grass;* feeding upon their sins until you are fat and strong, not ceasing to bite and devour, taking part with the *accuser of the brethren* against those whom God hath justified.

But unto every soul who hath a right apprehension of Jesus, *he* is precious in his people; and they know what it is to discern the body of the Lord, and not as those Corinthians, who having respect of persons amongst them, came unworthily to the table of the Lord, as though they could partake of that, and the *table of devils* also.

There is nothing so powerfully excites to brotherly love and kindness, yea, to universal kindness and compassion to mankind, as a gospel view of Jesus Christ our Lord.

Do we in heart believe that whatsoever is done to his *children* is done unto *him?* how tender shall we *then be* of grieving and oppressing them; can we then hate them, whisper against them, envy them, and uncharitably condemn them? O God forbid! it is utterly inconsistent with

with a true veneration for Jesus Christ. Can we see them hungry, and not feed them; thirsty, and not give them drink; naked, and not cloath them; in prison, and not visit them? Doth not he say, forasmuch as we *do it not to them*, yea to the least of *them*, we do it not to *him*? what a robbing of Jesus would this be, a keeping back from him what he hath given us in trust for the use of all his children. Are any of them despised, sorrowful, troubled on every side, and grievously tempted, and will we be shy of them, shun them and disown them? Will not this be to be ashamed of the humiliation of *Jesus*, and to leave *him* and forsake *him* in the day of his temptation, as the affliction of his people is a filling up of the sufferings of Jesus which are behind? Let us not stumble at *him* now, as sundry did, on the *first* day of his distress; but a soul, who glories in his humiliation, and draws all his comfort from those deep *wells of salvation*, can never be offended at him, in his despised suffering members, as he will, under every form and appearance, be precious to all such.

He is precious in his children to every one who walketh in the light, for there we love our brethren, *and see none occasion of stumbling in them*. Whosoever can see Jesus as *he is*, can see his children like him; for the King's daughter is all glorious within. O happy, happy spouse and bride of Jesus! whom God loves, for whom Jesus hath died, whom angels

gels with joy attend. Let my tongue for ever cleave to the roof of my mouth, ere I speak evil of *Thee*; and let my right hand forget its cunning, ere I grow weary of waiting upon *Thee*, or of being an useful, as I am a living member in *thy* body; or ere I cease to deliver *Thee* affectionately and faithfully, the whole of every message our common Head and Husband shall intrust me with to *thee*; for in *thee* I behold thy Husband's beauty, love and grace, yea all the glories of that eternal redemption and salvation, which *He* obtained for *thee*. Therefore, I summon all my powers to join with *thee* in ascribing all praise, might, majesty, dominion, honour, power, and glory, unto *Jesus*, the Lord of life and glory, in time and to eternity. *Amen.*

THE
SALT of the SACRIFICE;

OR, THE TRUE

Christian Baptism

DELINEATED,

According to REASON and SPIRIT:

As gathered from sundry Discourses on that Subject.

By JAMES RELLY.

HAVING *abolished in his flesh the enmity, the law of commandments, contained in ordinances, for to make in himself, of twain, one new man, so making peace,* Eph. ii. 15.—*Blotting out the hand-writing of ordinances, that was against us, which was contrary to us, and took it out of the way, nailing it to his cross,* Col. ii. 14.

LONDON:

Printed for the AUTHOR; and sold by S. BLADON, Bookseller, in *Paternoster-row.*—Price Two Shillings.

TO THE READER.

AMONG those who may read the following treatise, on the Reason and Spirit of Baptism, there will be many who, instead of attending to argument, or of submitting to the conviction of truth, will be challenging the reasons of such a publication; as if it were extremely difficult, if not totally impossible, for the author to propose to himself, or to the community, any valuable end, by writing on such a subject.

Prepossession disqualifies men for reading with candour and impartiality; and even irritates them to condemn, where they have not yet heard: to prevent, if possible, the lead of such a spirit, I shall endeavour in this preface to the reader, to render such reasons for my writing and publishing on the subject of ordinances, as will, I trust, satisfy the truly candid, that I have not acted in it altogether without reason.

Satisfied

Satisfied with a positive testimony, concerning Jesus the Son of God, as the perfected and final salvation, set forth before the face of all people; many years elapsed before I saw it needful to treat negatively of the matter; by an attempt to shew, that certain usages in the church, which are judged to contain the essence of christianity, are not perfectly consistent with the truth of Christ.

The things, which I and others were taught to abstain from, as weak and beggarly elements, were never animadverted on in my discourses, only when justice to such passages of scripture as I happened to treat on absolutely required it; and then they were touched with all possible brevity, and tenderness.

The use of ordinances amongst others, I never inveighed against; nor did I at any time attempt, either publicly or privately, to dissuade men from subjection to them: nay, so far was I from desiring to impose my faith on others, that I rather discouraged their abstinence from those things, when it appeared that their conviction was not from above.

Under this influence, faithfully following the light that directed my own path, I should
have

have rested well content that all mankind should do the same, however they might differ from me; nor was it possible for me to censure any man for thinking otherwise than my self; having these words engraven on my heart, " No man can receive any thing, except it be given him from above."

The utmost that my friends and I sought for was, that having faith, we might be permitted to have it to ourselves; and this we thought we had a right to expect: but, alas, we were taught by experience, that our hopes were by much too sanguine; and that, considering the attachments of men to externals in religion, we had but little reason to expect such a toleration as exempted us from their censure.

We were calumniated as evil-doers; and loaded with reproaches, as neglecters and contemners of divine ordinances; the most rigorous, and even severe censures, were estimated as mild, in comparison of our deserts, so very atrocious were our errors judged to be. That we might possibly err from mistake, or that we had the least degree of good-meaning among us, or that we were able to render but the shadow of a reason for our conduct, were hypotheses much too favourable for our indulgence.

It was constantly insinuated, and even affirmed, That we, bidding defiance to revelation and reason, neglected the ordinances of God, and poured contempt on them, only because they were commanded, and the continual observance of them enjoined us, in the Bible; and, that having no colourable plea for our proceedings, we affected to treat all reproof, and every attempt to regulate our sentiments, with wanton sneering and ridicule.

Our adversaries continued challenging, and even defying us to render a reason of our faith; and our forbearance made them not only conclude, but affirm, that we had no reason to render. Hence, we were registered as obstinate hereticks, rejected and cut off from the Christian name, in their judgment; and exposed to feel the smart of every rod of power, but that which providence has not put into their hands.

I could yet have been well satisfied, to have possessed my soul in patience, and peaceably to have endured what I esteemed as the reproaches of Christ; but some sincere hearts stumbling, and others growing uneasy, it was judged needful that a defence should be made, by rendering a reason of the hope that is in us, respecting these matters.

This induced me from time to time to treat on the subject of ordinances; and at last it was thought right that I should print those discourses, as a proof that we had a foundation for our faith: but, as I had no notes by me, to assist my memory in recapitulating by the pen, what without pre-meditation I had delivered in the congregation, it may not be expected, that I should recollect, with any precifeness, what I had thus delivered; therefore, I chose to entitle it, as a gathering from sundry discourses, &c.

I can propose none other advantage to myself from this publication, than what consists in taking up the cross of Christ, and in following Him. But as mankind, in proportion as they are subject to ordinances, as they are bigoted to externals under the idea of real christianity, are, in my judgment, deprived of the sweet felicity of the gospel; and are either strangers to, or greatly estranged from, the adorable Person, and imbibed Spirit of our Saviour. So if by means of this, or by any other, they may be brought to see that Jesus is All and in All—That He is before all things,

things, and that by Him all things confist—That in Him, as the First and the Last, the curse is removed—That in Him all the promises are yea, and amen—That He is the Spirit, the Substance, the Accomplishment, and Final End of every ordinance; the advantage is great, as the comfort is real, both in him who communicates, and in him who receiveth.

If these matters, so well attested, and explicitly taught in the holy Scriptures, are, as the things of Christ, shewn to us by the Spirit of Truth; they will not only endear the Person and Salvation of Christ to us, but they will endear all his creatures to us also, for his sake; and herein consists the true spirit of morality; for if love thinketh no evil, much less will it injure its neighbour.

He who believeth doth not make haste—Nor is this a hasty publication.—The manuscript has lain by me these three years; during which time, I have often seriously read it over; and though my frames of mind at such times have been various, yet I have always found, in the reading of it, a full conviction of its truth; my conscience also always bearing me witness, that it was writ-

ten

ten with a single eye, to the glory and honour of our Lord Jesus Christ.

But, as the love of Jesus renders the mind exceedingly tender, I have hitherto delayed printing it, lest, though some approved of it, other sincere hearts might possibly feel an uneasiness, to them unknown before; this I considered as a certain misery to my self, as the unfeigned sorrow of my fellow creature is really my own.

Therefore, nothing but the conviction, that I seek not myself, but Christ Jesus the Lord; and that my witness is on high, that I had nothing in view in writing it, nor have I any thing in view in publishing it, but the glory of Divine Grace, as exhibited by Jesus Christ our Lord; and that I believe it to be really Spirit and Truth; and that as such, it may be useful in turning men from darkness to light, and from touching, tasting, and handling what perishes with the using, to the incorruptible bread of life: these, I say, with the judgment of my friends, are the only considerations which could possibly induce me to print on the subject of ordinances.

If there be yet other objections to the doctrine contained in this treatise, than those which

which I have already noticed, and anfwered, or at leaft, have attempted to anfwer, I declare I know them not: therefore, let it not be imputed to a timid, or deceitful filence in me, that I have not noticed them; for I here promife, that when I do know them, as I feel my heart is not incorrigible, I will pay a ferious and due attention to them.

J. R.

ONE BAPTISM.

One Baptism. Ephes. iv. 5.

THE Apostle to the Hebrews speaks of the doctrine of Baptisms, as of many; but in the text before us, he emphatically mentions "One Baptism." "One Baptism," as only necessary; "One Baptism," as comprehensive of the many; and as that wherein every other Baptism hath had its final period.

The Baptism mentioned in the text is, not only simply and invariably one, but the only one; and this is manifest, not only from the emphatic "One Baptism," but also from the articles wherewith it is classed; "One Lord, One Faith," each of which, is in truth, unchangeably one, and excluding all others.

What this one necessary Christian Baptism is, remains still to be a matter of dispute among men. There are a few indeed who believe the one Baptism to be spiritual, and that (relating to what hath been accomplished in Christ) it operates upon the mind and conscience, through the faith of him: but these are but few. The multitude are on the other side of the question, and believe, or pretend to believe, that it is external, and intends the Baptism of water only.

To investigate the truth of this One Baptism, and to hold it up to public view, is my present design: and as it is impossible, in my judgment, for us to attain to truth in things of this nature, while we follow the lead of custom, tradition, and human authorities, I purpose to set very lightly by these, and to confine myself to the scriptures, and to sound reason; and this I promise to do, at least, in truth and faithfulness; not courting the favour of any man, nor dreading his frown. As I am well aware of the reception this attempt will meet with in the world from man's native ignorance of truth, and from his attachment to the works of his own hands, however external and consisting of bodily exercise, I shall feel no disappointment from that quarter. Thus anticipating their fury, but with a view to their instruction and happiness, and as a witness of the glory of Christ, I shall cease from care and fear, and persist in speaking the words of truth and soberness.

That Water-baptism was not an ordinance of our Lord's appointing, is manifest, from its being used by John Baptist, before our Saviour entred upon his office; and that it was not an ordinance of Moses, or of the prophets, is as manifest, from its not being once mentioned in all their writings: and yet,

yet, something similar to Water-baptism seems to have been practised among the Jews, before the days of John Baptist. They are said, to have enjoined the washing of water, as a necessary circumstance towards making a complete proselyte.

It is not improbable, but that the Jews might have taken the custom from the law of Moses; where ablutions of that kind are commanded to the priests, and to such who had the plague of leprosy; or, who had defiled themselves by contact with any thing unclean. Hence the Jews, regarding the Gentiles as unclean, would not admit them as complete proselytes, until they had been thus washed, or baptized. Accordingly, when John Baptist came baptizing with water, the Jews were so far from considering his practice as novel, or as an innovation, that they rather seemed as people accustomed to the usage; and consequently, in their various ranks and degrees, attended to be baptized of him, in Jordan. But I do not mean to insinuate, that John Baptist took his mission and pattern from the Jewish custom: nay, but John had a divine warrant for what he did, both respecting the thing, and the manner of it.

Our Saviour bears an honourable testimony of John, where he says, "Verily I say unto you, among them that are born of women, there hath not risen a greater than John the Baptist." But except some other meaning

meaning be tolerated here, than what appears upon the face of the letter, it will more than imply that Jesus himself was not greater than John the Baptist, since he also was born of a woman; than which nothing can be more absurd, or a more palpable contradiction to the testimony of all the prophets and apostles concerning him.

But our Lord's meaning in the proposition, is, as I conceive, to be understood as follows: Women, in the scriptures, are often considered as a symbol of weakness; hence the prophet, " My people, children are their oppressors, and women rule over them." And in the above, they are emblematical of the darkness and weakness of the Old Testament dispensation; and to be born of women, in the text, denotes a being under that dispensation; which dispensation, under various administrations, extended from Adam to Christ. The kingdom of heaven, contrasted to this state in the text, intends the Christian dispensation; or, our Saviour must have (only) taught that the least angelic power, was greater than John; since all human beings, however glorified, (Adam and Eve excepted) were literally born of women. But it doth not appear to have been our Lord's design, to teach that angels were greater than John the Baptist; but that the kingdom of heaven intends the gospel state; and that the being born of women signifies the law; which

was

was weak, and had but the shadow of good things; and that the greatest, under the latter state, was not equal to the least under the former, in point of righteousness, peace, and joy in the Holy Ghost.

Thus the Old Testament dispensation is represented as a state of bondage and fear; whilst the New Testament, or Christian dispensation, is that of the spirit of adoption, where we cry Abba, Father. Again, the former is said to contain but the pattern of heavenly things, but the latter contains the heavenly things themselves: under the former, they are said to be born of women, alluding to their imperfect means of instruction, and to that scantiness, in point of real happiness, unto which they attained; but under the latter, they are said (i. e. believers) to be in the kingdom of heaven, where they are born of God. And in this latter, the least, as born of God, is greater than the greatest under the former, as born of women.

Thus, from Adam to Christ, there was none greater than John the Baptist; no, not Moses, nor Elias, nor any one of the prophets. The greatness of the prophets and apostles is not estimated by creature-excellence, or by any advantage of person or station, which one possessed above another, but this was always to be determined of by the Divine Presence; he who had the greatest measure of the Spirit of Christ, and who was most peculiarly taught of him, was ever esteemed of in the church as the greatest; in which sense, none of those who went before Him were greater than John the Baptist: For John came in the full spirit and power of Elias, and had also the additional honour of pointing out in person, the Lamb of God, who took away the sins of the world. But the least in the kingdom of heaven is greater than John; by which we are to understand, either Christians in general, or rather (as I conceive) the apostles, &c. in particular, the least of whom had more of the Spirit of Christ, and was more immediately acquainted with the glories of his person, and the nature of his kingdom, than John the Baptist was. Our Lord's design in supporting the dignity of the Baptist was to shew, that though his practice was not perfectly correspondent with that of Moses, and of the prophets; yet that he, being inferior to none of them, might have an immediate and particular mission from God, and which was not limited to their rules; thereby accounting for his using Water-baptism, which they did not.

I have said, that under the Old Testament there were various administrations; as from Adam to the flood; from the flood to Moses; from Moses to the prophets; from the prophets to John the Baptist; and from John the Baptist to the accomplishment of all things in Christ. It is possible that they
might

might be much more varied, but the above being sufficient to anfwer my purpofe, I decline attempting it. It may be obferved that thefe, as the times of the Mefliah drew nigher, continued to brighten upon the church, from one degree of brightnefs unto another. From Adam to the flood, they had the promife of the Mefliah, the ufe of facrifices, &c; from the flood to Mofes, their fprings of faith, and its directory to its object, received fome additions, in fundry promifes and figures, and in the appearances of the divine prefence, with the inftitution of circumcifion, the feaft of the Pafchal Lamb, &c. all which were properly digefted in Mofes' code, with many additions ftill, all written by the finger of God. As an addition to this, ftill coming on to perfection, fucceeded the prophets, with new inftructions, promifes, &c. enforced by fimilitudes not contained in the former; unto thefe fucceeded John the Baptift, as a prophet, yea, and more than a prophet, being the immediate forerunner of the Mefliah, the meffenger before his face to prepare his way; and he, by the divine direction, added to all the former figures of Chrift, and to the fymbol of man's falvation and purity in him, the article of Water-baptifm; which, as an outward wafhing and cleanfing, was ftill more fignificant of that promifed purification of the people, now foon to be accomplifhed through the offering up of the Mefliah. Upon which

I build the following propositions;—1. That Water-baptism was not practised, by divine authority, before John;—2. That John the Baptism did practise it by divine authority;—3. That it was temporary, and that John was apprized of this, and had the signs of its period given him;—4. That it was an addition to the ceremonial law, and a figure of Christ, and cannot in reason, nor spirit, extend beyond the accomplishment of all things in Him. To prove the first, the silence of the scriptures is sufficient. To prove the second, we have not only our Lord's vindication of John, as before recited, but we have also the testimony of the Baptist himself, who says, "But he that sent me to baptize with water, the same said unto me, &c." Here we learn, that he who distinguished to the Baptist's notice, the person of Jesus, was the same that sent him to baptize with water; but as none but the Spirit of truth could glorify the one, so none but the same Spirit could send him to administer the other. The third proposition, I conceive to be also proveable from the Baptist's own confession, "And I knew him not: but he that sent me to baptize with water, the same said unto me, Upon whom thou shalt see the Spirit descending and remaining on him, the same is he which baptizeth with the Holy Ghost;" those words contain at least a tacit acknowledgment, that John, upon being sent to baptize with water, was

given

given to understand, that his ministry and Baptism should be of no long continuance; for that the Lord's Messiah, or the kingdom of heaven was at hand; who, as the spirit and substance of his ministry, and as the true administrator of spiritual Baptism, (of which his Baptism of water was only a figure) should totally supersede and make void his commission. Which commission, in its original intention, was only an introduction to our Lord's coming, a preparation of his way, and therefore ceasing of course upon his being made manifest unto Israel. I say, it may be gathered from John's own confession, that he was apprized of this, upon his being sent out to baptize with water; hence also his testimony concerning Jesus, "He must increase, but I must decrease." Yea, and he had a certain infallible sign given him withal, whereby he was not only to distinguish the person who was to baptize with the Holy Ghost, but also the date of that epoch; "Upon whom thou shalt see the "Spirit descending and remaining on him, "the same is he which baptizeth with the "Holy Ghost;" but this sign did not appear until Christ himself was baptized with water: as we read, "And Jesus when he "was baptized, went up straightway out of "the water: and lo, the heavens were open-"ed unto him, and he saw the Spirit of "God descending like a dove, and lighting "upon him." The spirit, and the meaning

ing of which, I shall have an occasion to speak of in another place.

I have proposed, that Water-baptism was an aggregate to the ceremonial law, and typical of man's salvation in Christ; which is synonimous with the Baptism of the Holy Ghost: and here it will be expected that I should give my reasons.

Whatsoever is commanded in the scriptures belongs to the decalogue, or moral law, or to the ceremonial or typical law; or otherwise, to some new law of commandment, given by Christ, or his apostles. I have chosen to make those distinctions, not that they all exist in my own sentiment, but as they are the common received rules, by which men determine of the scripture precepts.

The whole of the moral law, as the eternal invariable rule of righteousness, is contained in the Old Testament; but Water-baptism is not found in the Old Testament, therefore Water-baptism is no part of the moral law. Again, the decalogue or moral law, as written by the finger of God, was unalterable, permanent, and perfect in its extension and circumscription, and therefore cannot admit of diminution; no, not from the consideration of any change of circumstance in man, to whom it was given: neither can it admit of interpolations nor additions. Therefore, the New Testament contains no mitigation of the moral law, nor doth it contain any additions to it; but the New Testament is rather an elucidation and fulfilling of the law, gloriously magnifying it, and making it honourable. Hence my argument—Water-baptism's being mentioned or even commanded in the New Testament, as it is only mentioned or commanded there, is so far from being a proof of its being contained in the decalogue or moral law, that it infallibly proves the contrary. Again, if Water-baptism was implied in the moral law, then, without the consideration of faith in Christ, it would be the duty of all men to submit to it. But this is contrary to the scriptures, and to the generally-received sense of things, and therefore needs none other confutation.

The most generally received sense of Water-baptism is, that it is an ordinance of Christ, a new-testament or gospel command, and independent of the law of Moses. I have already thrown out a hint relative to this matter, but I shall now treat it more explicitly: Water-baptism, as I have already shewn, was practised by John the Baptist, before the Lord Christ was manifest unto Israel; therefore, Water-baptism hath not its original from the doctrine nor practice of Christ; hence it cannot be an ordinance of Christ. To this it will be replied, that though Water-baptism be not originally an ordinance of Christ's institution, yet he approved

proved of it, adopted it, and commanded his disciples to practise it.

To this I answer—The various usages in the church until Christ, had doubtless their significancy, and were adapted to their particular dispensations, nor could the faithful but approve of those usages: hence our Lord approved of Water-baptism as a significant mystery, and a practice suited to that dispensation. But this proves not that he intended its continuance in the church, nor indeed that it should continue longer than until the Baptism of the Holy Ghost took place. That our Lord adopted the practice of Water-baptism, is so far from being plain, that I think the contrary appears; this we are certain of, that Jesus himself baptized none, and therefore it cannot be said that he personally adopted the practice. It is true, that the disciples of our Lord Jesus Christ, are not required to imitate him in all things, there being many particulars in his life, and death, which were peculiar to himself; yet I cannot but conclude, that the practice of every gospel minister, is so perfectly exhibited and circumscribed in the example of the Holy Jesus, that no man is left at liberty to practise innovations. But Jesus himself baptized none, therefore no man, following his steps, can find from his example any authority to use Water-baptism. Hence, the Apostle to the Gentiles says, that he " was not sent
" to

"to baptize, but to preach the gospel;" which is an intimation by the way, that Water-baptism is no part of the gospel; or the administration of Water-baptism would, in some sense, be to preach the gospel.

It is confidently asserted, and generally taken for granted, that our Lord commanded his disciples to practise Water-baptism: I have carefully and candidly searched the four Evangelists, but cannot find this commandment; and indeed, it would be a thing not easily accounted for, to find our Saviour commanding them to practise actively, what himself never practised but passively.

But I suppose the commandment generally meant, is in that commission which our Saviour after his resurrection, gave to his disciples; as follows, "Go ye therefore and teach all nations, baptizing them in the name of the Father, and of the Son, and of the Holy Ghost." But laying tradition aside, it becomes questionable, whether Water-baptism be the Baptism meant in the commission. To me, it appears reasonable to conclude the contrary, both from what I have already mentioned, and from what I have yet to say upon the subject. John the Baptist hath very explicitly shewn, that Water-baptism was a dispensation committed to him in particular; " I indeed baptize you with water:" but that the dispensation committed to Christ, was the Baptism of the Holy Ghost; " He
" shall

" shall baptize you with the Holy Ghost and with fire." It is surely impossible to read those words, with an unprejudiced and candid mind, without perceiving that Water-baptism was a figure, and but a figure of spiritual Baptism; and that as such, it was only to continue until the spiritual Baptism took place. And moreover, that as John Baptist was the despenser of the figure, so was Jesus Christ the sole administrator of the substance. These things considered, the proposition that our Lord sent forth his disciples to baptize with water, appears arbitrary, forced, and deformed; not beautified with reason, nor intitled to the shadow of propriety.

Teaching and baptizing are inseparably connected, in our Lord's commission to his disciples; and more than an implication contained, that teaching and even believing, without Baptism, are inefficacious and useless. But of Water-baptism it cannot be said, that it is thus absolutely necessary to the salvation and happiness of mankind; therefore the Baptism of water, is not the Baptism which our Saviour connected with teaching, in his commission to his disciples; but a baptism, rather, without which man in the midst of all his uprightnesses would be yet impure, and though abounding in knowledge, would be still unhappy.

Again, if Water-baptism was the Baptism intended in our Lord's commission to his
apostles,

apostles, then were all the apostles unto whom this commission extended, under a necessity of administring Water-baptism: but our Lord's commission extended unto Paul, his call to the office of an apostle was immediately from Christ, and his commission as ample as that of the other apostles, none excepted: but Paul says, "Christ "sent me not to baptize, but to preach the "gospel." Therefore Water-baptism was not the Baptism intended in our Lord's commission to his apostles.

Again, the commission above mentioned, was given by our Lord after his resurrection, when he had exhibited undeniable proof of his having fulfilled all righteousness: therefore the Baptism contained therein, could not possibly be figurative, nor relate to any thing that was to have its period, but with the present world. But it was manifestly designed, as a perfect invariable rule of apostleship, not only to such who were already thus importantly imployed, but to all those also who should hereafter be dignified with the office. Paul was chosen to the office of an apostle, nor was he a whit behind the chiefest of them, and yet he declares that he was not sent to baptize; (i. e. with water) therefore the Baptism contained in our Lord's commission to his apostles, was not Water-baptism, but something more divine and spiritual.

Having

Having thus contrasted Paul's testimony, to the generally-received sense of our Lord's commission to his apostles, I shall now in their harmony, endeavour to fix a criterion whereby to determine of the truth of this matter. I suppose the term Baptism, in the apostle Paul's declaration, to be of different import from the same term in our Lord's commission to his disciples; by the former is manifestly understood Water-baptism, which the apostle says, he was not sent to practise; and, in my judgment, by the latter is as manifestly intended spiritual Baptism, or that washing and purification of the conscience to God, through the Blood of Jesus; which is ever attendant on the belief of the truth: now, if the apostles were originally sent forth to baptize with the Spirit, as the fruit or consequence of their preaching the pure gospel, which they certainly were, then was their commission the same with that of the apostle Paul; but where any of them mistook the Baptism of the Spirit contained in their commission, for the Baptism of water, the apostle Paul still sets us right, by declaring that it was not contained in his commission; therefore, we must necessarily reason that it was not contained in theirs.

All the apostles were sent to baptize with the Spirit, which they successfully effected by the word of truth; they were all agreed as to spiritual Baptism, that they were sent to administer it by preaching the gospel; but

but with respect to Water-baptism, they were not all satisfied of their being sent to administer it. Nay, the contrary is manifest, from him who says, that he was not sent to baptize, &c. Therefore, the Baptism contained in their commission was that about which they were all agreed, and to the administration of which, each of them was clear of his call. This proves that the apostles were sent to baptize with the Spirit, and not with Water.

To this it will be objected—That the apostle Paul had no intention to deny the practice and utility of Water-baptism, in saying that he was not sent to baptize, &c. in thanking God that he baptized none but a few particulars, &c. but that his design was to check the spirit of party and faction, at that time beginning to lift up its head in the church of Corinth, and which had its rise as follows: For the work of the ministry, for the perfecting of the saints, for the edifying of the body of Christ, God was pleased to send some apostles, some pastors, some teachers, as Paul, Cephas, Apollos, &c. who (though they preached the same gospel, and were under the influence of the same Spirit) might yet in many respects be very differently gifted; with some, Paul's gifts and manner took most, whilst with others, those of Cephas, or of Apollos were most taking. Thus, as they were differently attach'd, and especially if they had received

Water-baptism by their hands, they cried out for Paul, or for Cephas, or Apollos, to the exclusion of the other apostles. Yea, matters were carried so far among them, in the party way, that some pretended to be for Christ, as though he was divided against himself. And though it be very probable, that (by much) the greater part were for Paul, as the person who had first preached the gospel among them, yet it recommended not their proceedings to this apostle, who, to convince them of their error, reasons with them as follows; " Is Christ divided? Was " Paul crucified for you? Or were ye bap-" tized in the name of Paul? I thank God, " that I baptized none of you but Crispus " and Gaius, lest any should say that I had " baptized in mine own name: and I bap-" tized also the houshold of Stephanas: " besides I know not whether I baptized " any other. For Christ sent me not to bap-" tize, but to preach the gospel." Here (say some) the apostle's words are so far from containing a denial of Water-baptism, that they rather intend an excuse for his conduct in not practising it; as is evident from his saying, " Lest any should say that I had baptized in mine own name."

To this I reply, had the apostle judged it prudent to desist from practising such particulars of his office, as either gave offence to mankind, or an occasion to enmity, divisions, and faction to the professors of Jesus, he
would

would have defisted not only from baptizing, but from preaching the gospel also; since (without controversy) wherever it proved a favour of death, as it did to some, it always produced the above effects: but "Woe be "to me (saith he) if I preach not the gos-"pel." Wherefore? Because Christ sent him to preach it. And had he been sent to baptize with water, the same woe would have been to him upon his declining that also; nor could he then have said, I thank God I baptized none of you.

Again—Had it been the apostle's duty to have used Water-baptism, he ought to have administered it at all events, nor is it to be doubted but he would have done so. If the ordinance be divine, mens abuse of it is no reasonable plea for ministers neglect of it: nay, it should rather stir them up to a more diligent and conscientious exercise of themselves in such matters.

Is it enough, is it reasonable to say, I will not do my duty, lest it be misrepresented? Nay, though God our Saviour hath commanded that Water-baptism should be observed, as an ordinance in the church for ever, yet I will not administer it, lest it should be said that I did it in mine own name? Can any man suppose such reasoning as this worthy of an apostle? Or will any man presumptuously impute such palpable chicanery to that Spirit, who is infinite in wisdom and simplicity? God forbid! rather let

let the voice of truth be heard, though it be to the condemnation of our moſt darling opinions.

But yet, ſomething of this nature muſt neceſſarily be ſuppoſed, from the apoſtle's ſaying as recited above, by all ſuch who affirm that Water-baptiſm is a divine ordinance, to be obſerved in the church for ever; or I ſee not that they have any pretenſion, or even the ſhadow of a pretenſion, to a conformity in their ſentiments to the apoſtle's declaration.

To diſpenſe with the commandments of God, for fear of conſequences, would be not only to impeach the divine œconomy, but alſo to aſcribe ſuperior wiſdom, foreknowledge, purity, and prudence to the creature; than which nothing can be more abſurd and blaſphemous. But yet, ſome man will poſſibly aſk me, Did not the apoſtle mean to excuſe his conduct, in receding from the adminiſtration of Water-baptiſm, where he ſays, " Leſt any ſhould ſay that I " had baptized in mine own name?" To which I anſwer—The apoſtle's conduct in the above was free from error, and therefore he could mean nothing leſs than an extenuation of his conduct in the words: he did not only know that it was not his duty to baptize with water, but he alſo knew that it would be contrary to his commiſſion, (if not to the truth itſelf) for him to practiſe Water-baptiſm: hence he ſays, " I thank God " that I baptized none of you," &c. I can

eaſily

easily conceive the reason, and even the expediency of giving God thanks, for my having escaped error, in judgment or practice: but the propriety of giving God thanks for what I have done amiss, or even for my leaving undone the things which I ought to have done, is totally inconceivable to me; and therefore, it is impossible for me to impute that to an apostle, which in myself would be so unreasonable, and senseless.

The apostle's giving God thanks that he baptized none, &c. is so far from supposing that it was right for him to baptize, that it supposes quite the contrary; he was convinced that it would have been wrong in him to have administered it; he knew that Water-baptism teem'd with creature-righteousness, faction, and party in the church; but that it answered no one valuable purpose to counter-balance these: and therefore, he could with much propriety, thank God that he had practised it but little; nor was it possible that his conduct in receding from the practice of it, should need an excuse.

It may indeed be supposed, that the Christians of that day, ignorant of the design of Water-baptism, not knowing unto what it tended, nor yet distinguishing where it had received its accomplishment, were very tenacious of it, as they were of circumcision, and of other typical matters; and therefore, that they were not a little alarmed, when they perceived him, who to the

Gentiles

Gentiles was the first and principal apostle, to decline the administration of it. This might render it needful in some degree, for him to give them a reason of his conduct; which he does, by declaring that Christ had not sent him to baptize, thereby indicating that it was not neglect of duty, novelty, or a desire of being singular, that occasioned his giving up Water-baptism, but his knowledge of his commission, he was not sent to baptize with water. And, that though tradition, the general voice, and even his own popularity required that he should baptize with water, yet he would not go beyond his commission, he would not practise what he was not called unto, upon any consideration whatever; "Christ sent me not to baptize, "(saith he) but to preach the gospel." Here we learn, that the true gospel minister knows what he is called to practise, and what not to practise; and that all who are called to preach the gospel, are not called to baptize with water. But these are things that our modern preachers, and teachers, give themselves little trouble about: there are but few of them who can prove that they are sent of Christ at all. But where, from selfish purposes, or from the heat of imagination, they persuade themselves they are sent, they make no inquiry as to the particulars of their commission, but take it for granted, that being preachers, or teachers, they have authority to administer Water-baptism, the Lord's-

Lord's-supper, with other supposed peculiarities of the office. Thus it is very difficult to find *one* among them, who does not suppose his commission to be much more enlarged, than that of the great apostle to the Gentiles; he was sent only to preach the gospel, and not to baptize; but they, almost to a man, suppose themselves sent to perform all things.

I am aware that this is generally imputed to enthusiasm, and I believe it may be the case with many at the first, but I have long observed that enthusiasm is but short-lived; the human system cannot possible admit of its long reign: reproveable enthusiasm consists in mistaking the passions, a heated imagination, &c. for divine inspiration; under such a deception, men are so full of themselves (while they think they are filled with the Spirit) that they never permit a doubt of their own knowledge, wisdom, faith, and holiness; in their own conceit, their abilities are equal to the most difficult undertakings; their zeal is hot and full of temerity; in doing, and suffering, their fortitude is often amazing, and they think they have nothing in view but the glory of God, and the good of mankind. It is easy to conceive, that men thus tinctured think themselves the particular favourites of heaven, and that their commission is equal, if not more than equal, to the apostles.

This occasions their pretensions to infallibility,

bility, in preaching what they call the gospel; these towering imaginations are they that occasion their rushing into the administration of what they call the Gospel ordinances, without once inquiring, whether Christ hath sent them to administer them, or not: without their practising these things they think their office would be defective in dignity, and possibly they may judge them necessary to salvation; and therefore, they are generally very earnest upon this head. But, by degrees, the simplicity, sincerity and zeal, which seemingly influenced their spirits at the first, dwindle and degenerate into more selfish motives; until self-importance, and the love of profit, swallow up all. Then the administration of ordinances is necessary to complete the ministerial character; ordinances are then judged necessary to gather congregations, and when the congregation is gathered, ordinances are deemed a proper cement to hold it together; ordinances are made use of to serve worldly purposes; in brief, ordinances are used as if our Saviour's kingdom was of this world, in manifest contradiction to his own sacred testimony.

Before the apostle made his declaration as above, our Lord's disciples had so practised Water-baptism, that it was considered as part of their office, and it was taken for granted, that all the apostles were sent to baptize, as well as to teach; and therefore, there must have been some especial reason for Paul's being

being sent to preach only, and not to baptize. To me it appears, that the apostle viewed Water-baptism, as having in its original a reference to what was to be accomplished in the person of Christ, thro' his sacrifice; and therefore, that he, blessed with this view of things, knew that he was not sent to baptize, but to preach the gospel. To elucidate this proposition, I would yet propose, that the apostle Paul, at his being first sent out to preach, did not know that he was not sent to baptize; but as he grew in grace, and in the knowledge of our Lord and Saviour Jesus Christ, he was able to distinguish as above, and consequently was convinced that he was not sent to baptize. To prove the first, I would observe, that for a time after his being sent out to preach, he used the Baptism of water as the others did, for by his own confession he baptized some; which we cannot suppose he would have done, had he then known that it was not included in his commission: therefore, the apostle did not at first know that he was not sent to baptize. The second is clearly proveable from his own testimony, where, in a period future to that of his practising Water-baptism, he positively says, that he was not sent to baptize: therefore, this was a point that the apostle was convinced of in process of time, as he knew more perfectly the mystery and mind of Christ. Hence, we may account for his baptizing some at the

first;

first, and for his receding from the practice afterwards, and declaring that he was not sent to baptize.

A minister of truth (though assured of his call, and that Christ hath sent him to preach the gospel) may, not being closely attentive to the particulars of his call, practise for a season, such things as are commonly thought to belong to such an office, though these things are abrogated in Christ, and have now none other importance than what tradition or custom gives them. But here their ministry is always spiritless, and without that favour to themselves, which attends their practice in what they are positively called to; and from their own feelings, from the absence of the Holy Ghost, in his witness and unction, as neither bearing witness to these things, nor rendering them unctious in their use, they may be assured, that they are now of no real importance. And tho', during this period, ministers may not be able to render an explicit reason wherefore such practices should cease, by shewing the original end or design of them to have been fully answered, yet may their minds be free from doubtfulness in this matter: for tho' they may not be able, distinctly and clearly, to assign the reason or cause of the death, yet from the spirit's being fled, they may be perfectly assured of the body's being dead.

In things of this nature, a minister of the gospel cannot act with zeal and spirit; he

may

may poffibly from cuftom, form, or infirmity, drag heavily on in the ufe of thefe things for a feafon, calling them by the name of things indifferent, &c. becaufe he thinks they merit no name of more importance: but thefe are things that he will not adminifter at all events, particularly where they are abufed, and made to clafh with what he is pofitively fent to adminifter; nay, he will then totally ceafe from them, and fay, I thank God, I never was forward in the ufe of them; I have exercifed myfelf but very little in them, left any fhould fay that I baptized, &c. in mine own name.

Thefe may ferve to illuftrate the meaning of the apoftle in the words, " I thank God, " that I baptized none of you but Crifpus " and Gaius, left any fhould fay that I had " baptized in mine own name," which in my judgment, is equal to his faying, " Now I know and declare, that Chrift did not fend me to baptize with water; but before I knew this, or had made any fuch declaration, and confequently ufed Water-baptifm occafionally, I ufed it fparingly, I only baptized Crifpus and Gaius, and the houfhold of Stephanas, left any fhould fay that I baptized in mine own name; for againft fuch an evil, fo highly derogatory to the name and honour of the bleffed Jefus, as is that of being thought to baptize in mine own name, there remained no remedy equal to that of totally renouncing the practice that occafioned it:

and

and this I could do the more eafily, becaufe I faw no honour to Chrift, no good, no advantage to mankind, could poffibly be propofed from the ufe of Water-baptifm, as a counter-balance to the evil occafioned thereby; and therefore, I thank God, that I baptized none of you: it is to me now a delightful reflection, that I ufed it fo fparingly, that I abftained from the adminiftration of it fo much as I did." Thus, in my judgment, it may fairly be gathered from the teftimony of this apoftle, that Water-baptifm was not the Baptifm intended in the commiffion which our Lord gave to his difciples, after his refurrection from the dead; but that the Baptifm of the Holy Ghoft was what was there intended: " Go ye, there-
" fore, and teach all nations, baptizing them
" in the name of the Father, and of the
" Son, and of the Holy Ghoft." Our Saviour, in thefe words, did indeed command his apoftles to teach all nations; to teach them, I fuppofe, the things concerning himfelf, as the things that belonged to their peace; but Baptizing is here fpoken of as a neceffary confequence, or fruit of the divine teaching, as what was to be effected by means of fuch teaching. The apoftle to the Ephefians fays, that " Chrift loved the
" church, and gave himfelf for it: that he
" might fanctify and cleanfe it with the
" wafhing of water by the word." The wafhing of water here, by which the church

is

is sanctified and cleansed, and which is by the Word, must, in my judgment, most certainly denote the purification of the mind, and conscience, from the filth and guilt of sin, which is by the Word of Truth's being preached, and believed on; this is figuratively called the washing of water, from the well-known property of that element to cleanse and purify. Thus, the Baptism intended in our Lord's commission, is the same with what is here called the washing of water by the Word; and which from reason, and spirit, cannot possibly be conceived to be external. Briefly, our Lord's commission to his apostles, contains Teaching as the cause, and Baptism as the effect. The former they are commanded to do, the latter is shewn to be dependent thereon, promised thereto, and joined to it, by Infinite Wisdom and Goodness, as the effect to the cause.

Having shewn that Water-baptism is not expresly commanded in the decalogue, and that it is not a law-commandment, nor an ordinance of our Saviour's; it remains for me to shew what law, dispensation, or period, it did belong to, with its reason and use. And here I would propose, that Water-baptism was an appendix to the ceremonial law, and that it bare a strong figurative resemblance to the salvation by Jesus Christ. What I have here, conforming to custom, called the ceremonial law, the apostle somewhere calls the "law of commandments

"ments contained in ordinances;" and which, he says, Chrift abolifhed in the flefh, as the fource of the enmity that fubfifted between Jew and Gentile. This law of commandments contained in ordinances, may be thus diftinguifhed from the decalogue, or moral law.—That, as a tranfcript of the divine nature, is confidered as the perfect rule of righteoufnefs, the infallible ftandard, whereby to determine of good or evil, and the only balance of moral rectitude: but this, as a rule of worfhip, and a directory to the faith of the worfhipper, according to the covenant of promife. That entered, that the offence might abound; it was given for the knowledge of fin, and that the whole world might ftand guilty before God: but this was ordained to manifeft the method of falvation by Jefus Chrift, according to the divine purpofe, revealed in the original promife. That was extended, and circumfcribed in perfection from the firft, fo as neither to admit of any new commandment being added to it, nor of one jot or tittle thereof being taken away: but this, as I have already hinted, was capable of augmentation, and under each difpenfation, from Adam to Chrift, as times and exigencies required, it was ftill increafed and improved. The laft ceremonial difpenfation, was that of John the Baptift; which, as it immediately preceded the Meffiah, and the accomplifhment of all things in him,

was

was enriched with a symbol of salvation, not practised nor known under any former dispensation: this was Water-baptism, which the Holy Ghost sent John to administer, as the messenger before the Saviour's face; who, whilst he proclaimed the approach of the Messiah's kingdom, was to exhibit the nature and properties thereof under that figure.

The Baptism of water, as practised by John the Baptist, may be considered as consisting of three particulars: I. The requisite in the subjects thereof; II. The matter; and III. The manner thereof. The requisite was repentance, which consisted in, 1st, confession of sins, 2dly, a forsaking of them, and 3dly, newness of life. The material of this Baptism was water, and which, as a similitude used in holy writ, hath various senses assigned it; sometimes it is used as a metaphor of the deepest sufferings, sorrows, and distress: thus the Psalmist, "Save me, O God, for the "waters are come in unto my soul." And again, " All thy waves and thy billows are "gone over me." And, in sundry other passages of scripture, it is put for troubles and afflictions. So doth it also certainly denote the means of cleansing, purifying, and refreshing. Hence, the promises to wash them with clean water, &c. and the invitations in the Old and New Testament, to come unto Christ and drink. The manner, form or mode of John's Baptism, was to immerse and overwhelm the baptized in the water: this is sufficiently manifest, from his making choice of such places to perform his baptism where there was much water; and from the accounts we have of their going down into the water, coming up out of it, &c.

From the above remarks, I propose to shew, that John's Baptism was, as a figure, both propitiatory and purifying: that it was propitiatory, appears from the confession of sin, which the candidates for this Baptism were required to make at their being baptized; as we read, " Then went out to him " Jerusalem, and all Judea, and all the re- " gion round about Jordan, and were bap- " tized of John in Jordan, confessing their " sins." So, in the case of the sin-offering, and of the scape-goat, both which were expiatory, it was required that the sin of the people should be confessed over them; which intended a transfering of sin from the people to the sacrifice, in that to be chastised and cancel'd. But to cancel, or blot out the sin of the people by adequate chastisement, is in the scriptures term'd a washing, a being washed, &c. which is of equal import with the term Baptism.

Again—The washing of water in John's Baptism implied, in a figure, the putting away of sin; and that the Baptist himself thought so, is manifest enough, according to my judgment, from his speech to our Saviour upon that occasion; " then cometh Jesus " from Galilee to Jordan, unto John to be
" baptized

"baptized of him. But John forbad him, "saying, I have need to be baptized of thee, "and comest thou to me?" Here it is plain, that John saw no propriety in Christ's submitting to his Baptism; and wherefore, but because he conceived of Christ, as of a person perfect in innocence and holiness? Therefore John looked upon his Baptism to be a figurative purgation of sin, and that it had no signification but to sinners. Again, that the washing of water, in John's Baptism, implied a cleansing from sin by a legal chastisement, may also be gathered from its sinonymals in the scriptures: to be in the water, in the deep waters, to have the waves and billows thereof pass over us, &c. are figures used in holy writ, for such troubles, afflictions, and distresses as denote chastisement for sin, as I have hinted above. Thus the Baptism of John was, in my judgment, a figure of the sufferings of Jesus, and of the expiation of sin thereby.

Hence the comers thereunto were obliged to confess their sins, as over the sin-offering, &c. signifying that their sin, thus confessed, was transfer'd, from the sinner's person, to the person and sacrifice of Christ, as represented by these; for which purpose, contact was as necessary as confession; nor would confession, without contact, have availed them any thing at all: thus it was necessary for them to lay their hand upon the head of the sacrifice; so also in Baptism, it was equally necessary

necessary for them to go into the water; and it may be supposed, that they did not make their confession until they were in the water; it was also needful, that they should go *down into* the water, in such sort as to cover the whole surface of the body, that the whole man might in this figure be united to the punishment and propitiation. It is said of John's Baptism, that it was the Baptism of repentance, and that he baptized with water unto repentance: but I cannot think, that by repentance Here is intended the sorrows, contritions, and repentances, which his disciples might express at their baptism; because those who were only baptized with his Baptism received not the Holy Ghost; they knew not Christ, and consequently their repentance was not of faith; and what is not of faith is sin. Again, their repentance in such a state, could not possibly extend farther than to the putting away of the filth of the flesh, or to a meer reform of conduct; they were incapable of bringing forth fruits, meet for such a repentance as God required for sin; nor indeed are any of *our* humiliations equal to such a repentance. But that repentance which is not to be repented of, that repentance which is equal in its merit to the demerit of sin, and without which we must all have perished, consisted in those strong cries and tears, wherewith the Saviour called upon God in the days of his flesh, and was heard in that he feared: this repentance
Unto

Unto Life confifted in thofe unknown forrows that overwhelmed his righteous foul, when it was forrowful even unto the death; in thofe wounds and diftreffes of fpirit, which befides himfelf none could poffibly bear: all which was more than equal to the hell, the death, and punifhment which fin deferved, and wherewith the iniquities of mankind had been threatned. This repentance, in figure, was held forth in John's Baptifm; this was that whereunto they were baptized, where it is faid that they were baptized with water unto repentance, though the comers thereunto were not yet made perfect, pertaining to the confcience; That being referved for another difpenfation, when Jefus, exalted as a Prince and as a Saviour, fhould give repentance and remiffion of fins unto Ifrael.

It is confefs'd, by even the warmeft advocates for Water-baptifm, that it was in the hands of the Baptift an outward and vifible fign of inward fpiritual purity: to this I alfo affent, and explain it in the following manner. John's Baptifm, refpecting both the neceffary confeffion and reformation in the baptized, and alfo the wafhing of their bodies with water, was typical of fpiritual purity; which purity, was to be effected in Chrift, legally and phyfically, by his forrows, facrifice, and death; both which were manifeft at his refurrection from the dead: there he gave proof of his having fuftained sustained the adequate chastisement, by which he had legally purified mankind; and there, in his own holy and purified person, he exhibited them as naturally and personally purified from all sin and iniquity. These things being first true in him, are also true in every faithful worshipper, who being once purged, hath no more conscience of sin, and which an apostle describes as follows; "Unto the like figure whereunto "Baptism now saves us, not the putting "away of the filth of the flesh, but the "answer of a good conscience towards God, "by the resurrection of Jesus Christ."

Here, by putting away the filth of the flesh, we must either understand the putting away of bodily filth, by the washing of water, or otherwise the filth of the former conversation, put away by contrition and a reformed conduct; nor can the most sanguine and bigotted to ordinances propose any thing beyond this, from their use of Water-baptism now. But the Baptism spoken of by the apostle above, doth not consist in the putting away of the filth of the flesh; it is the Baptism of salvation which he speaks of, nor does that depend on any external purification of the body, nor reformation of conduct, nay, nor yet upon any inward change in man; but the true Christian Baptism here spoken of, and which relates to the purity, peace, and joy of each individual worshipper, consists simply, and at
all

all times, and in every condition of life, in the anfwer of a good confcience towards God, by the refurrection of Jefus Chrift. A good confcience certainly implies a confcience free from filthinefs, guilt, and fear; a confcience perfect in righteoufnefs and true holinefs, and which is only attainable through the perfect work of Chrift, as manifeft by his refurrection.

The Lord, the Redeemer, and Saviour of mankind having, from kindred, relation, and union to the people, the right and office of redemption invefted in him, undertook, on behalf of the people, to do the will of God, which will was their fanctification: to baptize, wafh, purify, or to fave them from all their fins, was his errand into this world; in order to which, he took on him their nature, perfons, and condition, and was confidered in all refpects as the people: hence, through his obedience, fufferings, death, and purification, he legally, fpiritually, and gracioufly effected what he undertook. But, as the proof of this refts upon his refurrection, as his refurrection is our affurance of his having fucceeded in his undertakings, the anfwer of the good confcience is particularly afcribed to that. And the fame apoftle propofes, that this Baptifm, as the fubftance, anfwers to Noah's flood as the figure; the latter was the purification of the world, through the punifhment of their iniquities: the falvation of Noah and his family

mily by water denotes, that what was the means of destruction to the world, was the means of salvation to them. The eight persons mentioned in the text, as partakers of this salvation, were a figure of the whole church; and the world, destroyed by the flood, were figurative of the sins, and sinner character of the church; the chastisement and destruction of the latter, being the salvation and purity of the former: according to which figure, the true Christian Baptism now saves us.

Of this Spiritual Baptism another apostle speaks, and under another figure, as follows: " Moreover, brethren, I would not that you " should be ignorant, how that our fathers " were under the cloud, and all passed " through the sea; and were all baptized " unto Moses in the cloud, and in the sea." It is indeed amazing to think, what wranglings and disputings are among religious people, about the apostle's meaning in those words, as if they were only calculated to settle the form or mode of Baptism. There are some who pretend, from hence, to have authority for the mode of sprinkling in Baptism; and this they ground upon its being said " They were all baptized unto Moses in " the cloud, and in the sea." The Baptism of the cloud, they suppose, intends the rain wherewith the people were sprinkled while they passed under it; and that, during their passage through the sea, the waters being
gathered

gathered together on each hand, and raised as a wall, much higher than their heads, the wind sweeping over the surface of the waters, sprinkled them with the spray of the sea, as they passed on: and by these means, they imagine the exact mode and form of Baptism to be ascertained.

But there are others, who as stiffly maintain the contrary, and say, that while the waters of the sea were raised on each hand of them on an heap, the cloud was over their heads, so that being surrounded with the waters denoted immersion, and shewed That to be the true form and mode of Baptism. But all disputes of this kind may, in my judgment, with the utmost propriety, be termed a vain jangling, a disputing about trifles; and therefore, unworthy of farther notice.

I am ready to acknowledge, that by the cloud spoken of in the text is literally intended that pillar of a cloud, which God gave the Hebrews at their departure out of Egypt, to direct them in their march; this cloudy pillar was commonly in the front of their army, but on the appearance of the Egyptian army, behind them: on the borders of the Red-sea, the pillar of the cloud placed itself between the two armies, having a bright side towards the Israelites, that they might see to pass the channel opened for them through the midst of the sea; but to the Egyptians it had a dark side, which we may suppose

suppose greatly added to the darkness of the night, so that they could not come near the Israelites all the night; but in the morning, when the Egyptians perceived the channel by which the Hebrews had entred the sea, they pursued and went in after them to the midst of the sea, even all Pharoah's horses, his chariots, and his horsemen; but still the rear of the Israelitish army was protected and secured by the cloudy pillar: and the Lord looking unto the host of the Egyptians, through the pillar of fire, and of the cloud, troubled the host of the Egyptians; it is said, that he took off their chariot wheels, so that they drave them heavily; which denotes, as I suppose, that he dispirited them, he planted terrors in their bosoms, and sowed the snares of death thick amongst them; the face of the Lord, in the fire and in the cloudy pillar, unmann'd them; it loosed the girdle of their reins, and made them to feel the pangs of the second death. Then would they have fled from his face, but the toils of death were laid for them by an unerring hand; at the voice of the Omnipotent the floods clap'd their hands, and, swifter than the chariots of Pharoah, came rushing upon the Egyptians, to their utter destruction; not one of them escaping. Thus the means of salvation to Israel, were the means of ruin and perdition to the Egyptians.

Egypt, spiritually, is the state of involved nature; and therefore, one of the names of
the

the great city, where our Lord was crucified: from its wifdom and learning, it denoted flefhly excellence. Hence, the Egyptians are faid to be men great with flefh; full of the wifdom of this world, of its knowledge, learning, and religion, and of confequence conceited; puffed up and inflated with pride and arrogance. Egypt was alfo the houfe of bondage, and intends fpiritually, the miferable and perplexed condition of human nature; as men are without hope, and without God in the world. The tafk-mafters, in Egypt, without making the leaft allowance for imbecility, and even without allowing them materials for the work, continued to exact the fame tale of bricks of the Hebrews, daily correcting in them with many ftripes, what they deemed them faulty in, though the fuppofed fault was from abfolute neceffity. Such is the natural ftate of man; according to the firft awakenings of his confcience, he apprehends the law, as demanding perfect obedience of him, without making the leaft allowance for his frailties; and as perpetually curfing him for his mifcarriages, without adminiftring to him the leaft degree of wifdom, or power, to do that which is right: nay, it rather enfeebles him with its terrors, and irritates him to wrath and enmity.

Hence, the deliverance of the Ifraelites out of Egypt, under the conduct of Mofes, hath

hath always been viewed, as a figure of man's salvation, by Jesus Christ our Lord.

In brief, Egypt is spiritually the state of corruption, bondage, and misery, a strange land; the Egyptians, as the natives of this land, are the iniquities and fruits of the flesh. The Israelites were a figure of mankind, or the church in general, who, for a season, were sojourners in the strange land; during which season, the natives of the land polluted and oppressed them. But when God would deliver his church out of this strange land, and from all the iniquities thereof, it must be done by punishing their sins, and yet sparing their persons; as a skilful physician destroys the disease, but saves the patient. I have already shewn, that the waters, particularly the deep waters, indicate punishment, or afflictive chastisement; nor does the fire, and darkness of the cloud, intend any thing less; under, and through these, did the Israelites, or the church, pass unhurt; whilst their iniquities, i. e. Egyptians, were totally **destroyed**. Thus were they purged, washed, or purified from the filth and fear of Egypt, through the chastisement of their sins exemplified in that figure, and are therefore said to have been baptized unto Moses, in the cloud, and in the sea: the spirit of which is, "God in Christ, reconciling the world unto himself, not imputing their trespasses unto them."

Thus,

Thus, from the relation that the term Baptiſm, as uſed by the apoſtle, bears to the ſalvation of mankind in Jeſus Chriſt, and from the affinity of Water-baptiſm as the figure, to the great ſalvation as the ſubſtance, it is manifeſt enough to me, that the former belonged to the ceremonial law, and therefore had its accompliſhment and final end in the latter.

Again—That Water-baptiſm belonged to the ceremonial law, and was intended as a figure or type of what Chriſt was to accompliſh in himſelf, is farther manifeſt, from our Lord's ſubmitting to it in his own perſon, and from his ever memorable ſaying on that occaſion.

John the Baptiſt conceiv'd ſo highly of the Perſon and Baptiſm of Chriſt, in compariſon of himſelf, and of the Baptiſm which he adminiſtered, that when our Lord came to him to be baptized, he not only judged it unneceſſary, but forbad him: nor was he prevailed on to do it, until our Saviour ſaid, "ſuffer it to be ſo now, for thus it becometh "us to fulfil all righteouſneſs." The righteouſneſs which it became our Lord to fulfil, may be diſtinguiſhed into active, and paſſive; the former conſiſted of what the decalogue, or moral law, commanded and required; but Water-baptiſm was no part of this obedience, becauſe not commanded nor required in that law; therefore, our Saviour did not intend it this ſenſe. His paſſive obedience,

or

or righteousness, consisted in his patient submitting to endure such pains and penalties, as the sins of mankind had merited at the hand of God: which punishments of sin, and the purification of the people thereby, were represented under the various figures, contained in the ceremonial law; and among these I would consider Water-baptism, and that it was in this sense the Saviour spake of it, when he said, "it becometh us to fulfil "all righteousness," i. e. passive as well as active. Thus rendering a reason, why a person so pure, and perfectly holy in all active obedience, should yet submit to Water-baptism, because, as belonging to the ceremonial law, it related to his passive obedience, or righteousness; hence the emphatic ALL righteousness. Our Lord in acknowledging that it became him to fulfil all righteousness, confesseth himself under an obligation so to do: which is true, from his kindred relation to the people; and again, from his covenant engagements, and also from the joy that was set before him, as the reward of his toil.

But our Lord speaks in the plural, "It "becometh us to fulfil," &c. which intends, as I conceive, that he personated mankind, and containing the people in himself, through all his active and passive obedience, they are considered as having fulfilled all righteousness in him, and with him, and that from thence they are intitled to the benefits of the whole;

whole; hence the saying, "it becometh us to fulfil." Thus, the Saviour, from his oneness with the people, is pleased to consider them as co-workers, and sufferers with himself, agreeable to his testimony elsewhere; "And the glory which thou gavest me, I have given them: that they may be one, even as we are one, I in them, and thou in me, that they may be made perfect in one." From the above remarks, I thus argue—Water-baptism was an article of righteousness, and of that righteousness which Christ, as the Representative and Saviour of mankind, was under an obligation to fulfil; but Water-baptism was not commanded, nor required by the law, and therefore, no part of righteousness in that sense: it follows of necessity then to conclude, that Water-baptism was an article of ceremonial righteousness. And this the Saviour, for reasons already offered, was obliged to fulfil, and that in a twofold sense; first, typically, in the letter or figure, and finally, in the spirit and substance. The first he was obliged to, as he was one of the people, "Made of a woman, made under the law." As the certainty and method of man's salvation by Jesus Christ was proved, and exhibited under the particulars of what is called the law of ceremonies, it may be viewed, as the gospel preached to the Jews, and the obedience thereof, as the obedience of faith; since it was not only requisite,

quisite, that the worshipper should punctually perform what was literally required of him, but it was also necessary, that he should be able to look unto the end of what was to be abolished; for, an obedience meerly literal and implicit to these things, rendered them an abomination even to him who commanded them: and it is hence we find practices literally commanded, so often censured in the scriptures. In all the sacrifices, washings, festivals, &c. it was needful that they should have the Messiah and his salvation in view, as the origin of their appointment, as their final accomplishment, and the end of them all for righteousness. But, for their ignorance and unbelief in these, there was an atonement to be made, as for the sin of their holy things; plainly denoting, their inequality to the knowledge and faith required in the performance of these things. Hence also a reason of our Lord's submitting to the practice of the law of ceremonies; the people were unequal to the perfection required in the practice of it: but this perfection of faith and knowledge was necessary. Therefore, Jesus being, in the mystery of his person, and in the spirit of his office, the complete assemblage of all the nations of the earth, judged it becoming Him, both for Himself and them, to fulfil all righteousness with a perfect heart; hence the saying, "It becometh us," &c. But again—The Saviour was obliged to fulfil all

in

in a higher fenfe: if we apply the term righteoufnefs to the things which our Saviour fuffered, it may intend an exertion of Divine Juftice, in the punifhment of our fins in Him; where fin, confidered as criminal, is expiated and cancell'd by an adequate chaftifement: or, viewing it as a debt, it is paid to the uttermoft farthing; unto which righteoufnefs, I will fuppofe, our Saviour had a particular reference, in the words before mentioned, And it may be urged, as a reafon of our Lord's fubmiffion to Water-baptifm, that it was a figure of this righteoufnefs.

In brief, our Saviour's words to John the Baptift, on this occafion, are words of great grace and fpirit; they contained a full anfwer to his objection, and a perfect refolution of his doubts concerning this matter. John thought his Baptifm to be calculated only for finners, for fuch as needed repentance, purification, &c. and therefore it was, that conceiving of Jefus, as holy and free from fin, he at firft forbad him; but our Lord's anfwer taught him, that though in Himfelf he was pure and undefiled, yet, as bearing the fins of the people, as fuftaining the finner character, he needed repentance and purification, and therefore would fubmit to Water-baptifm, as an acknowledgment of it; and that as the reprefentative of mankind, and as the captain of their falvation, he was to be made perfect through fufferings.

ings. Hence, he said, suffer it to be so now; partly intimating thereby, that there would be no necessity of repeating it; and moreover, that he was under an obligation to fulfil all righteousness, both in its figure and substance. He had, from eight days old, submitted unto, and practised the law of commandments, contained in ordinances, in all its ceremonies; and Water-baptism being one of these, he would also submit to that. And having submitted unto, and practised with a perfect heart, the whole of what was figurative, he, when the time was fully come, entered upon the substance, and there fulfilling and accomplishing in spirit and truth the whole of what was represented under the figure, he put a final end to the figure, totally abolishing in his flesh the law of commandments, contained in ordinances. And here, as I conclude, Water-baptism had its period, in reason and spirit. For if so it be that we are washed, that we are sanctified, that we are justified, in the name of the Lord Jesus, and by the Spirit of our God; external washings will not only appear to us unnecessary, and unmeaning, when used for religious purposes, but inconsistent and antichristian. Thus have I shewn, or have endeavoured to shew, that Water-baptism is to be numbered among those ceremonies, or ordinances, that were appointed and used as figures of Christ,

and

and of his falvation; and therefore of courſe abrogated, according to real chriſtianity.

But, to all that I have yet ſaid on this ſubject it will be replied, That the apoſtles practiſed Water-baptiſm, after our Lord was received into glory; and therefore, it could not relate to what was accompliſhed in his deceaſe at Jeruſalem, but it was deſigned as an ordinance, to remain in the church to the end of time.

To this I anſwer, That the practice of the apoſtles during a certain period, and even after our Lord's reſurrection, is not in all things an abſolute rule for Chriſtians now. The apoſtles attended to the Jewiſh worſhip, though it was aboliſhed in the fleſh of Jeſus; they practiſed circumciſion, though totally abrogated in Chriſt; they continued to diſtinguiſh between Jew and Gentile, between meats and drinks, as clean and unclean, though the middle wall of partition was broken down, and all theſe diſtinctions removed. In like manner, they might practiſe Water-baptiſm, notwithſtanding its being diſannul'd, as having had its accompliſhment in Chriſt.

There appears to have been a time fixed with God, when the things already fulfilled and perfected in Chriſt ſhould ceaſe to be literally obſerved, or uſed among believers; and of this time, our Saviour often ſpake, as the End, &c. the beginning of which, very probably related to the ſubverſion of the

Jewiſh

Jewish church and polity; and until which, the apostles seem to have kept up, in many particulars, an outward conformity to the manner of the Jews.

Though the apostles succeeded to our Saviour's humiliation, and to the accomplishment of all things in him, as his ambassadors, and the publishers of glad tidings, yet it does not follow, that they immediately knew the reason and spirit of such things as they published for truth; nay, the contrary is manifest, and therefore, it was only in proportion to their enlightnings, and to the purging of the conscience, through the accomplishment of all things in Christ, that they ceased from ordinances; there being degrees in faith, and in the knowledge of our Lord and Saviour Jesus Christ: hence saith an apostle, "When I was a child, I "spake as a Child, I thought as a child, "but when I became a man, I put away "childish things:" and again, "Not as "though I had already attained, or were al- "ready perfect."

The Spirit of Truth expressly declares, that "God was in Christ, reconciling the "world unto himself, not imputing their "trespasses unto them." And that Jesus reconciled Jew and Gentile in "one body "on the cross," that he brake down the middle wall of partition that was between them, and that of twain he made "one new "man, so making peace." Consequently, in the commission before recited, which our Lord gave to his apostles, after his triumphant resurrection, he commanded them to go into all the world, and to preach the gospel unto all nations. But the apostles did not comprehend these things at first, there was some time elapsed before this grace was clearly revealed to them; nor did they easily come into it at last: such were their prejudices as Jews, and their self-righteous maxims, as being not yet fully instructed in the nature of the Messiah's kingdom.

In the article of meats and drinks, how much they were for a season at a loss, both respecting the reason and spirit of the distinction, between clean and unclean; and also, of the annihilation of those distinctions in Christ; I say, how far behind they were respecting those things for a season, is obvious enough from Peter's scruples at Joppa, and afterwards from his conduct at Antioch; and indeed, from their general voice, in their great council at Jerusalem, where they decreed that the Christians should abstain from blood, and from things strangled, &c. it does not appear, that they then saw the lawfulness of eating whatsoever was sold in the shambles; nor, that when they were bidden to a feast, they were to eat whatsoever was set before them, asking no questions for conscience-sake. The correspondence between their faith and practice, respecting the oneness of Jew and Gentile in Christ, was very irregular

irregular and unstedfast; of which there are many instances. And though their commission ran expressly, that they should preach the gospel to "all nations," yet it was some time before they saw the expediency, or even the lawfulness, of preaching salvation to the Gentiles. Nor, were they generally agreed that the Gentiles had a title to salvation, until the gift of God to the Gentiles rendered it impossible for them to deny it, without a refusal of his favour to themselves. From all which, it appears to me, that during a certain period, the practice of the apostles consisted not with the reason and spirit of christianity, in many things; nor, with their own positive testimony under another dispensation. When Paul would have Timothy to go forth with him, he took him and circumcised him; and yet, Paul himself says afterwards, "if ye will be circumcised, Christ shall profit you nothing." Peter was taught, that he ought not to call any man common, or unclean; but the part which he acted at Antioch, was very different from this teaching.

Let it not be falsely surmised, that I aim by these remarks, at depreciating the apostolic character: God forbid! But I distinguish between the apostles testimony, and their conduct; for this, I have authority from the scriptures, even from their own writing: and I trust that I do it, with the same faithful view to the glory of Christ.

The

The doctrine of the apostles hath certainly much more authority than their example; the one is infallible, the other was not so: their doctrine was Christ Jesus the Lord, the same yesterday, to-day, and for ever, holy and irreproveable: but being, personally, men subject to like passions with others, their conduct exhibiting infirmity, and therefore, beneath the standard of perfection, they merit not an implicit and universal imitation; this being only due to their doctrine, and to him who was the subject of their doctrine. Hence he, who was not a whit behind the very chiefest of them, exhorts the church, to follow him but as he followed Christ.

For some time after the resurrection and ascension of the Lord Jesus, his apostles seemed to countenance the things that were abolished in him; and which in their epistles, written afterwards to the churches, they declared to be abolished, and pronounced it antichristian to observe them. Hence it follows, that their example, during this period, was not a perfect pattern for their successors. But it is from the example of the apostles during this period, that the generality of the people called christians draw their copy: and hence it is, that there is so much of the old leaven retained amongst them.

It is true, there are some of those that use Water-baptism, who reckon it among things indifferent

indifferent, and who (though they be incapable of giving a reason of their hope in the use thereof) think they may with safety comply with such usages; yea, and who think they ought to comply with them, rather than give offence, or suffer any inconvenience for their singularity. But let such remember, that whatsoever is not of faith is sin; and that whatsoever a person does doubtingly, he is condemned in the doing of it. Nor are there any such things in the true worship of God our Saviour, as things indifferent; the things which are not for him, are against him; what leads not to the faith and obedience of Christ tends to idolatry, and, as such, ought to be disused and exposed by every faithful worshipper: as we may learn from the examples of Hezekiah king of Judah, and the apostle Paul.

When the children of Israel, for their rebellious murmurings, were bitten by the fiery serpents, and the dreadful King of Terrors with awful strides marched thro' their camp, the heart of the people failed them for fear; until, overwhelmed with distress, they cried out, "We have sinned," and besought Moses to pray for them. Immediately upon his intercession, the Lord commanded, and Moses made a Serpent of brass, and set it upon a pole; and it came to pass, that if a serpent had bitten any man, when he beheld the serpent of brass he lived. Our Lord himself makes honourable mention

tion of that serpent, as an eminent type of his person and salvation; and as such it stood, witnessing the great deliverance, for more than seven hundred years, even unto the days of Hezekiah king of Judah, who utterly destroyed it. For a long season before its destruction, the people of the land, mistaking its real use and design, idolatrously offered it divine honours, by burning incense to it. This gave the royal reformer such indignation against it, that though it was originally formed, and set up by divine direction; yea, though God had wrought by it a great salvation in Israel, yet King Hezekiah would not spare it; nor did he think it sufficient to destroy it, but that it was also needful to pour the most public contempt upon it, by calling it Nehushtan, (which is interpreted, a trifle of brass;) thus shewing, at once, the unimportance, the worthlesness, yea, even the impiety of all things in the use thereof, though of a divine ordination, when profaned to a wrong use, or made to be competitors with God. In like manner, the apostle, when he saw that Water-baptism interfered with the glory of Divine Grace, and that men were rather discipled to men, and to the works of their own hands thereby, than to the person and salvation of Jesus Christ; I say, upon this conviction and view of things, the great apostle seems to treat Water-baptism, as Hezekiah did the serpent, where he says, " I
" thank

"thank God, I baptized none of you;" &c. thus in effect calling it (though not a trifle of brass) a trifle of water.

But possibly it will yet be urged, that Water-baptism is more than an empty form, or a meer figure of things, as being not only of a divine appointment, but also attended originally with such spirit and power as sufficiently evidenced its being of God; and therefore, to be retained and practised in the church at all events.

Unto this I reply, that nothing could be more expresly commanded of God, than the making and setting up of the brazen serpent, as noted above; infinite wisdom itself drew the model of it, and directed how it should be lifted up or exalted. And O how unparallel'd was the power attendant on that very significant figure! merely the sight of it expell'd the poison and terrors of death, drawing back from the brink of the grave, and instantly recruiting with life and strength, such who but a moment before were grinding between the jaws of the devourer.

And to shew that the virtue of life and healing was not in any bodily or mental act of the patient, but altogether in the ordinance, and power of God, it is to be noted, that a simple looking, or turning of the eye to this serpent, without the use of physical means, and even without any preparation of the mind, perfectly effected the cure, and
delivered

delivered out of their diſtreſs, the moſt miſerable of mortals.

That the origin of this ordinance was divine, that it was of the utmoſt benefit to the afflicted, and that it was an almoſt unparallel'd diſplay of the glory, power, and goodneſs of God; and that it was withal a ſtriking figure, and an eminent type of Jeſus Chriſt our Lord, is undeniable. But when that great end, for which it was formed, was ſerved, when the divine efficacy and power no longer attended the ordinance, it not only ſunk into a ſtate of worthleſsneſs, but became the object of an idolatrous worſhip; and therefore, it richly merited the deſtruction it met with.

In like manner, if Water-baptiſm was at any time a means, by which proper ſubjects received the Holy Ghoſt, (though I cannot perceive from the ſcriptures that it ever was thus bleſt) it is not ſo now: this I conclude is manifeſt enough; and therefore, being now an unmeaning lifeleſs form, it can only ſerve to purpoſes of idolatry.

While Water-baptiſm retained its ſignificancy, as a figure of the Chriſtian ſalvation, I doubt not but the ſincere worſhipper might receive conſolation through the uſe of it: but, that ſalvation being perfected, the reaſon of the uſe of Water-baptiſm no longer remains; nor does the Spirit *now* bear witneſs to it. And, ſuppoſing it to be ſtill a ſignificant figure of ſome future grace, if those who use it do not use it simply to that purpose, it becomes in its use, either the shiboleth of a party, by which men are discipled and proselyted to men, or the worship of ignorance, blindly following the lead of tradition; or otherwise, it is practised as an article of righteousness, and by sundry, made to be the new-birth, justification, sanctification, &c. and, though external, and altogether a bodily exercise, yet substituted in place, not only of the true spiritual worship, but even in the place of Christ, and of his salvation. Thus, like the serpent abovementioned, being profaned to a wrong use, it merits a similar respect.

That there are some who pretend, that the Holy Ghost is yet given by their hands, in the administration of Water-baptism, I am well aware. But these, in general, are men particularly concerned for their craft, which is in great danger, if outward ordinances be superseded; for the administration of these (as to the function of clerical men) may be considered as the principal support of their order, their ground, and pillar of dignity. Hence, until they are content to let themselves down to a level with the unhallowed laity, impartiality, in things of this nature especially, is not to be expected from them; being scrupulously tenacious of every thing they deem essential to their authority.

One of those gentlemen, in a printed letter which I have lately seen, expresses himself

self thus: 'I know this, from plain fact; 'many have received a sense of pardon, 'when I baptized them.' But I am constrained to conclude, that this is much too confidently spoken. How should this gentleman know, that the persons whom he baptized, received a sense of pardon? He could know this only from their ownnfession; but infants are incapable of making such a confession, therefore, their Baptism is out of the question here: and the good man's assertion must of necessity relate to his Baptism of adult persons only; and this admits of various questions. Was it by the act of Baptism, or by what he spake to them on the occasion, that their faith and the sense of pardon came? Is it not possible for a person to receive a sense of pardon, by the preaching of the gospel, without the administration of Baptism? This, I suppose will be granted. But may the same be asserted of Baptism without the Word? Or is it necessary to a person's receiving a sense of pardon, that both be joined? The latter is denied, from the practice of the apostle Paul, who was not sent to baptize, but to preach the gospel: and yet it is not to be disputed, but that many received a sense of pardon under his ministry. Hence we argue, that Water-baptism is no part of the gospel; nor may the administration of it, *in any sense*, be considered *now*, as preaching the gospel. By the preaching of the gospel, the Spirit operates

rates upon the heart of the hearer, to a sense of pardon; but, by that which is not the gospel, the Spirit does not thus operate: Water-baptism is not the gospel, therefore, the Spirit does not thus operate by Water-baptism. What is not the gospel, does not preach Christ, does not manifest him; and what does not preach Christ, conveys no sense of pardon: but Water-baptism is not the gospel, it does not preach Christ, therefore, it conveys no sense of pardon.

If, as he asserts, many received the sense of pardon when he baptized them, it does not follow that they received it by the means of Baptism: why may it not be supposed that their faith came by hearing, and their hearing by the word of God? This is certainly more eligible, and consistent with revealed truth, than that any external application should effect it.

But the time when they received the sense of pardon: 'When I baptized them,' says the person above mentioned: this proves nothing relative to the point in hand yet; it neither proves that they received the sense of pardon by means of Water-baptism, nor by the sanctity of him who administred it. Perhaps it would not be very difficult to produce instances of such who have received a sense of pardon, at a time when the circumstances of their then employment were by no means hallowed thereby; no, nor recommended by divine authority to others, as a means whereby they also might receive the same sense of pardon. Thus the Lord is found of them who seek him not, and reveals himself to such who have not asked after him. But it does not follow, that such a wretched, ignorant, supine state, is the means of attaining the knowledge of the Only True God, and of Jesus Christ whom he hath sent. Nor does it follow, because a person received a sense of pardon at the time of being baptized, that he received it by means of Baptism; or, that Water-baptism is enriched with such gifts.

From the whole, I cannot but conclude, that Water-baptism is now an unmeaning spiritless ceremony. All usages and forms, when their end is answered, and the Spirit hath left them, are no more than the dead body; rather tending to defile, than to purify, all who touch, taste, or handle. Where the soul and spirit is departed, the corpse should be buried out of the sight of the living. But where men retain the form, when the reason and spirit of it is no more, they do in effect embrace the dead body, and keep it among them, to the reasonable dislike of many, who on that account are constrained to leave them.

There are also such, who pretend that Water-baptism succeeded to circumcision; and upon this hypothesis, their authority for Infant-baptism is in a great measure founded: but how inconsistent with true reason and

and spirit, I shall now proceed to shew. Water-baptism cannot be said to succeed circumcision, by divine appointment, for various reasons: 1st, Water-baptism took place before circumcision was abolished, and they both were observed by the same persons. 2d, Circumcision was typical of what was to be accomplished in Christ, and therefore it remained but until Christ. But it would be absurd to suppose, that one type was succeeded by another, and especially after that end was answered for which it was originally appointed. Where the apostle saith, " if ye be circumcised Christ shal " profit you nothing," it is manifest enough, that he does not speak this with a view to introduce Water-baptism, as an ordinance that was to take place of circumcision; but his design was to shew, that circumcision being abolished in Christ, as a matter which, in its reason and spirit, had always referred to him, the use of it now (supposing it to have had such a reference to Christ) would be in effect to deny that Christ was come in the flesh; or, that though he was come in the flesh, it would be to say, he had not fulfilled that for which he was promised; and therefore, the things which as figures related only to him, and to what he was to fulfil, were not yet abolished. Or otherwise, the use of circumcision then would be, to suppose it an ordinance independent of Christ, and without the least reference to
his

his salvation; which would be at once to establish it as an article of human righteousness. The use of it, in either of these senses, would imply a rejection of Christ, and such an affront put upon his salvation, as would naturally exclude the offender from its benefits. To suppose then that Water-baptism was appointed to succeed circumcision, is either to make it an article of human righteousness, or to deny that Christ, by coming in the flesh, hath fulfilled all righteousness; for if circumcision was a figure of what was to be accomplished in Christ, wherefore should it, when it was thus accomplished, be succeeded by another figure? But, if it was not a figure of Christ, it must of necessity be an article of the moral law; or otherwise, a political institution. But that it is not an article of the moral law is manifest, from its abrogation by divine authority; nor, had it belonged to that law, could it have been mitigated, or succeeded by a milder ordinance, such as Water-baptism. And, as I have only to do at present with such who profess the scriptures to be their rule of faith, I need not waste time, nor words, to shew that circumcision was more than a political institution, and therefore of necessity it must be considered as typical: but every type refers to its antitype, in whom it hath its reason and spirit; and is not to be succeeded by another pattern of heavenly things, but by the heavenly things themselves.

But to all that I have yet said upon this subject, it will possibly be replied—That circumcision was a seal of " the covenant " which God made with Abraham, where " he commanded him and all his seed to be " circumcised; and ordained that, for the " future, they should undergo the operation " at eight days old: but this being a yoke, " which neither we nor our fathers were " able to bear, the Lord took it out of the " way, and substituted Water-baptism, as " less grievous; and yet perfectly answering " the same end." In answer to this, let us first consider the nature of the covenant which God entered into with Abraham:—The promise was unto Abraham, and unto his seed, that he should be heir of the world. By this seed, " Christ was intended," who was to proceed from the loins of Abraham according to the flesh, and in whom all the nations of the earth were to be blessed. In these promises, Abraham saw the salvation of mankind in his seed Christ, and believing this, it was counted unto him for righteousness; and this was the righteousness of faith which he had, being yet uncircumcised. But in this covenant, it was required of him, and of his posterity, that they should receive the sign of circumcision, as a seal of the righteousness of faith. As it was to be worn in their flesh, a sign, testimony, or witness for God, of his goodness in promising, and of his faithfulness in performing, so was it

also

also ordained a sign of the grace promised; consisting of a separation between them and their sins. Righteousness supposes a privation of sin, and the righteousness of faith implies such a state effected by Christ alone, without works of righteousness as done by us. And of this righteousness circumcision is said to be the seal; confirming and securing under a covering, the grace and salvation thus promised, until the seed should come. Circumcision was a sign and seal of this righteousness: first, in itself, as it consisted in a cutting off the superfluous; thereby denoting, that its antitype, or spirit, consisted in putting away the body of the sins of our flesh; in separating our sins from us as the east is from the west. Secondly, the part circumcised shewing, until the promised seed should come, that he was to be a descendant of Abraham, who should effect such a separation between mankind and their sins. Thirdly, the manner of circumcision; it was painful and bloody, to shew, that this salvation was to be effected by the sheding of the blood of Jesus, and by his enduring the pains and penalties due to sin. Fourthly, the subjects, infants eight days old, having not sinned after the similitude of Adam's transgression; implying the innocence of the sufferer in his individual right: " he who knew no sin was made sin for us, " that we might be made the righteousness " of God in him." Thus was circumcision significant, a sign and seal, respecting both the method and matter of the righteousness of faith.

This accounts for circumcision's being abolished in Christ; or for its being taken out of the flesh and the letter, into the heart and spirit; as is manifest from the New Testament: "And ye are complete in him, "which is the head of all principality and "power. In whom also ye are circumcised "with the circumcision made without "hands, in puting off the body of the sins "of the flesh, by the circumcision of "Christ." And again, "We are the true "circumcision, who worship God in the "Spirit, who rejoice in Christ Jesus, and "who have no confidence in the flesh." "And circumcision is that of the heart, in "the spirit, and not of the letter, whose "praise is not of men, but of God." These testimonies are so plain, as to need no comment: the vail is here taken off from the face of Moses, so that we are able to look to the end of circumcision, and to see it abolished in Christ. But that man who first invented the hypothesis, of circumcision's being a figure of Water-baptism, had an unreasonable warm side to ceremonies, and a fruitful imagination indeed; since it is contrary to revelation, and even to common sense. And I may also venture to say, that his followers in this sentiment are no less famous
for

for tame credulity, or for being under the influence of the same craft.

Thus have I shewn, or at least I have endeavoured to shew, that Water-baptism orginally pertained to the law of ceremonies, as a type or figure of the purification of mankind by Jesus Christ; which being accomplished in Him, Water-baptism is no longer a reasonable service. Nor is Baptism of the Letter now, but of the Spirit; which Spiritual Baptism, I would here propose to be that ONE Baptism mentioned in the text: and of which Baptism I shall now proceed to speak. And here, uninfluenced by the favours or fear of man, I shall faithfully follow the lead of that light, which God my Saviour hath given me; and which, in conjunction with the sacred records, shall ever be the guide of my judgment, and the purity and peace of my conscience.

The apostle says, " For as many of you " as have been baptized into Christ have " put on Christ." Men but lightly tinctured with truth may possibly aver, that being baptized into Christ intends no more than a being baptized with water, into the name, religion, and church of Christ; and that to put on Christ, in consequence of such a Baptism, implies only a putting on the profession of christianity; or, that it can intend no more at farthest, than a putting on of Christ by an imitation of his spirit and conduct.

But in anſwer to this, I would obſerve, it is highly probable, that all the members of the Roman church, whoſe faith at that time was ſpoken of throughout the world, were baptized with water: they publicly profeſſed Chriſt, and in their meaſure were all zealous imitators of him: I take it for granted, that the generality of Chriſtians make no doubt of this. But the apoſtle's words imply a doubtfulneſs of their being all baptized into Chriſt: this appears from a manifeſt caution in the text—" As many " of us." And again to the Galatians, " As " many of you as have been baptized into " Chriſt, &c." All are agreed, that thoſe epiſtles were written to particular churches, or ſocieties of people called Chriſtians. But none were intitled to this ſacred appellative, much leſs to church-fellowſhip, until they had not only believed, but alſo conformed, and ſubmitted to ſuch rules and ordinances, as were at That time judged to be a proper teſt of faith in Chriſt; and in the very front of theſe ſtood Water-baptiſm. But, tho' thoſe people profeſſed to believe on the Lord Jeſus, though they ſubmitted themſelves to the ordinances, and conſequently had been baptized with water, yet the apoſtle ſpeaks with great warineſs and reſtriction about their being baptized into Chriſt, and of their having put on Chriſt.

If it may be ſuppoſed, that there were no unbaptized perſons in the churches of Rome and

and Galatia, unto whom those epistles were immediately written, wherefore does the apostle fix these limits, "As many of us,"—"As many of you," &c? Is there not a distinction manifestly supposed in the words, between such who had been equally partakers of the outward Baptism? Would not the apostle's words be defective in sense and propriety, if he intended the Baptism of water, wherewith they all had been baptized, where he says, "As many of us,"—"As many of you as have been baptized into Christ," &c? The words plainly imply, that the apostle thought it possible, that some of the people to whom he spake them, might not be baptized into Christ; but they had been all baptized with water: therefore, the apostle intended not the Baptism of water, when he spake of being baptized into Christ.

But what he meant by being baptized into Christ, may be known by this criterion, "They put on Christ." How This is to be understood, I shall have an occasion to shew in the sequel; but in the interim, I shall just take notice of some general opinions relating to this matter, and of these in their variety, as abounding amongst men of different complexions, attachments, and sentiments.

The more remote from the Spirit of Truth, in this matter, are such who make nothing more of it than to have the sign of the cross drawn upon the forehead with a wet finger.

Hence, they pretend to have put on Christ from their infancy; and that they were then made members of Christ, children of God, and inheritors of the kingdom of heaven; that they were then regenerated, born again, and made Christians, and all without their own knowledge of the matter.

This is that which hath filled the world with ignorant Christians, who know not wherefore they are so called: from hence proceeds the innumerable swarm of unbelieving Christians, who have just as much confidence in Jesus Christ, as they have in Mahomet: hence, that notorious contradiction, that abominable lye against the truth, the persecuting Christians; such who (from the delight which they have in blood) are promised blood to drink: hence also, the fighting Christians, whose kingdom is of this world, and who therefore delight in war. In brief, from hence proceeds such who are Christians without faith, who are good without holiness, who are fruitful without works, who, having the form of godliness, deny the power thereof, and who imagine Christianity to consist of external ceremonies. The proposition, that Christ is put on in Infant-baptism, is so unreasonable, and unscriptural, that (but for the consequences attendant thereon, a few of which I have mentioned, and which need none other confutation than barely to mention them) it merits not my notice.

But

But there are others who, totally rejecting the above as an invention of Antichrist, propose, that an imitation of Christ is what the apostle means by putting him on. This I confess, hath a much greater air of probability than the above; and if an imitation of Christ in truth and perfection could be produced, it would have great weight, and a fair claim to the meaning of the apostle: but neither the scriptures nor experience will permit the conclusion, that there is any such imitation of Christ to be found among mankind. The scriptures teach that all men are sinners; that there is none among them who doth good, no not one; that in many things all offend: and if any man say that he hath no sin he deceives himself, and the truth is not in him. The knowledge of ourselves, and of mankind in general, from one degree thereof unto another, serves more and more to confirm us in this truth. Among such who profess themselves the followers of Jesus, there are indeed high pretensions to an uniform imitation of him; but they are meer pretensions. For whoso is capable of delineating what they call their new-creature, their resemblance to Christ, &c. is as capable of shewing that it hath not one similar feature to the great original. All pretended Christ-like appearances in man, when properly sifted, will be found to be altogether chaff; not partaking in the least degree of the true substance.

To

To begin with the motives to holiness, or to what they call an imitation of Jesus Christ; these in man are self-seeking, self-love, &c. and therefore, wholly corrupt; as not partaking of the disinterested, or of that which flows perfectly from love. It is impossible that man should divest himself of self, and selfish principles, whilst he is an inhabitant of this world; let him do what he will, let him disguise himself as he can, it will still be discoverable, that these are his springs of action: whether vice or virtue distinguish his choice, these are still his leading principles. For where a man rushes into vice as the horse into the battle, it is under the influence of self-love, self-pleasing, self-gratification, &c; these triumphing over his reason, so perfectly lord it over him, that there is no law, be it divine or human, civil or social, that he will not break through, and trample under foot to indulge and gratify these.

Again, where the paths of virtue (as called) are the choice, it is but a transformation of the same principles; to avoid punishment, to gain the reward, to court the praise of men, to please himself by reflecting on his own actions and manner, where he becomes his own idol. Some, or all of these, are still the source of his virtue, and his motives to piety: and, under this consideration, his virtue and piety (however excellent in their appearances) stand exposed to the

the cenfure of revelation and right reafon, as flavifh, mercenary, vain-glorious, and idolatrous.

To fuch who know mankind, it is fufficiently notorious, that all friendfhip, love, goodwill, and kindnefs, fubfifting among men, have their foundation in felf only. In ftrict propriety, mankind know no other love than the love of themfelves; and their diflike is governed by the fame principle: whom do you at any time make choofe of for your friend, but him, whofe perfonal accomplifhments, or manner, or fentiments, or piety, &c. pleafe you? And wherefore do you make choice of fuch, but becaufe he pleafes you? Thus from your own will you choice nothing but what gives you delight; nor have you any other motive for choofing it, than that it gives you delight. If we love a friend, it is for our own fake; and if we hate an enemy, it is from the fame motive: every act of benevolence which we do, it is for our own fake that we do it, and where we withhold our hand, we are influenced by the fame principle. In every action of life, mankind ftill facrifice to their own net, and burn incenfe to their own drag. And where they contend for acting difintereftedly, generoufly, and without mercenary motives; and that they love virtue, or holinefs purely for its own fake, they are ftill pleading the caufe of felf-love, and exhibiting proof, beyond exception, of its abfolute dominion over them.

But

But this by no means agrees with the scripture-account of our Saviour's virtue and obedience; that consisted of disinterested love, self-denial, and doing the will of him who sent him. But this (i. e. human virtue) being perfectly the reverse, cannot, with any shadow of justice, be called an imitation of Christ.

Perhaps, as an objection to what I have said upon the subject, it will be asked, if man be so fully under the power and influence of self-love, as you have represented him to be, to what purpose do the scriptures require him to love his neighbour as himself, yea, to esteem of others as better than himself; to love his enemies, and to render good for evil, &c? I answer—The scriptures do not require this of man, as supposing him capable of it; for the coming of Jesus Christ into the world to save sinners, proves the contrary: the law was given that the offence might abound, and the commandment took place, that man might die. It was to distinguish to man, between good and evil, and to make him sensible that he could not perform the good; to prepare the way of the Lord, by proving the necessity and utility of our Saviour's appearance, as the fulfiller of all righteousness, that the law took place: but Christ being come in the flesh, and having fulfilled all, In us, and For us, his virtue and glory is ours, and we are taught to reckon by him, and not by the works

works of our own hands: thus we stand perfected in his love to God, and to his neighbour; whilst we are conscious that self-love still predominates in our persons, and in all our personal fruits.

But it will yet be objected probably, that these things are not only required of men in the law, before the coming of Christ, but that the Christians are also exhorted to them in the New Testament, by the apostles themselves. To which I answer—Though the law be fulfilled in Christ, and we delivered from the curse thereof, by his being made a curse for us; so that it hath Now no authority to inflict pains and penalties on us, as such who cannot personally fulfil its precepts, forasmuch as we are not under it; yet the nature and the properties of the law are the same, its voice is the same, and it is of singular use in the house of God, not as a master indeed, but yet as a servant faithful in all the house; and as such it is made use of by the Spirit of Truth to gracious purposes.

The law, in the New Testament, is made to detect, expose, and censure all human righteousness; and that it doth continually, lest at any time the Christian man, forgetting the hole of the pit from whence he was digged, and the rock from whence he was hewn, should grow wise in his own eyes, and holy in his own conceit. Hence it is, that such who are far gone in those matters

will

will not, by any means, allow their fanctification to be tried by the law; but are obliged to have recourfe to many inventions, to keep up their fpirits in this particular: but fuch who do allow of the law here, are ever fenfible of their own nothingnefs, and that it is in the Lord only that they have righteoufnefs and ftrength. Again, where the apoftles urge the voice of the law, in the reproofs, precepts, and exhortations which we find in their epiftles, it is not that they fuppofe the people to whom they write, capable of fulfilling it; nor is it with a view to mitigate the feverity of the fpiritual law, by eftablifhing an imperfect righteoufnefs, confifting of fincerity, of mens beft endeavours, and of obeying from a good intention, from a peculiar principle, &c. thefe were not the defign of the Spirit, fpeaking by the apoftles. But his intention, by holding up the purity of the perfect law before them, was to keep low the fpirit of conceit and felf-importance; and that they might feel themfelves under the neceffity of a continual looking unto Jefus. To people in their circumftances, in whofe principles, conduct, and confcience, fo great a change had been wrought, it was natural to conclude, that they increafed in goods; and that they had more wifdom, ftrength, and righteoufnefs, according to the works of their own hands, than they had before they believed: in proportion to thefe thoughts,
they

they muſt neceſſarily be lifted up, and wander from the right way. To prevent which, by ſhewing them that they are in themſelves as weak and inſufficient as ever, the law is in its precepts and ſpirit ſet before them, that they might have no confidence in the fleſh, nor any rejoicing but in Chriſt Jeſus: thus is Chriſt the end of the law for righteouſneſs, to every one that believeth.

But to return from this digreſſion—As man's pretended imitation of Chriſt is corrupt in its ſource, it is yet more ſo in the ſtream: the obedience and holineſs of Chriſt have continuance in them; his purity is conſtant, invariable, and everlaſting; but man's goodneſs is as the morning cloud, and as the early dew it paſſeth away, and hath no continuance in it. Again, the obedience, or holineſs of Chriſt is comprehenſive, univerſal, and uniform: but ſuch is not the holineſs of the moſt upright among men; their goodneſs is very contracted, confined to particulars, generally conſiſting of uſeleſs peculiarities, very irregular, and full of chaſms and contrarieties. Again, the holineſs of Jeſus is all perfection; it was pure in the fountain, it was unpolluted in the ſtream, nor could it admit of any corrupt mixture: but ſuch is not the holineſs of man; that, as I have ſhewn, is corrupt in the fountain, becomes more ſo in the ſtream, and admits of abominable mixtures; ſuch as pride, revenge,

venge, the love of money, deceit, and many more such, too tedious to mention at present.

With what propriety can it then be said, that man's holiness is like Christ's holiness, when the nature and properties of the latter are not, in any degree, discernible in the former? Man is not only defective under the predominancy of his particular foible, but his very wisdom is folly, and his greatest strength is weakness itself; he is extremely defective in that wherein he most excels; as daily experience, and the examples of the holy men of old, recorded in sacred writ, plainly teach.

But some man will ask me—Do not the scriptures speak of following Christ's example, of walking in his steps, of being in his likeness, &c? I answer—They certainly do, nor do they speak in vain. But of this I shall have occasion to treat, when I come positively to describe the True Baptism; and to shew that the putting on of Christ is a spiritual act; my design here being only to shew, that it is not of the flesh. For as to man's pretended likeness to Christ, in his imitation of him, it is not *more* than equal to an actor's mouthing and strutting upon the stage, in the character of some hero of ancient story; where there is neither identity, or similarity, but in the whim of folly and romantic fancy.

Man's fleshly imitations of Christ, may be farther explained, by that beautiful and inimitable

mitable simile of the prophet; where he says, "That the day of the Lord shall be upon all pleasant pictures." A picture, however well executed, however strong the resemblance, has not the properties essential to the original. The most pleasant picture, as it is only a shadowy representation of the original, so is it a representation to one sense only; nor are there any of them so perfect, as in this particular to deceive the eye of the judicious, that they should mistake them for real life.

Nor can the most specious appearances of holiness in man so far impose upon the judgment of such as know mankind, and who are not unacquainted with the scriptures, and with the power of God, that they should at any time mistake such appearances for the same with the holiness of Christ; or ever suppose, that they amount to what is intended by putting on Christ. It is impossible for men to put on Christ, according to their own righteousness, or by such imitations of him as they are capable of; but as the comedian puts on his hero, or as the dead picture wears the living original; and which none but children and fools can mistake for reality.

The term Baptism is applied, in the New Testament, with propriety and consistency to spiritual things; sometimes to the sufferings and death of Jesus, and again to the belief of the truth, in its effects on the mind and conscience of the believer: the death and sufferings

ferings of our Lord Jesus Christ were designed to wash and purify the people. Hence, He Himself terms it a Baptism, where he says, "But I have a Baptism to be baptized with, and how am I straitned till it be accomplished?" This was the Baptism which he spake of to his disciples, when he promised them that they should drink of the same cup with himself, and be baptized with the same Baptism. This is also called the Baptism of fire, and with much reason and spirit; as it implies a purification obtained by enduring the penalty. Fire is used for various purposes of agriculture; sometimes to purge the land from thorns, briars, thistles, and other noxious lumber; and at other times, to burn the face of the ground, in order to its fruitfulness; particularly, such ground as is naturally barren and difficult in its culture.

Fire is also a purifier of putrid and corrupt air, by purging it of impure animalcula, and noisom vapours, thereby restoring it to health and sweetness.

It is also the property of fire to purify metals, by separating the precious from the vile; and to distinguish the true ore by consuming the dross. Upon these, and other similar accounts, we may suppose the metaphor was made use of to denote, that the Lord having laid upon Jesus the iniquities of us all, He, as comprehending us in Himself, did through his death and passion purge

our

our sins, He consumed our transgressions and purified our nature. Hence, it is called a Baptism, and the Baptism of fire; and hath the preference in the doctrine of Baptisms.

For, though the washing of water implies the putting away the filth of the flesh, yet this filth is again contracted, and soon; which urges the necessity of repeated washings. But the Baptism of fire doth not only separate between us and our sins, but it also consumes them; so that we may not be defiled with the guilt nor filth thereof any more. This is true in Christ, who being the captain of our salvation, and comprehending us in Himself, was made perfect through sufferings. Thus the fire of his Baptism was both penal and purifying, the latter in consequence of the former; and occupying the nature and persons of mankind throughout the whole of his sufferings and death, they were baptized with the Baptism wherewith He was baptized, they drank of the cup which he drank of, and were together with Him perfected through the same sufferings: Christ being with respect to the people, through the things which he suffered, as the fuller's sope, and as the refiner's fire.

To elucidate which, let us notice the following passage from the words of the apostle, " For as the body is one, and hath " many members, and all the members of " that one body, being many, are one body, "so also is Christ:" Thus runs the proposition, and the parallel as follows: Christ being one, hath many children, or members, these being many are one Christ. The substance, or doctrine of which is—The church is Christ diffused, or in the many, in variety; and Christ is the church in one, in unity, and perfection: and as Christ was thus the church, it was that He fulfilled all righteousness, in the holiness of His life, through the sharpness of His suffering and death, attested by the power and purity of His resurrection.

Jesus, by perfecting himself through sufferings, from the character of the wicked which he sustained, from the iniquities of us all, which were laid upon him, and thus in knowledge and experience qualifying himself to preside over the house of God, hath brought life and immortality to light; and has given assurance unto all men, that they shall be judged by Him; that every threatning, wherewith fallen men have been threatned from the beginning, has been executed upon Him, to their final exemption from all; and that He hath intitled them, together with Himself, to every benefit resulting from his obedience and sufferings. All which (from his natural care for them, and from his perfect knowledge and qualification, through a sameness of experience with them) He, as the appointed, stands engaged

gaged to render useful to them, through all the vicissitudes of their mortal life.

In the holy gospel we are taught, that Christ sanctified the church, By and In Himself; and that, as her substitute and surety, he blessed her with the opening of the prison, and cloathed her with the garments of salvation: He put the robe of legal innocence upon her, and not only so, but comprehending her, with all her infirmities about her, in Himself, He really and physically purified her, by eradicating the evil, and by conforming her in Nature and in Person to the holy Image of God.

The Lord Jesus, having taken on him the maladies and person of mankind, He, as the physician of value, destroyed the disease, and saved the patient; He made an end of sin, He finished transgression, but saved the people with an everlasting salvation. This, as having the people in Himself, he effected through his obedience unto death, without the consideration of any thing done by them; or, any thing wrought within them, in their individual simple persons: of which He exhibited undeniable proof at his resurrection from the dead, when he was declared to be the Son of God with power, according to the spirit of holiness. And this salvation is further described by the apostle, as follows: " Not by works of " righteousness which we have done, but " according to his mercy he saved us, by " the washing of regeneration, and renew-
" ing

"ing of the Holy Ghost, which he shed on us abundantly through Jesus Christ our Saviour."

Thus are mankind, together with and in Jesus their forerunner, baptized unto the Father. In this grace the church is presented a glorious church, not having spot or wrinkle, or any such thing; but holy and without blemish. The apostle, in ascribing glory and dominion to Him who loved us, and who washed us from our sins in His own blood, hath doubtless a reference to this Baptism; for he manifestly places not only the pardon of sin, but the being purified, or washed from them, to the account of our Lord's death and sufferings, where he says, "He washed us from our sins in His own blood:" which not only implies a legal purification, by a chastisement proportioned to the offence, but a radical cleansing of our nature also; not only a forgiveness of sin, and an exemption from future punishment, but a conformity to the Divine Nature also; a meetness to be partakers of a glorious inheritance among the saints in light.

This was the Baptism of the Holy Ghost and of fire, with which it was said that the Saviour should Baptize the people; for as the fire denotes penal sufferings, and justification and legal innocence in consequence thereof, so the Baptism of the Holy Ghost intends sanctification, or such a spiritual purification, as renders us partakers of the Divine

vine Nature. And that our blessed Lord hath effected this, that he hath baptized us with the Holy Ghost and with fire, is sufficiently proved from his own state at his resurrection from the dead, where he appeared the second time without sin unto salvation; having by himself purged our sins, he sat down on the right-hand of the Majesty on high.

In brief, I am constrained to conclude—That the Baptism of the Holy Ghost and of fire, of which John the Baptist declared our Saviour to be the administrator, and likewise that Baptism which our Lord Himself spake of, as a Baptism which he had yet to be baptized with, and for the accomplishment of which he was straitned, and in which he promised his disciples a participation with himself; I say, I must necessarily conclude, that these all related to what was to have its accomplishment through the obedience, sufferings, and death of Christ; and that they have their perfect reason and spirit in the finished work of Jesus.

Hence, in consequence of what Jesus accomplished through his one offering upon the cross, Peter was taught to call no man common or unclean, because God had cleansed them. The apostle Paul taught that God had of the Jew and Gentile made one New-man, so making peace; that he might reconcile both unto God in one body by the cross, having slain the enmity thereby, and came and preached to you which were afar off,

off, and to them that were nigh; and that God was in Christ reconciling the world to himself: with many other similar passages. All which, according to my judgment, plainly indicate, and even positively teach, that mankind, notwithstanding contrasting appearances in them as individuals, are washed, cleansed, and reconciled unto God in Christ Jesus; which being wrought in the Name of the Lord Jesus, and by the Spirit of our God, is that True Baptism of the Holy Ghost wherewith Jesus was to baptize the people.

But here I expect it will be asked me—'Is this the *whole* of what the scriptures 'mean, by being baptized with the Holy 'Ghost?' Unto which I reply—This is the primary meaning of the scriptures respecting the matter; but I am so far from denying, that they speak of the Baptism of the Holy Ghost in a second sense, as consisting of a divine operation upon the human mind, that I believe and affirm that the things which are true in Christ, are also true in them who believe on him. If in pursuit of this subject, I have first spoken of truth as it is in Christ, it is but a mite of that infinite sum which is due to His name; He, as head over all things unto his body the church, hath in all things the pre-eminence. Besides, in Christ is the fountain of the waters of life, but in man a stream only; the stream may be suspended, cut off, or dried up, but the

fountain

ountain is always full, inexhauftible, never failing; the ftream, while it flows, is comfortable, refrefhing, and chearing to our fenfes, but in the fountain is our hope, truft, and delight; we know that There we are ever filled, That can never fail us, becaufe Jefus Chrift is the fame yefterday, to-day, and for ever; in Him is the ftability of our times, and the ftrength of our falvation: nor is it confiftent with truth, that any attainments, confolations, or fpiritual fruits in ourfelves, fhould ever render us independant of Him, or make us unmindful of the honours which are due to His Name.

The Baptifm of the Holy Ghoft, as relating to his operations on the human mind, or on the heart of individuals, is fpoken of in the fcriptures fometimes in an extraordinary, and at other times in an ordinary fenfe; the one limited to the age of the apoftles, but the other familiar to all true believers to the end of time; the former confifted of fuch an effufion of the Holy Ghoft, as did not only include the witnefs of falvation, with righteoufnefs, peace, and joy; but miraculous gifts and powers alfo: and this was it which the Lord promifed the apoftles after his refurrection, faying, "For John "truly baptized with water, but ye fhall be "baptized with the Holy Ghoft not many "days hence;" and for the accomplifhment of which they were to wait at Jerufalem. And of this fame Baptifm fpeaks the apoftle

Peter,

Peter, in vindication of his conduct, when accused of preaching the gospel unto the gentiles; where he says, "And as I began to speak, the Holy Ghost fell on them as on us at the beginning: then remembered I the word of the Lord, how that he said John indeed baptized with water, but ye shall be baptized with the Holy Ghost." This falling of the Holy Ghost on the Gentile converts, was according to his miraculous gifts and powers, as is manifest from the following reasons: First, It was according to the manner of his falling on the apostles on the day of Pentecost; which was not as a spirit of faith in Christ, for that they had before; nor as a witnessing spirit of their interest in Christ, for this we may suppose them possessed of before; nor as a sanctifying spirit, which they certainly had from their first faith in Christ; it therefore follows, that the Holy Ghost fell on them that day in his miraculous gifts and powers, speaking with tongues as the Spirit gave them utterance; according to which was the manner of his falling on the people to whom Peter preached. Again—That it was so is farther evident, from the instantaneous proof they gave of it; the apostle discerned it immediately, which had not been the case had their Baptism of the Holy Ghost here spoken of intended his sanctifying influences; as to have ascertained this, some time of probation and perseverance would have been necessary:

and

and as both our Saviour and his apoſtles have taught, that men may have extraordinary joys, and even from hearing the word of truth preached, and yet give no certain proof of their being the good ground, or of their being ſuch who are baptized with the Holy Ghoſt, and who ſhall endure to the end, there can be nothing inferred with certainty from ſuch appearances; nor could the apoſtle determine from their expreſſed comfort, that the Holy Ghoſt was fallen on thoſe Gentiles, as he did at the beginning on the apoſtles. It follows then, that Peter determined of the Gentiles having received the Holy Ghoſt, by proofs ſimilar to what were exhibited on the day of Pentecoſt in himſelf and the other apoſtles, when they received the Holy Ghoſt: and this out-pouring of the Spirit is termed by our Saviour and his apoſtles " the Baptiſm of the Holy Ghoſt."

By this Baptiſm were the diſciples of Jeſus diſtinguiſhed in the ſight of men, and undeniable proof given that they were of the truth, under the influence of this Spirit; they neither thought their own thoughts, nor ſpake their own words; but they thought and ſpake as they were moved by the Holy Ghoſt: though they were men compaſſed about with infirmity, and ſubject to like paſſions with other men, yet purified with the Spirit, immerſed in the Holy Ghoſt, they were cleanſed from themſelves, ſo that their perſonal weakneſſes could neither prevent nor impede the
. Divine

Divine Power which wrought In and By them. Thus were the apoſtles and other eminent believers of that epoch baptized with the Holy Ghoſt; they were by this means ſeparated, purified, and influenced to the glory of Chriſt, as his diſciples and unerring witneſſes; the truth of which they demonſtrated and confirmed by many ſigns and wonders, which they wrought in the name of Jeſus by the ſame Spirit. But the Baptiſm of the Holy Ghoſt, conſidered in this ſenſe, was extraordinary, as hinted above, and peculiar to the apoſtles and Chriſtians of the firſt claſs in that age; nor doth it appear, with any degree of certainty, that this fulneſs of Spirit and Power extended beyond that age. But though modern Chriſtianity can make no juſt pretenſions to the Baptiſm of the Holy Ghoſt in this extraordintry manner, yet every true believer in Jeſus is ſtill, in ſome ſenſe, baptized with the Holy Ghoſt; nor without this, is it poſſible for men to enjoy either ſpiritual purity, or true conſolation: the truth of this hypotheſis is granted by all that have any right of claim to the Chriſtian name (as a doctrine very explicitly taught in the New Teſtament), who are yet far from being agreed as to the nature and properties of the thing itſelf.

There are ſome who unreaſonably, and unſcripturally, reſt the doctrine altogether upon externals, pretending that the Baptiſm of the Holy Ghoſt operates In and By bodily exerciſe, cife, or by the ufe of outward things; as by the wafhing of water, and the formal ufe of words on that occafion; and that fuch a Baptifm may be, where no fubfequent change can be proved, nor any correfpondent fruit produced; as in the cafe of infants, who are fuppofed to be baptized with the Holy Ghoft, when they are baptized with water.

Others fuppofe it to confift in a reformation of manners and fentiment, &c. and having in their own eftimate experienced fuch a change in themfelves, they conclude themfelves regenerated, baptized with the Holy Ghoft, and changed into the image of the Lord from glory to glory, even as by the Spirit of the Lord.

There are yet others, who elated with the conceit of perfonal purity, and abounding with affurances, joys, and extatic feelings (in confequence thereof) eafily miftake their paffions for divine infpiration, and their imaginary purity for the Baptifm of the Holy Ghoft: but this partakes fo much of the nature of fpiritual pride, and which is fo perfectly repugnant to the gofpel purity, that it is impoffible for the chafte virgin to Chrift to be deceived by it, by miftaking it for the Spiritual Baptifm. And fo far are the above from being authenticated by the fcriptures, that they ftand rather expofed to the cenfure of the divine word, as inventions of men; and as having their foundation in ignorance and pride.

Again—

Again—There are some who not distinguishing between being baptized With and By the Holy Ghost, conceive of the Holy Ghost in an active sense; or under the notion of spiritual agency in this Baptism: contrary to the scriptures, except it be granted that the Lord Christ is that Spirit, and that He baptizes His disciples with Himself.

The plain scripture-account of this matter is, That Jesus is the agent or administrator of Spiritual Baptism, and that the Holy Ghost is that wherewith he baptizes us, or the material of this Baptism to the soul or spirit, as water is to the body in the external washing. The Holy Ghost is not spoken of in an active sense, as the Baptizer or Purifier; but passively, rather as the element of purification, as that innocence, life, and purity, wherewith Jesus was to wash mankind; and which, in the first sense of the promise, He hath perfectly accomplished in Himself, as I have already shewn.

The name Ghost, in its common acceptation, signifies the spirit or existence of a deceased person, and the epithet of Holy added to it, shews it to be a ghost or spirit divinely pure. This may be applied, and not improperly, to the resurrection of our Lord Jesus Christ; where that which was sown natural was raised spiritual. Mankind, as comprehended in Jesus, died in his death; but whether this death was their eternal loss, or whether it was propitiatory, and consequently

consequently the gate of life, did not immediately appear: for while Jesus lay in the sepulchre, both men and angels were seemingly in a state of suspence with respect to the Deceased; but in His resurrection, not only the Ghost, but the Holy Ghost of the Deceased made its appearance, and gave proof, not only of His existence with God, but of His acceptance with Him also. In brief—I would here propose, that the terms Spirit and Holy Ghost, are not always personally applied in the scriptures; but that sometimes they denote truth, in opposition to falshood: and again, they intend reason and substance, in opposition to shadows outward ordinances, and literal appointments; they also design supernatural influence and operations, in contradistinction to lifeless forms, and to the heats of imagination: but more especially, they intend the reason and purity of redemption by our Lord Jesus Christ, which is the Spirit that giveth life, in opposition to the dead and killing Letter.

The reason of our redemption by our Lord Jesus Christ, which is the Spirit that giveth life, consists, First, In the Divine Decree, wherein the glory and honour of being the Redeemer was assigned him; and again, In that union, or oneness, subsisting between the Redeemer and the Redeemed: hence, the Redeemer had His right of redemption, and His capacity of sustaining their persons and condition; and hence also appears, the equity

of

of their maladies being healed by His stripes. The purity of this redemption was manifested and ascertained in our Lord's resurrection, by which he was declared to be the Son of God with power, according to the spirit of holiness; and by which, mankind also were begotten unto a lively hope. Briefly, The resurrection of our Lord Jesus Christ exhibits, in holiness, the redemption of mankind by His blood and death; and may (not improperly) be called, the Holy Spirit or Ghost of every promise, ordinance, or shadow, relating to this promised salvation. And to have the mind and conscience brought up into contact with the resurrection-state of Christ, so as to answer to the purity of that state, as face answers to face in the glass, is true Spiritual Baptism; it is to be baptized, washed, or purified with the Holy Ghost; that is—with the resurrection-power and purity of our Lord Jesus Christ.

This may be supposed to be what the apostle had in view, when he was desirous of knowing the power of our Lord's resurrection; its power to discharge him from all guilt and impurity, and to perfect him pertaining to the conscience: but more particularly, where he says, " If by any means
" I might attain unto the resurrection of
" the dead; not as though I had already at-
" tained, either were already perfect; but
" I follow after, if that I may apprehend
" that

" that for which alſo I am apprehended
" of Chriſt Jeſus." Here, in my judgment, the apoſtle plainly ſheweth, that as the people comprehended in Chriſt were raiſed from the dead, together with Him, in His reſurrection, ſo the true Chriſtian perfection conſiſts in attaining according to the heart, or to the harmony of our faculties, to that reſurrection, power, and purity; Where we are to the teſtimony of our own conſcience, What we are to the eye of the Father, as accepted in the Beloved.

The diſtinction between what Chriſt hath perfected For us in Himſelf, and that of the revelation of this matter In us, for the Baptiſm or purification of the conſcience, is not a deviſed fable, but a truth authenticated by the ſcriptures. It is not only propoſed that Jeſus loved us, and waſhed us from our ſins in his own blood; and that by Himſelf He purged our ſins, &c. which intends the ſalvation that He wrought out and perfected for us, in His own perſon; but it is alſo propoſed, that the blood of Chriſt ſhall purge the conſcience from dead works to ſerve the living God: the former intends our ſalvation finiſhed in Chriſt; and the latter implies its power or efficacy in the human heart, when known and believed; and which may be conſidered, as a Baptiſm with the Holy Ghoſt, that is, in common to all believers in Jeſus, even unto the end of the world.

I

I have already aimed at shewing, that the material of this Baptism, or that wherewith we are baptized, is the Holy Ghost; or the finished work of Christ, as brought to light and ascertained in His resurrection; and that this grace and truth, through its knowledge and faith, purifies the heart from the filth, guilt, and fear of an evil conscience: hence, the apostle calls it " the washing of water by " the Word."

The Spiritual Word hath, to the mind or conscience, the same property of baptizing, washing, or purifying, as water hath to the external man. The Word is that which by the gospel is preached unto us, it is that which endureth for ever; though all flesh be but as grass, and the goodliness thereof, but as the flower of the grass: the Word is the Spirit and Truth of the scriptures; the Facts of salvation, distinguished from the Report. This Word, in its baptizing virtue, was what our Saviour intended when he said to his disciples, " Now ye are clean through " the Word which I have spoken to you." THE WORD is indiscriminately applied to the person, and salvation of Christ; and is that which the apostles were sent forth to preach, by the gospel, to all nations: and wheresoever it was received, and proved a favour of life, the receiver was baptized, or purified thereby, in the name of the Father, and of the Son, and of the Holy Ghost.

This

This Baptism may be considered, in the Name of the Father, as the origin of love, who gave us to the Son, and decreed our salvation by him; and in the Name of the Son, as he redeemed and saved us; and in the Name of the Holy Ghost, as he convinces of this grace, shews it to us, bears witness of it, and keep us in the truth of it. Again, as the Father teaches us and draws us to the Son; the Son justifies us, saves us, and speaks peace to us; the Holy Ghost, as glorifying Jesus before the eyes of our minds, distinguishing his beauties, and unsearchable riches, and as influencing those discoveries to our hearts: or, we are baptized in the Name of the Father, as Him of whom are all things, and we in Him; and in the Name of the Son, as the One Lord Jesus, by whom are all things, and we by Him; and in the Name of the Holy Ghost, as the precious testimony and influence of that love to our spirits; until we come up to the acknowledgment of the mystery of God, and of the Father, and of Christ; that is, to the revelation and consciousness of the grace concealed under each sacred appellative, as relating to our happiness in time and in eternity.

This Baptism (as I have already proposed) is called a being baptized into Christ; and is evidenced by the baptized's putting on Christ: to put on Christ is a spiritual act, and intends the exercise and appeal of

H the

the soul to God. We are taught in the scriptures, that our Lord Jesus Christ is not only our friend, our benefactor, our kinsman, our brother, but ourselves; one flesh, one blood, one spirit with us: the people, as many, make one Christ; as the members, being many, make one body. Christ and the church are considered in the scriptures, throughout the whole of his undertakings and attainments, as but one person; in the articles of his sufferings and death as the guilty sinner, whose soul was doom'd to die; and in his resurrection, as the righteous, the sanctified, made perfect through sufferings. Jesus being thus made of God unto us wisdom, righteousness, sanctification, and redemption; He being the New-creature, the perfect Man, not only for Himself, but for the people; they, as many as believe on his Name, have power given them to become the sons of God, by putting on the Son.

Christ is put on by appropriation founded upon right, arising from the ordinance and gift of God, and from his union or oneness with the people; from hence, we have an undoubted right, to consider him as our New-man; and to deny every self, in our appeal to the Highest, but Him who is our perfect self.

Before Jacob could inherit his father's blessing, he found it needful to put on his elder brother; he not only put on his apparel,

rel, and assumed his name, but he clad himself with his person in a figure, where he drew on him a similar skin to that of his brother's; and taking on him withal the name of his elder brother, he asked and obtained the blessing in his person and name.

The reason and spirit of which is, the elder brother is Christ; to whom pertains the birth-right, the father's blessing, the inhetance, the office of prophet, priest, and king in the family: it is true, He is not ashamed to call us brethren, because both He and we are of one, of one original, of one parent-root; but, as the younger brethren, we have no inheritance but by Him, being ordained to a state of dependence on Him; He gives us leave to ask in his Name, that our joy may be full, with an assurance of receiving what we so ask.

But how can we ask in his Name, except we are found in Him; by entering into, and appropriating his Person, as Jacob entered into the person of Esau? The gospel exhibits our right of appropriation, from the ordinance of God; from the elder brother's love, consent, and desire; and from the oneness subsisting between Him and us in all His undertakings. It was the will of God, that Jesus should be the Saviour and Salvation of mankind; therefore, were they the body prepared for Him to do that will in: in consequence of which, they were to look unto Him, to come unto Him, to believe on Him,

Him, to put Him on; and to reckon of their
state and condition, in time and in eternity,
both to their own confcience, and to God the
judge of all men, by Him; faithfully con-
cluding, that as He is, even fo are they in
this prefent world. Thus was He ordained
to have the pre-eminence, and that no man
fhould glory before God but in Him.

To this Jefus confented, faying, " Lo I
" come to do thy will, O my God;" fo in-
tenfe was his love, and fo fully was his heart
fet upon the reftoration of the people, that
it was the joy which was before him, when
he endured the crofs, and defpifed the fhame.
He took on Him the feed of Abraham, and
faved them In and With Himfelf, with an
everlafting falvation; and now calls upon
them to be of good cheer, in that he has
overcome; affuring them that his grace is
fufficient for them, that his ftrength is perfected in their weaknefs, and that they fhall
have peace in Him, whilft in the world
they have tribulation: yea, to as many as
believe on him, He gives power to become
the fons of God; requires them to reckon
themfelves indeed dead unto fin, and alive
unto God by Him; to put Him on, to
walk in Him; and to affure themfelves,
that becaufe He lives, they fhall live alfo.

We are alfo inftructed in the gofpel, that
there was fuch a gathering of the people into
One, into the Name, Perfon, and Office of the
Lord Jefus, as rendered them His body, His
fulnefs,

fulness, members of his body, of his flesh and of his bones; and indeed the reason and equity of his humiliation, obedience, sufferings, and death: here the Many were made perfect in One, and a reason rendered, wherefore no man should be called common, or unclean, because God had cleansed them. Here Jesus appears to be our New-man, our perfect Man, our New-creation; and from all these considerations, our right of appropriation takes its rise.

We put on Christ—We put him on for the adoption of sons—We put him on for our title and claim to the love of God—We put him on as our wisdom, and righteousness, and sanctification, and redemption—We put him on as our deliverance from all evil, as our final perseverance, and eternal life.

To put on Christ is an act of the mind, and purely spiritual: it supposes without doubtfulness, such a kindred-relation to Christ, such a oneness with Christ, and such a decreed real and full representation of us, in all His doings and sufferings, as clearly entitles us, together with Him, to all the benefits which He has obtained through His doings and sufferings.

Thus we go out of the consideration of what we are in our individual existence, as from the things which are behind, to the simple, faithful consideration of what God hath wrought in Christ, and in us as com- p-ehended prehended in Him. This is the mark of the prize of our high calling in Chrift Jefus; which is fet before us, and unto which we are required to prefs forward.

Here the real believer in Chrift is confcious of being as Chrift is, yea, even in this world: he is righteous in Chrift's righteoufnefs, as Chrift is righteous; holy as He is holy, and in the fame holinefs; and accepted of God in Him, with the fame acceptance which he hath obtained. As this implies a wafhing, or purification from all human righteoufnefs, and an immerfion in Spirit and Truth, it is term'd a being baptized into Chrift, a putting on of Chrift, and anfwers to the true Spiritual Baptifm.

This in the language of the holy fcriptures fignifies, " A change into the fame image
" (with the Lord) from glory to glory, even
" as by the Spirit of the Lord: as He is fo
" are we in this world—Perfect, pertaining
" to the confcience—Becaufe that the wor-
" fhippers once purged, fhould have no more
" confcience of fin.—Therefore, if any man
" be in Chrift, he is a new creature; old
" things are paft away, behold, all things
" are become new.—Be ye therefore perfect,
" even as your Father which is in heaven is
" perfect—Till we all come in the unity of
" the faith, and of the knowledge of the Son
" of God, unto a perfect man; unto the
" meafure of the ftature of the fulnefs of
" Chrift." Nor are thefe paffages to be expounded

pounded as outward, and in the flesh: "But he is a Jew, which is one inwardly, and circumcision is that of the heart, in the spirit, and not in the letter, whose praise is not of men, but of God."

The benefits attendant on the true Spiritual Baptism are many, and great; and may, by comparison, be thus illustrated:

The Baptism of water hath no higher claim than that of putting away the filth of the flesh; but the Baptism of the Spirit is a cleansing from all filthiness, both of flesh and spirit.

Outward Baptism is a meer bodily exercise, and cannot possibly contain any argument of profitableness in it, beyond mens false conceptions of the Divine Being; for while they think Him to be such a one as themselves, they will also imagine Him to be delighted with the like kind of homage. But the Inward Baptism, which is of the heart, is a spiritual operation; a purity and worship suitable to the properties of that God, who is a Spirit, and who seeketh such to worship him, as worship him in spirit and truth.

The Letter-baptism, as it is a creature-act, leads men to glory in themselves; as the ancient Pharisee, who boasted of being circumcised on the eighth day; or as the modern Pharisee (unto whom the face of Moses is yet vailed) boasts of his submission to ordinances. But the Spiritual Baptism, as

it

it is an act of Christ, purging the conscience from dead works by his own blood, that men might serve the living God in the newness of the Spirit, is a Baptism that baptizes us out of ourselves into Christ, where rejoicing in Him we worship God in the Spirit, and have no confidence in the flesh.

The External Baptism leaves its subjects where it found them, whether infants or adults; it produceth no change in them, they are as much in their ignorance, unbelief, or self-righteousness afterwards, as they were before. But the Internal Baptism is a deliverance from the power of darkness, and a translation of men into the kingdom of God's dear Son.

The Fleshly, or Water-baptism, does not only permit bigotry, but even makes men bigots; for as they are either led to think, that to baptize with water is to christianize, or that it is essential to Christian obedience; so are they taught to censure, and condemn as hereticks, and heathen men, all those who refuse submission to their Baptism; and this lays a foundation for the injurious spirit.

But the Baptism with the Holy Ghost gives men very different ideas; this Baptism expels the spirit of bigotry from the heart, and teaches the Christian to determine of real christianity in men; not from their use of ceremonies, from their subjection to ordinances, but from their having their faith,
hope,

hope, and rejoicing in Christ Jesus; and from their having imbibed his Spirit.

And as to those, whom the spiritually-baptized cannot as yet (on these grounds) call Christians; they are taught to consider them as beloved of God, as redeemed by Jesus Christ; and therefore, such who may sooner or later be blessed with the One Spiritual Baptism.

Hence, they are taught to treat them as their neighbour, yea, as their brother, according to the Word of Truth, which says, "For this end Christ both died, and rose "and revived, that he might be Lord both "of the dead and the living. But why dost "thou judge thy brother, or why dost thou "set at nought thy brother? We shall all "stand before the judgment-seat of Christ: "For it is written, As I live, saith the Lord, "every knee shall bow to me, and every "tongue shall confess to God."

Thus does the Baptism with the Holy Ghost, purify the Christian man to the love of God, and of his neighbour; it so deeply tinctures his heart with the compassions of the Lord, that he cannot oppress, he cannot injure; nor does harshness, or severity, consist with the Christian character; nor can he consider any man so remote, as to behold his miseries with an unpitying eye: but according to the Spirit of Him who hath baptized him, he is influenced by tenderness, and good-will to all; and as a child of the higheſt, he is kind even unto the unthankful, and to the evil.

Theſe, and many more, are the advantages attendant on the Baptiſm with the Holy Ghoſt; which is ſufficient to ſhew its importance, and to prove beyond all diſpute, that this Baptiſm of the Spirit, is that One Baptiſm, which the apoſtle ſpeaks of in unity with the One Lord, and the One Faith.

As I am now drawing nigh to a concluſion, it will not be improper to take ſome notice of what might otherwiſe, in a prejudiced and critical reader, give a ſeemingly plauſible occaſion to charge me with ſelf-contradiction and inconſiſtency; from my defining the Spiritual Baptiſm to be firſt what Chriſt has effected on behalf of mankind in Himſelf, through his doings and ſufferings, having exhibited undeniable proof through his reſurrection, of his having purified and ſaved the people in Himſelf, with an everlaſting ſalvation. And again, to be a divine operation on the hearts of ſuch who believe on Jeſus; whereby they are waſhed from their filthineſs, and purified to the anſwer of a good conſcience towards God, by our Lord's reſurrection.

If, by a few brief hints, I can free the above diſtinctions from the charge of contradiction, by ſhewing, that though I have diſtinguiſhed the Baptiſm with the Holy Ghoſt, wherewith Chriſt was to baptize the people, into what he hath perfected in Himself, and again, into the operations of His grace on the heart of the believer; yet that these distinctions are truly in unity in the one Spiritual Baptism; I shall attempt saying nothing more on the subject.

The great salvation, in every gracious particular, is wrought out, finished, and perfected for ever in Jesus Christ: to this all the prophets, who have been since the world began, bear witness, that " Israel should be " saved in the Lord, with an everlasting sal- " vation." That In the Lord all the seed of Israel shall be justified, and shall glory, were the leading doctrines of the Old Testament; and to this faith, every particular of the ceremonial law was appointed to be a directory.

This also is the doctrine of the apostles— Christ is the seed to whom the promises were made; made to Him as comprehending mankind in Himself, on condition of perfect obedience, actively and passively; made to Him, as the Spirit and Truth of every blessing contained in the promise. Christ having succeeded in all his undertakings, all the promises of God are in Him now, yea and amen. Whether it was forgiveness of sin, or righteousness, or holiness, or that spiritual effusion, which answers to the Baptism with the Holy Ghost, that was contained in the promise; they are all fulfilled upon the people as comprehended in Christ Jesus.

Thus

Thus we affirm, that Christ baptized us in Himself with the Holy Ghost, and that in Him the beloved, we are made accepted, having redemption in His blood, the forgiveness of sins; and this is surely true in Him, when we .... and unbelief, as when we live in .... ge and enjoyment thereof; no .... ing but this record's being a pe......th, ever convince the world of sin, because they believe not. Thus stands the truth in Christ, and thus are we seen of God in Him, whatever situation we may be in respecting our own consciousnesses.

But when it pleases God to reveal his Son in us, when we are brought up to the knowledge and faith of the Truth, as it is in Christ, our state of mind, respecting purity, peace, and joy, answers to the particulars of Grace and Truth in Christ, as face answers to face in a glass.

Thus that Baptism of the Holy Ghost, wherewith Christ has baptized us in Himself, becoming intelligible to us, we believe it, appropriate it, and purify ourselves in it; so as to be free from guilt, and fear, and filthiness. Thus, in our measure, we experience that Baptism of the Holy Ghost, wherewith Christ baptized us in Himself; but we can no longer experience this, than we are found believing, and rejoicing in the truth as it is in Him: hence, the necessity of a continual looking unto Jesus.

As the sacred writings often speak indiscriminately of the truth as it is in Christ, and the manifestation and effects of the truth as in us, as the kingdom of God, the salvation of God, &c. without ever intending that any thing besides Jesus Christ alone is the salvation of God; so I, (where I have defined the Truth as in Christ, to be the Baptism with the Holy Ghost, and the same of this Truth's operation on the Christian heart) have had none other view than to testify of the Salvation that is in Christ, and of the knowledge and experience of it, as in every one who believeth.

F I N I S.

⁎⁎ *Shortly will be published by the same* AUTHOR, *by Subscription, A* TREATISE *on the* LORD's SUPPER; *another on the* MINISTRY *of the* NEW TESTAMENT; *and a third on the* CHERUBIMICAL MYSTERY, *or an Essay on the* MISSION *of* EZEKIEL *the Prophet. Subscriptions will be taken in by the* Author, *and* S. Bladon, *Bookseller, in* Paternoster-row.

THE SADDUCEE Detected and Refuted,

In REMARKS on the

WORKS

OF

RICHARD COPPIN.

BY
JAMES RELLY.

For the Sadducees *say, That there is no Resurrection, neither Angel, nor Spirit.* ACTS xxiii. 8.

LONDON:
Printed by M. LEWIS, at the *Bible and Dove,* in *Paternoster-Row.* 1764.
[Price One-Shilling.]

Though I greatly dislike the sentiments of *Richard Coppin*, yet their obsoleteness would have effectually secured them from my attacks: had they not been now re-published and sold, as it were under my nose; many of my hearers, being subscribers to the re-printing of them. From which circumstance, it being quite natural for the public to suppose that our doctrines are congenial; I thought it right to undeceive them: by giving them, in all these particulars, a specimen of my sentiments; which must necessarily be the sentiments of all such, who understand, and believe the doctrines which I preach. Unto this, with the desire of some friends, the following Remarks owe their existence: much rather then to any sanguine expectations by me entertained; of convincing such (of their error) who have already turned aside. For, where there is no heart for the authority of scripture, nor an ear to receive the arguments of reason, it is in vain for man to attempt the conviction and instruction of his brother: as objects of pity, all such must be left to the wisdom

dom, power, and goodnefs of him that made them: and who only can convince them of their error.

As I am rather confident of my matter, than of my manner, I hope the candid reader will pafs over all faults of the latter, and attend particularly to the former, honouring it with their credit, as far as it confifts with the fcriptures and right reafon.

THE
SADDUCEE
Detected and Refuted, &c.

My Dear FRIENDS,

CONTROVERSY is not my element: yet, if (in the smallest degree) it will contribute to your pleasure, and satisfaction, for me to cast my mite into the treasury, I shall readily comply with your desire.

You desire me to give you, and the public, my opinion of *Coppin*'s works; as they are now re-publishing.

That I might be able to do this sincerely and impartially, I applied myself with the utmost care, and candor, to the reading of them.—I read three numbers of a work, intitled, *Michael's opposing the dragon*, &c. and also another book by the same author, intitled, *The advancement of all things in Christ, and of Christ in all things*: prefaced with a warm recommendation by Mr. *Cayley*.

Having thus far qualified myself to give you an answer*, I shall first tell you, as a matter not at all foreign to your enquiry, that I was not in the least degree accessary, no, nor so much as privy, to the present re-publication of *Coppin*'s works, or to any part thereof.

As to the author, I think him unnecessarily abstruse: He labours to cloath himself with darkness as with a garment, and carefully avoids speaking intelligibly, except when he rails at his antagonists: and then he uses great plainness of speech. But, to darken counsel, with words without knowledge, is the grand arcanum of mysticism: and by some, reckoned to be the infallible criterion of spiritual teachings: witness Mr. *Cayley*'s preface, to part of this author's works.

Again, instead of submitting, when pinched by argument, or manifestly opposed by truth, he is very evasive: and often begs the question, that he may have an opportunity of bespattering his adversary, and of giving his own system an air of plausibility.

One instance of this, I shall give you, out of the many that may be gathered from his works, No. 3. chap. 12. of *Michael opposing the dragon*. Where, (because his opponents argue for the resurrection of the same body) he insinuates that they plead for the resurrection of a sinful body: whereas there was nothing farther from their thoughts: and this he very well knew.

If

---

* It was supposed by many, and even affirmed by some, that I privately encouraged the re-publication of *Coppin*'s works. Which accounts for my manner of speaking above.

If I affirm, that the same body that died, and was buried, shall rise again: doth it follow from thence, that it must rise a sinful body? I must deny it, except *Coppin* had proved, or, that his admirers will yet prove, that sin is a property, or part of the body, and essential to its existence—And that would be just the same as to say, that a leprosy, a fever, a delirium, being disorders in the body, are a part thereof; and that the body cannot exist without them.

Again, I think him opinionated, and conceited, even to sillyness: as appears from his boastings of light, knowledge, purity, *&c.* above his fellows; though there is not the least spark of this pre-eminence discoverable: neither in his spirit, nor manner.

As to that infallibility which he pretends to, in all his silly, unscriptural determinations; I believe every man of sense, will attribute it to pride and ignorance. Though he affects to treat his opponents in a very supercilious manner, yet he cannot help discovering, that their accusations give him smart. He betrays a much greater fondness for himself, than becomes an apostle: by complaining of his persecutions, *&c.* But I shall now leave the author, and take notice of his doctrines.

In his book, intitled, *The advancement of all things in Christ*; (the same which Mr. *Cayley* hath authorized, and blessed with the highest encomiums) he begins with this hypothesis: That there are two principles, or qualities, in man; which he calls good, and evil: and that these principles are the elect, and reprobate; the believer, and unbeliever; the saved, and the damned; the *Jacob* and *Esau*; the *Christ*, *&c.* in every man. And, that the Persons of mankind are not at all concerned in any of those characters. For saith he, " God hates " no man's person, but the evil in the person: " neither doth he love any man's person any " farther than as they shew forth something of " himself."

This is not only unsupported by scripture, and common sense; but diametrically opposite to both. Doth the word of truth ever affirm, or even suppose, that there is any good in man? did the prophets, our Saviour, or his apostles, ever bear such a testimony? Is it not their constant language, that the imaginations of man's heart are evil, and that continually? that there is none, who doth good, no not one? that we are all as an unclean thing, and all our righteousness are as filthy rags? that there is none good but one, even God? and that all the deeds of this world are evil? that in our flesh (or person) there dwells no good thing?

And as to the supposition of the principles of good, and evil, residing in man; the same word of truth enquires, *What fellowship hath righteousness with unrighteousness, and what communion hath light with darkness, what concord hath Christ with* Belial, *or what part hath he that believeth with an infidel?*.

If these cannot dwell together in the same house, much less can they dwell together in the same heart; in the same person. Our Saviour tells us, that the same person cannot serve two masters, *i. e.* God and mammon. The apostle saith, that the same fountain cannot send forth

bitter

bitter waters and sweet. Thus the scriptures detest, and explode, the notion of those principles being in man.

For, if the same person be an habitation in common; for God and the Devil, for *Christ* and *Belial*, for light and darkness; then would the apostles be found false witnesses: the same fountain would then send forth bitter waters and sweet: *Christ* and *Belial* would then have concord: and the believer would have part with an infidel.

Again, it is contrary to experience, to suppose the being of those two principles in man. The prophets, and apostles, all confessed, that they were sinners; and that there dwelt no good thing in them. Their good consisted wholly in that which dwelt in *Christ*: in what he was made of God unto them—and which was revealed in them by the Spirit of truth.

Every christian, in every age, who have truly known themselves; *have* confessed, and *do* confess, that according to the propensities of their own hearts, they are carnal and sold under sin: and that in them, in their flesh, or in their own persons; there dwelleth no good thing.

That all men are sinners, their actions, spirit, and manner, fully prove: We judge of this, according to what we are taught, to conceive of the nature, and properties, of the divine Being: and, if we are to judge by this rule, it is obvious even to common sense, that there is none that doth good, no not one.

The supposed good, in man; is quite invisible: If you believe it, you must believe it unseen: you must take their word, for what

they,

they, to a judicious eye, to an unbiassed judgment, can never make appear. So that if God loves no man, but in proportion to the good that is in him, we may look upon the eternal ruin of every creature as inevitable.

This antichristian invention, owes its original to that spirit, which attempts to investigate truth by the fluctuating passions: by frames, and visions, rather than by the testimony of the prophets and apostles.

The self-righteous spirit was also deeply concerned in the scheme: when fondly dreaming of goodness, and holiness, in the creature; and at the same time convinced of the evil, by scripture and experience; there remained no other way of solving the difficulty, but by proposing that there are two principles in man: or two distinct qualities, *i. e.* good, and evil.

Nor has opposition to the true *Christ* been wanting here. As appears from its ascribing to this phantasm in man; the whole of the salvation, and characters of the Lord *Jesus:* which I shall have occasion to shew, more particularly, in my following remarks.

Having denied, that the persons of mankind are either the objects of God's love, or hatred; that they are either the subjects of salvation, or condemnation, he, to maintain some shadow of consistency, denies also the resurrection of the body: No. 3. page 67.—So does he the ascension of our Saviour's body, if not his resurrection, in No. 2. ch. 9. in which, he has falsified the scriptures, and made void the hopes of the children of God from the beginning.

To

To do this, with impunity; he pretends that the scriptures are an allegory—that there are allegories in the scriptures, I deny not. But they do not destroy facts; and make void the truth of relation, and narrative, contained therein: *Paul*, speaking of *Abraham*'s affair with the bond-woman, calls it indeed an allegory—but *Paul*, in so saying, does not deny that there was such a person as *Abraham*, nor that he had a son by a slave: but his allegory consisted in a spiritual doctrine, concealed under that fact; until revealed to him by the Holy Ghost.

Where allegories have no affinity to facts, and to facts properly stated, and ascertained; the man who attempts to build by them, is as though he attempted to build castles in the air: Such kind of a building is *Coppin*'s: who will have it, that the resurrection, and ascension of the Lord *Christ*, is to be understood spiritually or allegorically only.

This brings to my remembrance, the dream of a certain visionary, who would be an instructor of others: This person, not long since, being in company where the siege of *Samaria* was talked of, of what distresses the inhabitants felt, how a woman in the rage and fury of hunger eat her own child, &c. The same person, then asked, with a contemptuous smile, whether they thought the thing *literally* true, or not? Upon their answering in the affirmative, the person replied: It is not true in your sense; I myself am the *Samaria*: and have been so very straitly besieged; that I was obliged to eat my first-born, *i. e.* that inward goodness

goodness, which I had brought forth in sorrow; and until then had nourished so carefully.

But to return; I confess myself simple enough to believe all things that are written in the law, and in the prophets; and that I have hope towards God, that there shall be a resurrection of the dead: I particularly reverence the testimony of the evangelists, concerning *Jesus Christ* our Lord. And in them we learn, that our Saviour was God incarnate, God manifest in the flesh, the word made flesh, &c. and that he was a real man; he had a reasonable soul, and a material body: that from infancy to a perfect state of manhood, he lived upon this earth; going about doing good, and fulfilling all righteousness. And, that as a man, he felt pain, sickness, weariness, hunger, thirst, joy, sorrow, &c. That in the article of his sufferings, his soul was sorrowful, even to death; whilst his body was scourged, crowned with thorns, spit upon, buffeted, and treated with the utmost indignity. And after all, by many wounds, he was nailed to a cross; where, having vented strong cries and tears, he expired under the torment. That, when dead, he was taken down from the cross and laid in a sepulchre, wherein never man was laid before—that a guard of soldiers was appointed to watch the tomb, lest his disciples should steal him away—that on the third morning, notwithstanding all their pre-caution, the angels descended; and smiting the keepers with deadly fear, rolled the stone from the mouth of the tomb: (this was altogether unnecessary if the material body did not rise again)—that the very identical body of
our

our Saviour, which was laid in that grave, did then arife; and fhewed himfelf alive to his difciples. All this I affuredly believe. He firft convinced his difciples of the truth of his refurrection, by his well-known form and features; by his voice, manner and matter of fpeech. He fecondly fhewed them the wounds in his hands and his feet, by which he had been nailed to the crofs: as they well knew how he had been treated; thofe marks, being perfectly correfpondent, fhewed them it was he. Thirdly, he propofed to *Thomas* (who was the moft incredulous of them all) in the prefence of the ten, that he fhould put his hand into his fide, and his fingers into the nail-prints: and to them all, he propofed that they fhould handle him, and fee, for that a fpirit had not flefh and bones, as they might perceive him to have.

He converfed with them, he eat and drank in their prefence; and gave them every poffible and neceffary proof of his refurrection, in that material, individual, identical body; which was crucified and laid in the fepulchre. After continuing with them for the fpace of forty days, he, (in their prefence, before their eyes) lifting up his hands and bleffing them, afcended up on high: an intervening cloud receiving him out of their fight. And they were then told, *that that fame* Jefus *fhould come in like manner as they had feen him afcend.*

Now, as it is manifeft, that he retained the identity, and corporeity of his body, to the moment of his afcenfion; it belongs to the oppofers to tell us what became of his body, if it did not afcend; what mountain, or hill,

was

was it found upon afterwards? did it diffolve into air? or is it preferved fomewhere until he come again? (becaufe they were taught, that he fhould come again, in like manner as they had feen him afcend) If it is, let them tell us where? Did not the manner wherein they faw him afcend, and in which he was to come again, relate to the reality of his perfon, and the method of his afcent? and alfo to their feeing him with their bodily eyes? I think it did: Let fuch who think the contrary, convince me of my error if they can.

Again, if the body of *Chrift* did not afcend, it will be pretty difficult to affix a meaning to the term: It cannot be applied to the godhead; the nature and properties of which, denies all circumfcription and paffibility: nor can it be applied to the human foul only, for reafons given below *.

To

---

* The terms *defcend*, and *afcend*, implies; either a change of ftate, or change of place, or both. But the godhead as omniprefent, impaffible, unchangeable, &c. cannot admit of change in either: Therefore, thefe terms cannot be applied to our Saviour refpecting his godhead only—Nor have they a limited application to his foul: becaufe it doth not appear, that our Saviour ever manifefted his perfon, his glory, his falvation, but as in the matter and form of a human body.—He is reprefented, as inhabitant in fuch a body, at the formation of *Adam*—when, as the image and likenefs of God; he was alfo the firft born, and the beginning of his creation; exhibiting in himfelf, the model after which man was to be created. In the form, and manner, of a human body, he appeared unto *Abraham*—in the fame manner, and form, he wreftled with *Jacob*—in the fame likenefs he appeared to *Mofes, Jofhua, Job, Ifaiah,* &c. And in fuch a body he always manifefted himfelf unto his apoftles, as well after his

refur-

To turn all the scripture-account of our Saviour's resurrection, and ascension, into such an allegory, as destroys the facts; is just the same, as if they denied that there ever was such a person as *Paul* the apostle: but that all that is said of him, relates to certain dispensations which mankind pass under in their own minds. And again, in history; it is as though we should aver, that there never was such a person as our king *Harry* the fifth: but, that the tradition of such a person, and of his battles, and victories in *France*; relate altogether to the good principle in man, the divine power fighting and conquering in the *France* of our nature.

What would be our conceptions of such a ranting spirit as this, madly drawing every thing into that devouring vortex, HIMSELF? I believe, that the most charitable constructions we

---

resurrection, as before: and in the same manner doth the Holy Ghost now reveal him: when he takes of the things which are his, and shews them unto us. Hence it is manifest, that the Lord Jesus always occupied a human body; both in matter, and form: particularly in his descension and ascension. When he descended to a fellow-feeling with the creatures, even to the lowest depth of human misery; it was in the whole man, consisting of body and soul. When he descended into torment, where the pangs of death encompassed him round about, and the pains of hell gat hold upon him; it was as the whole man, consisting of body and soul. In the same sense he descended into the chambers of death, exploring the sides of the pit; and sinking to the lower parts of the earth. The apostle assures us that, he that descended, is the same also that ascended, up far above all heavens. Upon which authority, we affirm; that the body of the Lord Jesus is risen from the dead, and ascended up on high—otherwise he who descended, is not the same that ascended.

we could possibly put upon such sentiments, would amount to this: The poor creature is altogether under the baneful influence of ignorance and pride.

And is not this the case with the author, whose writings are the subject of my present consideration, and indeed with the mystics in general? do not they pretend to account for the truth of all things in themselves? They certainly draw all scripture-facts, such as the incarnation, personality, birth, life, sufferings, death, resurrection, and ascension of *Christ*; into their own vortex: and deny their reality, or at least their usefulness in any other sense.

I need not use many arguments to prove, that whilst a man, by such a conduct, betrays the most wretched ignorance of himself: he also gives evidence sufficient, of his being one of the children of pride. The blessed *Jesus* saith of himself, I am the truth. But the person abovementioned, contests the point with him: by declaring that the truth of all things is to be looked for in man. And thus as a thief and a robber, he steals the brightest jewel in *Immanuel*'s crown; to ornament self with.

Allow but the facts of the resurrection, and ascension of our Saviour's body; and then you may spiritualize as much, as high, as refined as you please upon it; provided you always crown the head, by keeping the pre-eminence and exaltation of our Saviour's person in view: otherwise, the spirit which is in you, with all its niceties and appearances of piety, is but an antichrist.

If the resurrection of our Saviour's body, be ascertained in the scriptures; and guaranteed by all the apostles, as it surely is; we may easily come to a determination, concerning the resurrection and future state of our own bodies: for the apostle tells us, that our bodies shall be fashioned like unto the glorious body of the Son of God. The New-Testament teaches us, that the resurrection of the Lord *Jesus*, his state, as then appearing and manifesting himself, is the perfect pattern, and sample of our state and condition eternally with God.

What does the term resurrection imply, if not the rising again to life, of that which was subjected to death? But the soul is immortal, as proved from scripture and reason, and cannot die. It is the body *only* that dies: Therefore the future resurrection of the dead, if there be any, must be that of the body, and of the body only: otherwise there is no meaning in the term.

I confess that the term is sometimes used in the scriptures, as respecting the raising again of mankind in the second *Adam*; from that death of trespasses and sin, wherein they were involved in the first *Adam*. There are those also, who apply it to that quickening, or renewal, which is effected and wrought in the spirit of the mind, through the manifestation of the truth.

To limit and confine the term to this, is certainly to deny a future resurrection, and to commence disciples of *Hymeneus* and *Philetus*; of whom hear what the apostle *Paul* saith: *Their word will eat as doth a canker, who con-*

cerning the truth, have erred; saying, that the resurrection is passed already: and overthrow the faith of some. For an Infidel, a Deist, to set up his own opinions in opposition to the apostle, is not to be wondered at: but for people professing themselves Christians, who acknowledge the spirit speaking by the apostles, to be infallible: for such to prefer the instigations of a private spirit, to the public testimony of the divine word: is very strange and inconsistent.

For my own part, I do not see that death dissolves the union between soul and body, any more than what sleep doth. In sleep, the body is passive and inactive, as in a state of death: and yet the union of soul and body is discoverable in sleep.—So also in epileptic fits, &c. when the body is deprived of motion, and senseless as a corpse; when all the channels of advice are stopt, and the common sensorium deprived of intelligence: the soul doth *then* evidence her own existence; and confesses her union to the body, by retaining its organs: which she occupies in the spiritual world; (of which world the soul herself is a native) though according to things present, she hath ceased from the exercise of the material eye, ear, hands, &c.

Death being only a sleep, a state of suspension, respecting the exercise of bodily functions, destroys not the unity of soul and body; nor does it hinder, but that the soul possesses the bodily organs, in her consciousness of unity to the body.

Should

Should it be objected, that death is such a sleep as destroys the body: I answer, The change, or alteration of the body in death, respects form and manner only, and doth not imply the loss of matter: or that it loseth its identity: And therefore, I deny that death annihilates the body. The scriptures speak of man, as consisting of three parts: body, soul, and spirit. The body is meerly material, earthly, inactive and senseless: And yet the body itself, is fearfully and wonderfully made: That wisdom, power, and glory which manifest themselves, in the exquisite workmanship and structure of the human body, effectually demonstrate that it was built for eternity; and not for a moment of time only.

The second part of man, called his spirit, is his senses: This spirit, dwells *in*, and is united *unto* the whole body; even *in*, and unto every minute part thereof. This spirit, is guardian to the body, discovers bodily dangers, and concerns itself for the prevention of them. It also discovers what is good for the body, assenting to it, and chusing it. This is the spirit, that immediately occupies the bodily organs in this material world. It hears through the ear; it sees through the eye; it smells through the nostrils; it tastes through the palate; it feels through the skin: and swifter than lightning, it sends intelligence of all its discoveries to the common sensorium: where, in the head, as in the pre-eminent member, the spirit hath its highest residence: according to the determinations there, which are as speedily communicated

ted to the whole; the paſſions predominate: either love, joy, ſorrow, hatred, anger, &c. Thus far this ſpirit is in common to men and brutes.

But this ſpirit in man, as dwelling in, and united unto every minute part of his body, is alſo united to his ſoul: And thus becomes the medium of unity between ſoul and body, in the rational creature.

The ſoul in man, is an immortal conſciouſneſs of exiſtence, having the powers of thinking, reaſoning, reflection, will, reſolution, &c. —This ſoul, united to the animal ſpirit in man; improves, and raiſes that ſpirit in him, much above what it is in the brutes. Thus, though the faculty of ſpeech be in common to man and other creatures, as birds, &c: yet the latter has not the power of invention, order and reaſon, and can only ſpeak at random what they hear. But man has reaſon, invention, order and deſign in his ſpeech: which proves, that the principal, or head of the triad, in his compoſition; is a ſpiritual dignity.

As the ſoul in man, is immediately united to the ſpirit, and the ſpirit to the body; I would obſerve, that the ſoul always retains the ſpirit: Hence it is ſaid, that the ſpirit of a man goeth upward (*i. e.* in conjunction with the ſoul which is divine) whilſt the ſpirit of a beaſt (as not having a divine and immortal ſoul) goeth downward.

As the ſoul, in man, retains the ſpirit, and lifts it upward with herſelf—ſo does the Spirit alſo retain the body, in its organical ſyſtem: even

when

when the material machinery is subjected to corruption, and ferment in the grave *.

In a dream, when the body is as dead, the soul, by the medium of the animal spirit, occupies its organs; and feels the passions, sometimes to very great degree. Nor, doth the body's being in the grave, hinder the soul, (who by the medium of the spirit, holds the body in union through all its changes) from so retaining the organical system thereof, as to feel the passions; as perfectly at least as she does in a dream—for which reason, the apostle with the utmost propriety calls death a sleep.

And here, it may not be improper to observe, that sleep doth not always imply rest. There is a sleep; which, with very unpleasant dreams, extreamly troubles the mind; and fatigues the body: Tired, distressed, and tormented; we find gladness in awakening from such a sleep; and rest, in reflecting that our misery was but a dream.

I have been credibly informed, by some who have undergone the operation; that after the amputation of a diseased member, the patient has felt pain, (in every particular to their senses) as if in the separated limb: just as though it

---

* May we not suppose that the soul, by the medium of the animal spirit, may (even after death) retain the body: respecting its mode, and its necessary conjunction; for the operations of the soul: in a manner ineffable, and peculiar to such a state? whence through the organs thereof, as suited to the spiritual world; the soul may be capable of hearing, seeing, feeling, &c. and also of *appearance* in an ærial, or shadowy form: and of subjection to the passions—so far, as to render her susceptible of joy, or misery, in a future state?

it was yet in union with the body. The truth of this I shall not attempt to investigate here: Yet I profess to see no cause, why the soul, through the animal spirit, may not, according to the laws and powers of union; feel as *by* and *in* the body, though the latter according to sense be put off: And if so, the soul cannot but long for the time; when the body having undergone its necessary ferment, shall be raised in glory and immortality; like unto that of the son of God: a fit habitation for a spirit to dwell in.

We look for the reality of all the joys, and representations, which we have in dreams; unto those that we have when awake: when the whole machinery is in exercise. So may departed spirits look forwards, from their visionary enjoyments: for perfection, for consummate bliss, to the restitution of all things. When the body shall be raised; when the creature itself shall be restored from the bondage of corruption, and brought into the glorious liberty of the sons of God—when the redemption (to wit, that of the body) shall be fully come—when every seed shall have its own body.

The apostle saith, *If ye be Christ's, then are ye* Abram's *seed*—And elsewhere, speaking of our Saviour, he saith, that *he took upon him the seed of* Abram—And again, that we are *one flesh* with him—that we are *his fulness*—that we are *members of his body, of his flesh, and of his bones.* From these, and many other testimonies in the divine word, it appears that we are comprehended in *Christ:* our bodies, in his body; and our

our souls, in his soul: He being in himself, the fountain of lives.

If it be true then, that *Christ* saved himself, in the whole man, consisting of body and soul; as his resurrection sufficiently demonstrates: then were *our* bodies, saved in *his* body; and *our* souls, in *his* soul. Unto which salvation, *i. e.* of *our* souls, in *his* soul; we come up even in *this* life—when through the knowledge of the truth, we attain to the *end of our faith*. But we are yet obliged to wait, for the redemption: to wit, that of the body. We cannot come up, in the present state of things, according to our bodies, to the state of *Christ*'s perfect body: Therefore the apostle says, *We look for the Saviour, the Lord Jesus Christ; who shall change our vile body.*

But, if the redemption of our souls, in the soul of *Christ*, did not destroy their individuality; nor prevent their being brought up, through the knowledge of the truth, unto the enjoyment of that salvation, which they had in his soul: Wherefore, should it be supposed, that notwithstanding the redemption of our bodies, in his body, *they* must lose their individuality, *they* must not rise again, nor be brought up to inherit that salvation which they have in the body of *Christ?* Let me say, as there was a time for the one; so there remains a time for the other: when the whole man shall be saved; when both in body and soul, he shall be for ever with the Lord.

Again, the practice of those who deny the resurrection of the body, gives their opinion the lie. Why are they so remarkably fond of their bodies? to feed them, to dress them, to beautify them, to preserve them in health and vigour, to honour them—and to gratify their appetites, is the whole employment of life—what are all the cares, and toils of life, directed to, but to the body? Man, can reap no other advantage, than food, and cloathing, from all his labours beneath the sun.

What fools then, to make such a momentary being, as the body; the sole object of our care and concern! And to be so very unwilling to part with them; which excepting lunacy, is manifestly the case with every man: *No man hateth his own body.* I will suppose that the apostle, who bare this testimony, had at least, as much understanding as a man, and as much divine light and real piety, as a Christian; as *Ceppin*; his admirers; or, as any mystic whatever—And yet he, though he knew; that he had a building of God; an house not made with hands, eternal in the heavens: and was desirous of being cloathed upon, with that garment of immortality: (I say) though he was well assured of this, yet he says, *not for that we would be uncloathed—but cloathed upon, that mortality might be swallowed up of life.* By which, he means as I suppose, that he was not desirous of being found naked: by the loss of his body—but his desire was to be cloathed upon—both body, and soul, with that glory and immortality which God had prepared for him.

And again, he faith in another place, *Behold I shew you a mystery; we shall not all sleep, but we shall all be changed, in a moment, in the twinkling of an eye, at the last trump. (For the trumpet shall sound, and the dead shall be raised incorrupti-*
ble;

die; and we shall be changed.) I apprehend his meaning in those words, to be, that such who are alive, at the end of time, shall not die: but that they shall cease from all vile, earthly qualities, in a moment; in the twinkling of an eye: The body shall be purified, and changed, without putting it off: into an incorruptible state—*The dead shall be raised incorruptible, and we shall be changed.* He not only assures us here, of the body's being saved, and of its entering into glory; but also of its salvation, and entrance into bliss, without tasting death.

Should some poor anchorite in the desart, consumed with famine, exposed to cold, and nakedness, sinking under his infirmities, and whose whole life in the body, is one continual penance. I say, should such an one deny the resurrection of the body, as not feeling much consolation from its existence: it would have some appearance. But for those, whose time, labour, and study, are spent altogether on account of the body; and whose chief felicity in life, seems to consist in gratifying its appetites. I say, for such to deny its future bliss, and to treat it only as a pampered beast, whereon they ride for a season, is to act a very unreasonable, and inconsistent part.

But so it is: The child of affliction believing, that his poor famished or diseased body shall rise again, and be fashioned like unto the glorious body of the son of God; he lays it down in hope—whilst the worldly, jolly, pretended-spiritual man—the refined genius, as he would be thought—(though possibly he hath not one abstracted idea, of existence, separate from the

body)

body) unreasonably suggests, that the body being meerly brutal; shall as such, perish in death everlastingly.

Because the scriptures say, *That flesh and blood shall not inherit the kingdom of God.*—*And that being sown a natural body, it is raised a spiritual body:* there are those who infer, that the body shall not rise again. But I would observe, that the terms flesh, and blood, as used in the scriptures; doth not always imply, the material body. Sometimes it intends man's natural wisdom, understanding, and reason; as where our Saviour says to *Peter, Flesh and blood hath not revealed those things unto thee*—*but my Father which is in heaven.* Are there any so stupid, as to imagine that the Lord meant, thy body has not revealed those things unto thee? Upon a serious consideration I hope there are none such.

Again, the term intends ease, honour, and profit, according to this world. Hence the apostle tells us, that when it pleased God to reveal his son in him, he conferred not with flesh and blood: but gave himself up to preach *Jesus* unto the *Heathen.*

Again, it intends our own righteousnesses.— The apostle *Paul,* calls his circumcision on the eighth day—his being of the stock of *Israel*—his being of an orthodox, and respectable sect—his zeal in his religion—his blameless righteousness as touching the law. I say, he calls all this *flesh.* And in this sense the divine evangelist understood it: When speaking of the sons of God, he tells us, that *they were born, not of blood, nor of the will of the flesh, &c. Paul* uses the term flesh, in the same sense, in another place, where

he

he says, *So then, they that are in the flesh, cannot please God.* And again, *having begun in the Spirit, are ye now made perfect by the flesh.* But *Paul* does not mean, that they that are in the body, cannot please God—because he tells us elsewhere, that *Enoch, before his translation, had this testimony, that he pleased God.*

At other times the term is not limited to our supposed excellencies, &c. but used in a more indefinite sense; including all the weaknesses, frailties, and corruption of our mortal state—and in this sense it is used in the abovementioned text, *i. e.* flesh and blood cannot inherit the kingdom of God. It is evident, that the apostle does not apply the term in those words, to the material body; nor did he intend to deny the resurrection thereof. But his design was to shew the necessity of the body's being purged, through death, from all the base qualities and infirmities, which constitute what he terms flesh and blood; and which, he says, cannot inherit the kingdom of God.

He explains himself more fully in the following words—*Neither doth corruption inherit incorruption.* But we are not pleading for the resurrection of a corrupt body—nay, we should then gain nothing by the change. The body of man, as the immediate creation of God, was incorrupt—corruption as applied to man, in body or mind, certainly intends, the evil bias, and vile propensities of human nature. Or, if by a corrupt body, we understand, its purulency, its liableness to putrefaction—I would observe that the latter, is only an effect of the former. And that it neither is essential to the being, or existence,

istence, of the body nor soul: Corruption in the first sense, is an accident only in man, and no part of him; and disease, death, or corruption, in the second sense, is to be considered, meerly, as the effect or consequence of the former, and can only subsist by it; and *where* that is found. *Christ* being made sin for us, sustained corruption in the first sense; but as he totally eradicated it, put it away, and destroyed it; by his sufferings, and death, he did not see corruption in the second sense: that is, his body did not putrify, nor moulder to dust—Thou wilt not *suffer thy holy one to see corruption.*

But our bodies are not thus privileged, because they are vile, flesh and blood, or corruption dwells in them—They like the house that had the leprosy in the walls, must be taken down for the destruction of the plague. We who make our exit, before the time of the end, must see corruption, because our bodies are vile. But we are taught that they shall be raised in incorruption: yea, we have the pattern exhibited in perfection, in the glorious body of our divine *Immanuel:* In him, we view the glorious reality, of what we are *with* God, and *to* God, and of what we shall be, *in*, and *unto* ourselves, when raised from the dead.

As to the proposition, that the body is sown natural, and raised spiritual. I would observe, that natural and spiritual, are distinct and opposite *qualities* only; and not distinct beings. Therefore, the change from natural to spiritual, doth not imply, that one being is lost, nor that one being becomes another: but it implies, that all those qualities which constituted the natural character,

character, being destroyed in death, the body rises in the qualities which constitute the spiritual character. And thus the body is sown a natural body; and raised a spiritual body: First, the body is natural from its manner of subsisting, as by meats, drinks, sleep, &c. Again, it is natural from its infirmities; such as hunger, thirst, weariness, pain, sickness, and death. Again, the body is natural from its affections, and operations, as generation, augmentation, motion, &c.

The body as subject to these, is a natural body; but having put off (by death) all these, it becomes a spiritual body; a body subsisting without the use of natural means; such as meats, drinks, sleep, physic, &c. A body free from all infirmities, and from all earthly affections, and operations. A body, though retaining its materiality, yet in the resurrection as the angels of God.

Know you not, saith the apostle, that your bodies are members of *Christ?* Shall I then take the members of *Christ*, and make them the members of an harlot? God forbid. To which I may say, shall we take the members of *Christ* and destroy them? shall we assert, that they have no pre-eminence above a beast, but that they must perish everlastingly? God forbid.

When *Lazarus* died, and *Jesus* approached to raise him from the dead, one of the sisters of the deceased, went forth to meet him; and in reverence to the Saviour (whilst she bewailed her departed brother) she said, *Lord, if thou hadst been here, my brother had not died.* Unto which, the compassionate High-Priest answered,

ed, *Thy brother shall rise again. Yea Lord,* (said she) *I know that he shall rise again in the resurrection at the last day.* Jesus replied, *I am the resurrection and the life; he that believeth on me, though he were dead, yet shall he live: And whosoever liveth, and believeth on me, shall never die. Believest thus this?* She said unto him, *Yea Lord.* That *Martha* believed the resurrection of the body at the last day, is declared in words as expressive as can possibly be used: nor did our Saviour reprove her sentiment (for it is highly probable that she had received it from him) he only taught her, that the resurrection of the human body, doth not proceed from natural consequences, but that it depended altogether upon him. *I am the resurrection and the life,* saith he. The fact of our Saviour's resurrection, doth not only ascertain that of ours; exhibiting the most glorious and shining pattern thereof; but it is also the cause, the means and security of our resurrection. It may also denote that power, wherewith he, as the Son of man, stands invested by the Father. *Martha* believed that her brother should rise again at the last day: But our Saviour taught her, that as her brother could not rise *then,* without him who was the resurrection and the life: so neither was his power confined to that day; but that he could exert it when it pleased him so to do: and which he then intended to do, by raising her brother from the grave.

It is said of the apostles, that they *preached, through Jesus, the resurrection from the dead.* And again of *Paul,* that *he preached Jesus, and*

and the resurrection: and *when they heard of the resurrection, some mocked. Of the hope and resurrection of the dead,* (saith the same apostle) *am I called in question.* Again, *That there shall be a resurrection of the dead, both of the just, and of the unjust.* Our Saviour saith, *The hour is coming, in which all that are in their graves shall hear his voice, and shall come forth: they that have done good, unto the resurrection of life; and they that have done evil, unto the resurrection of damnation. And the graves were opened, and many bodies of saints which slept, arose and came out of the graves, and went into the holy city and appeared unto many.*—*If the dead rise not, then is not Christ raised; our faith is vain, and our preaching vain; ye are yet in your sins.* Abram *accounted, that God was able to raise up* Isaac, *even from the dead.* But not to multiply citations, it is manifest, that the resurrection of the body, is possitively and clearly taught in the New-Testament: and was a principal article in the preaching of the apostles.

But some man, such as *Coppin,* and his admirers, will say, How are the dead raised up? and with what body do they come? Thou fool, saith the apostle, that which thou sowest, is not quickened except it die. The intention of this answer is to teach us, that as the death and ferment of the grain sown in the ground, hinders not its rising again; but is rather absolutely necessary to its springing up in a plant: so the death of the human body, is no hindrance to it rising again. *And that which thou sowest, thou sowest not that body that shall be.*
This

This is to shew us, that the body being sown natural, and raised spiritual, is not the same in its resurrection, as it was in its death: because (as I have shewn before) all those qualities which constituted the natural character, are destroyed in death: and the spiritual character as no longer restrained, and concealed by the former, is now perfectly sustained in the resurrection. The body thus changed, is said, not to be the same body; that is, the comparison, which proves, that the sown body, is not the same as the risen body; doth not respect its materiality, or identical existence, but its *qualities*; or *mode* of existence only.

Where the apostle saith, Thou sowest not that body that shall be, but bare grain, &c. There are none so simple, I suppose, as to imagine that the apostle would not have us expect to reap wheat, where we sow wheat: or that by another body, we are to expect *barley* where wheat is sown. Nay, his design is to shew us, that though the grain sown be bare, and simple, yet it riseth a glorious body, producing many-fold: as an emblem of the body, which is sown in corruption, but raised in glory; even an hundred fold, when compared with what it has in this life.

The grain which is sown, respecting its substance, is not lost: for though it ferments and dies, it shoots upwards into the stalk. Were you *then* to take the stalk properly out of the earth, you shall find that the sown grain, is fast at the root in appearance: but upon examination, you may perceive, that all its substance, every material particle, containing all its genuine

ine qualities are spent; are risen in the plant; and nothing remains but the chaff, or husk, which is all of it that is lost. This is a simile of the resurrection: All the original genuine properties of the body are preserved; and nothing lost but the chaff: *i. e.* the base qualities that adhered to it. *But God giveth it a body, as it hath pleased him; and to every seed its own body.* The meaning of which, I apprehend to be, that God, without accounting for his ways to man, without their being able to comprehend the depths of his wisdom, and power, is pleased in an ineffable manner, to give a body to the sown seed. Bewildered, and lost, in the researches of reason, we are constrained to resolve all into the good pleasure of God. *God giveth it a body, as it hath pleased him; and to every seed, its own body.* But if God does not give a human body, to every human body sown, how can every seed be said to have its own body?

In the passages above-cited, the apostle is manifestly speaking of the future resurrection of the body: but Mr. *Coppin*, and his admirers, will not so understand him. They will make it out in such a manner, as says that the resurrection is past. Thus erring concerning the truth, and overthrowing the faith of some; in *The advancement of all things in Christ,* &c. Chap. 6. he speaks thus, "God hath sowed the seed,
" or planted the image of eternity, the image of
" the divine Being, the image of himself,
" which is *Jesus Christ,* in this world, as in
" general, so particularly in *Adam*— in the
" flesh of *Christ*—in the flesh of his saints—
"in

"in the whole world of things." What has this unscriptural, this unmeaning proposition, to do with the matter in hand? what hath it to do with that scripture-passage, of which it is a pretended exposition? what affinity has the phraseology, or sense, (if it has any sense) of his propositions, to this interrogation? *How are the dead raised, and with what body do they come?* And what relation doth it bear to the apostle's answer, *Thou fool*, &c. except an assertion of right, to appropriate the character?

The term, image; as applied to God, may be understood in various senses. Kings, and magistrates, from their power and rule, may be said to be the image of God. Any person, exercising himself in works of mercy, compassion, love, benevolence, &c. may be said, in so doing, to be an image of God.—The sun is an image of his brightness; the rock of his stability; the fire of his purity, &c. In this sense, all creatures may be considered as having somewhat of the divine image: The heavens declare thy power, and firmament sheweth forth thine handy work.

But, if by the image of God, we mean the assemblage of all divine perfections; represented, and reflected, as in a mirrour, which in the scripture, is the primary sense of the term: there is then, none other image of God, than *Jesus Christ:* He is the brightness of the glory of God, and the express image of his person. The light of the knowledge of the glory of God, is in the face of *Jesus Christ*. Coppin says, that God planted this divine image in *Adam:* but neither the prophets, nor apostles, say so.

Moses

Moses indeed tells us, that God made man in his own image, and after his own likeness. But this image, and likeness of God, *in* whom, and *after* whom, man was made; was *Jesus Christ*: the same yesterday, to-day, and forever.

God, eternal, invisible, immortal, incomprehensible, was pleased to exhibit an image of himself, of his own nature, and properties, in the person of his Son; who was with him, as one brought up with him from everlasting. By which medium he wrought all his works. And in which he was known, and his glories reflected on the angels, and on all the heavenly powers. In this image, and after his model and similitude (he being the head of mankind) was *Adam* formed. *Adam* was so far from being the express image of God in himself, or from having it planted, or sown in him; that he, in his brightest perfection and glory, was but an outward, shadowy, fleeting figure, of him who is the perfect, express, unchangeable, and eternal image of the invisible God.—Hence the apostle calls *Adam* the figure of him that was to come.

Again, instead of acknowledging *Christ* himself to be the image of God, he talks of the image of God, being sown, or planted in the human nature of *Christ*; and that when *Christ* laid down his flesh, by the death of the cross, this image was raised up into the divine nature, where it lives forever. Here he shews himself to be a divider of *Christ*, by distinguishing the *Christ*, from the person of Jesus of *Nazareth*. In this he seems to follow *Cerinthus*, a person who lived in the first century; who held, that *Jesus* was the son of *Joseph* and *Mary*; but that *Christ*

[36]

Christ, in the form of a dove, descended upon him at his baptism: and that when *Jesus* suffered death, *Christ* flew up into heaven, without being sensible of any inconvenience. To confute the errors of this heretic, and his followers, *John* is reported to have wrote his gospel. *Coppin* in his definition of the true *Christ*; says, he is to be in us, to redeem and save us as he was in the man *Christ Jesus*. He also says, that when *Jesus* laid down his flesh, by the death of the cross, (the *Christ*, or) the image of God, was raised up into the divine nature, where it lives forever.

By saying that the image of God which *Christ* had in his human nature, was at his death, raised up into the divine nature, where it lives forever: he affirms, either that the body, or flesh of *Christ*, did not rise again; but that his human nature perished and ceased to be in death: Or otherwise, that though his human nature doth now exist, it is not the image of God: nay, the image of God doth not so much as dwell in it *now*, according to him. But the image of God is raised up into the divine nature, where it lives forever. According to which, there is no exhibited image of God now. These things are so horribly blasphemous, and antichristian; that they need neither the argument of reason, nor scripture, to confute them.

Again, what a rant it is, to talk of the image of God being planted in the flesh of his saints! and then to quote sundry passages of scripture, in support thereof: which bear no more relation to *his* proposition, than they do to the *Coran*.

I have already shewn from scripture, experience, and reason, that there is no such thing as

the

the divine image, or good principle dwelling in the individuals of mankind: neither in their flesh, nor spirit; and therefore shall say no more to it here.

Nor will I spend my time, to shew the impropriety of asserting, that this image is sown in the whole world of things; but shall leave the superlatively enlightned, to admire, and worship the divine image, in dogs, swine, serpents, &c. which are not creatures of the *smallest* consequence, in the whole world of things.

Thus, according to this author, the dead, or the seed sown, is *Jesus Christ*, or the divine image. And that this seed, was sown, died, and was buried, in the human nature, or flesh of man; and in the whole world of things. —That God raises this dead seed, or *Christ*, by his voice; And being risen in us, it returns to God again: whilst the nature and persons of men, with the whole world of things, are all left behind to perish. " Thus, (saith he) God hath " carried the image of himself, through all " things in the world, and to the end of all " things again even to himself." (And again) " This is the last and general resurrection."

Without doing him any injury, I may venture to affirm: that his doctrines are unscriptural, and unreasonable: tending to the subversion of christianity in general. For first, with *Hymeneus* and *Philetus*, he affirms, that the resurrection is past already. Secondly, he denies that the body rises at all. Thirdly, he denies that man, or any part of him, is the object of salvation. Fourthly, he asserts that the persons of men, having no pre-eminence above a beast, shall perish everlastingly as the beast.

Whether this man understood the apostles, or payed any regard to their doctrine, or not, I leave the reader to judge: and shall here observe, that if the matter in hand, had related only to the resurrection of *our bodies*; I should not have meddled with it: but should have left *Coppin* and his admirers, to the time of the restitution of all things; when every man shall be restored to his right senses; at least, so far as to distinguish between truth and error. But the apostle shews us, that if the doctrine of the resurrection be not true, if there be no resurrection of the dead, then *Christ* is not raised: and if he be not risen, then our preaching is vain: our faith is vain: we are yet in our sins. Thus it appears to be, (not a meer opinion, a speculation, or fable; but) a matter of the utmost importance: the source, and evidence of our salvation: our happiness in time and in eternity.

Again, this author, denies the human nature of *Christ*, No. 2. page 26. where he scoffs at a corporal *Christ*: and No. 3. page 58, 59. where he more than once, treats the doctrine of our Saviour's having a body of flesh and bones, with sneers and derision: as also in sundry parts of his book, intitled, *The advancement of all things in Christ*, &c. How amazing! that any person who believes, or even pretends to believe the scriptures, should dispute the truth of our Saviour's having a body of flesh and bones: when the evangelists assure us, that the Lord *Jesus*, after his resurrection, was particularly careful, to give his disciples the fullest evidence, the most indisputable proof, of his

being

being risen; in the very same body wherein he suffered and died.

Of the truth of this, he convinced their eyes, their ears, their hands, and heart.—He who knew all things, foresaw that men of perverse minds would arise: who, (though they confessed themselves christians) would contest, and deny, the reality of his resurrection. His form, his features, his voice, his wounds, the materiality of his flesh and bones; all which were manifest, and proved to a demonstration; perfectly convinced his disciples, that the same, individual, material body of *Jesus*, which was crucified, died, and was buried, was risen from the dead; nor was it possible for them to be deceived, by any phantom or shadowy appearance; because he convinced them of his having flesh, and bones; which they very well knew, were not the properties of a spirit.

Behold my hands, and my feet, (saith our Saviour) *that it is I myself: handle me, and see, for a spirit hath not flesh and bones, as ye see me have.* And again to *Thomas, Reach hither thy finger, and behold my hands, and reach hither thy hand, and thrust it into my side: and be not faithless, but believing.* But the *Christ*, whom *Coppin*, and his admirers reverence, neither is, nor was capable of making any such proposal to his followers; because he has no body of flesh and bones; nor indeed has he any other existence, than in their antichristian conceit.

That the *Christ* whom the apostles preached, had a body of flesh and bones, is manifest: where *Paul* tells the church, that they are *members of his body, of his flesh, and of his bones.*

But

But this propofition, cannot poffibly be true, if *Chrift* has no body of flefh and bones; as this author afferts. Let God be true, and every man a liar. The word of truth affures us, that he has a body of flefh and bones; and that this body, notwithftanding all its wounds and bruifes, was fo preferved that not a bone thereof was broken. But it was preferved to no purpofe, if it did not rife again: or, if it was loft afterwards.—The Holy Ghoft, bearing witnefs of the Lord *Jefus*, by the prophets; teftifies, that a bone of him fhould not be broken. Speaking of the paffover, the type of *Chrift*; he fays, *Neither fhall ye break a bone thereof*, Exod. xii. 46. And again, *nor break any bone of it*, Num. ix. 12. And again, *He keepeth all his bones: not one of them is broken*, Pfal. xxxiv. 20. And, that this related to the body of the Lord *Jefus*, the evangelift *John* bare witnefs. Our Saviour, and thofe who fuffered with him, being crucified on the eve of an high fabbath among the Jews; the latter befought *Pilate* (as the crucified were long dying) that they might have leave to break their legs: and to take them down, that their bodies might not be feen on their croffes on the following day: To this he confented; upon which, they brake the legs of thofe who were crucified with our Lord; but when they came to *Jefus*, and faw that he was already dead, they brake not his legs. And the beloved difciple in his remarks upon this, fays, *for thefe things were done that the fcripture fhould be fulfilled, A bone of him fhall not be broken*, John xix. 36. Thus, the apoftle fhews that it was not accident, but

the

the purpose and council of God, that defeated the design of the *Jews:* when they would have broken his legs with the others. Nor are we to respect it as a trifling, or common occurrence: That would be to impeach the wisdom of God, who had so long before his sufferings, declared by his prophets, that a bone of him should not be broke

The preservation of our Saviour's body was for his own glory, and for the benefit and advantage of mankind. As mankind were comprehended in his body, flesh of his flesh, and bone of his bone; it denoted their final preservation and security in the same body: Not the smallest member, was to be separated from the whole; nor the body from the head: that we might live by him. It also denoted his faithfulness, power, and love, in preserving the whole body, all that had been committed to his trust.

Again, Mr. *Richard Coppin* by proposing *Christ* to be a meer quality in man, denies his person, No. 1. page 13. He says that *Christ* "is to " be in you to teach, redeem, and save you, " as he was in the man *Christ Jesus.*" Thus according to him, the man *Christ Jesus*, who was born at *Bethlehem* of a pure virgin, who wrought many miracles, and went about doing good; who suffered, and died upon a cross, in the reign of *Tiberias Cæsar*; and who rose again from the dead, on the third day; I say, according to *Coppin*, this person was not the *Christ*, in spirit, and truth: but that the true *Christ* was in him only, to redeem, and save him;

him; in like manner as he is to be in the people.

And No. 3. pag. 59. he says: "And you say, "When Christ, who is our life, shall appear; "then shall we also appear with him in glory: "and this life, even Christ, you say is eternal "life. Then I answer, this must not be meant "of a body of flesh, and bones, for that can- "not be our eternal life. And this life, the "apostles then waited for, and received; which "was a spiritual Christ, even Christ in them "the hope of glory: and not a fleshly personal "Christ as you say; for how can such a one be "in us to be our eternal life?"

If I mistake not, Mr. *Coppin* intitles his works, [in defence of which, that which now is a re-publishing in numbers, was written:] *A Blow at the Serpent*. But whether his admirers will excuse me or not, I am obliged to give it a new title; and as I think a very just one; *i. e.* A BLOW AT THE SEED OF THE WOMAN.

He says, that Christ as a person, or as having a body of flesh, and bones, cannot be our eternal life. That our Saviour hath a body of flesh, and bones, I have already proved from the scriptures. And I shall now endeavour to prove, that the person of Christ, as having such a body, is our eternal life.

Our Saviour, in the 6th of *John*; declares that his flesh is meat indeed, and that his blood is drink indeed. And saith, whoso eateth my flesh, and drinketh my blood, hath eternal life. But how can we eat or drink what hath no ex- istence? can a man fill his belly with the east wind?

wind? can he drink of a river, whofe waters are cut off, and whofe ftreams are perfectly dried up? We anfwer, he cannot. It is not meerly faying to the body, be fed, that feeds it; nor, will our bidding it be warm, adminifter any heat to it.

As the Lord *Jefus*, has propofed to all generations, that fuch who eat his flefh, and drink his blood, hath eternal life; fhall live thereby, &c. I think I may venture to propofe, with as much confidence, and upon much better grounds than *Coppin* afferts the contrary: that our Saviour always has a body, a material body, a body of flefh and bones. And that this body, as united with his foul, to the deity; in the glorious perfon of Immanuel, is the eternal life: Hence whofo eateth him, fhall live by him.

To eat and to drink his flefh and blood, certainly intends fuch an apprehenfion of our union and onenefs with Chrift; as infpires us with wifdom, refolution, and power to appropriate him. So to mingle with his flefh and blood; *i. e.* his human nature; that all his labours, fufferings, victories, and triumphs, being ours as they are his; we might eat his flefh, and drink his blood: that is derive life, purity, confidence, and blifs; from our being one flefh and blood with him; intitling us to his peace and joy, which is unfpeakable, and full of glory.

What a perfon eats and drinks, being properly digefted in the ftomach; the nutritive part, after chylification, becomes blood; and mingles with the whole mafs: adding health, ftrength, and magnitude to the body throughout,

out. Thus, what a person eats and drinks, becomes one with himself: and except it does so, the person is not nourished, nor can he live thereby.

In like manner, to eat the flesh, and drink the blood of the Son of man; is to apprehend our union with him, our membership in his body, even of his flesh and of his bones: in such sort, that becoming one with his flesh and blood, we rejoice together with him; in all the benefits of his humiliation, and exaltation in the body. And thus, that *Christ* who hath a body of flesh and bones, is our eternal life.

As *Coppin* tauntingly asks, how a personal *Christ* can be said to be in us, as our eternal life? I answer, Christ, in the scriptures, is said to be our eternal life, in a two fold sense; first, as he hath taken upon him the seed of *Abraham*, personating, and wearing the people in the body of his flesh: he was born in them, circumcised in them, baptized in them, tempted in them, fulfilled all righteousness in them; he suffered in them, died in them, rose again in them, ascended in them, and liveth forever in them. Thus saith the prophet: *Lord, thou wilt ordain peace for us: for thou also hast wrought all our works in us.* And thus is *Christ* in us, the hope of glory. Thus did *Job* behold God in his flesh. Thus all the promises, relative to God's dwelling in the people, to his coming in the flesh, *&c.* are fulfilled in him. In *Christ Jesus*, all the promises are yea and amen. Here we understand, how the personal *Christ* is in us, and is our eternal life, and hope of glory. The life which he lives, in his own person, he lives *in* us, and *for* us:

us: Hence the apostle tells us, that the eternal life which God, hath given us, is in his Son. And our Saviour says, *Because I live, you shall live also.*

Again, *Christ* is said to be in man by faith, by revelation, by manifestation, by his spirit, &c. In this sense, he is in us, according to our individual persons. Faith is the evidence of things unseen, &c. Therefore it is that witness; *in,* and *with* power, light, and love to our minds; of the glorious person, and salvation of *Christ:* Though we have not seen him, neither are we permitted to determine of him by what we feel, or know from ourselves; yet our understandings are enlightened to discern him, according to truth: our wills consent to his salvation, and submit to his glory: our affections rejoice in him: our conscience hath peace, purity, and perfection in him.

The *Christ,* thus explained to our judgment, thus glorious before the eyes of our mind, thus borne witness of in our hearts, by the Spirit of truth; is not some creature of fancy, or the offspring of enthusiasm: but a personal *Christ*; that very *Jesus* whom the apostles preached; that identical person who died upon the cross, without the gates of *Jerusalem:* who rose from the dead, who ascended up on high, and who liveth forever. This person, according to his personal properties, glory, grace, and salvation; being explained, revealed, and witnessed of, in, and unto our faculties, is *Christ,* dwelling in our hearts by faith: There, realized (though unseen) in his person, and benefits: dwelling there, as the object of our peace and purity. *Coppin*

Coppin cannot conceive how a perſonal *Chriſt* can be ſaid to dwell in our hearts, no more than the *Jews* could conceive, how he could give them his fleſh to eat: but this is certainly owing to his ignorance, both of the ſcriptures, and of the power of God: Where he has not a mind to believe any thing, he exerciſes his reaſonings, aſking, how can a perſonal Chriſt be in us? He might as well have aſked, how can the body, when dead, and mouldered to duſt, ever riſe again? how could the body of *Chriſt* aſcend in air; without ſteps, or ſome other convenience to go up by, *&c. &c.?* For theſe are matters which he poſitively denies, becauſe he cannot comprehend them: But with regard to his own ſyſtem, he is as far above all *reaſon* in his propoſitions, as the heavens are above the earth: he is there, all inſpiration, and infallibility: trampling the weak and beggarly elements of reaſon, and common ſenſe, under his feet.

I hope, I have ſufficiently proved, that our Saviour hath a material body; a body of fleſh and bones: and have alſo ſhewn, how he, as having ſuch a body, may be ſaid to be in us, as our eternal life. I would here obſerve of *Coppin*, and his admirers, that *their* Chriſt is *no body*: They will neither allow him to have a human body; nor to be a perſon. Conſequently, he is neither God nor man: nor is he a ſpirit of any kind; otherwiſe he muſt be perſonal. *Chriſt*, is by them, ſuppoſed to be a principle, or quality of good: originally implanted in every creature. This ſuppoſed good, he calls the *Jacob*, which is loved of God: the leſſ precious; the believer; the *Chriſt, &c.*

And

And the evil principle, or quality in man, he calls the *Esau*, which God hates; the reprobate, the unbeliever, the antichrist, &c.

If you compare the above, with the doctrines of the *Manichees*; you will soon perceive that *Coppin*'s sentiments, are only a revival of the *Manicheean* heresy. They held that there were two principles; the one of good, from which proceeded the good soul of man; and the other of evil, from which proceeded the bad soul, with the body; and all other corporeal, and perishable creatures. They, also held that the good soul, went to God, unto whom it was rejoined. They denied the resurrection of the body. They denied that *Christ* had a real body.—Whether *Coppin* gleaned his sentiments in the *Manicheean* field, or whether they were sown in him by the same hand which first sowed them in *Manes*, the leader of the sect; I shall not determine: But manifest it is, that they are perfectly similar; and that they raise the same inferences from them.

Hence it is, that in No. 2. page 45. he says "Man is become one with God, in all that "God was above man."—I hope I shall be able to cloath my ideas, properly; and if I am, I doubt not but to detect, and expose, the fallacy, and danger, of this blasphemous proposition. He pretends that this proposition follows of consequence, from man's reconciliation in *Christ*, to the Father: and thus denies the personality, pre-eminence, and medium of *Christ*. Excuse me, if I subjoin part of a letter, which I wrote to a person in the country, not long since, on a similar subject.

"I

" I cannot but greatly diflike that propofition in your letter, *of our being equal with God*. It is faid 'of our Saviour, indeed; that *he thought it no robbery to be equal with God*. This was intended as a proof of his real godhead: fince in a ftrict fenfe of the word, God has no equal. Whatever equality, our Saviour as a man, has to God; it is according to that grace, and favour only, which the deity hath conferred upon the human nature in his perfon. Hence he is called the man, God's fellow. That is, his companion, his friend, whom he hath exalted at his own right hand, to be a prince, and a Saviour: And unto whom he is fo clofely, myfterioufly, and eternally united; that the Lord *Jefus*, according to the properties of his human nature, ftands invefted by the godhead, with all divine perfections: fo that it was no robbery for *him* to think himfelf equal with God. But it does not follow from thence, that *we* are equal with God: It is manifeft robbery, for *us* to think in fuch a manner: we rob the fcriptures of their truth; for they declare the contrary: We rob that God of his honour; who fays, my glory I will not give to another: We rob our Lord *Jefus Chrift* of his pre-eminence, and are fchifmatics in the firft fenfe of the word. It is, as if the foot fhould fay, I am the head; therefore put the crown upon me; or at leaft, let me have a crown, as well as the head. If we claim a right to fay, that we are equal with God; becaufe *Chrift* is equal with him: Is it not as if the foot fhould fay, I muft needs be the feat of wifdom to the body; becaufe the head is fuch? Or, I muft needs

have

have the pre-eminence and crown, becaufe the head hath them? do not you perceive how groundlefs, and falfe, all fuch inferences are?

To infer that we are equal with God; becaufe *Chrift* thought it no robbery to be equal with God; is either to deny, that *Chrift* is any other perfon than the church, and, that the fcriptures have any other meaning than the people; in what they fpeak of him: Or, if we confefs him to be an individual, a diftinct perfon, wholly independent of mankind, in point of exiftence: I fay, if we thus confefs him, and yet infift on our being equal with God; becaufe he is fo: we certainly rob him of his preeminence, and deny him as the mediator between God and man. To fay, that *Chrift* hath none other body, or perfon, than the people; is the fame in argument, as if we faid, the head hath none other reality of exiftence, than what it hath in the hand, or in the foot.

The Lord *Jefus*, in his perfon, and in the myftery of his body, may be confidered as fimple, and aggregate. Simple, as he ftands alone, in an uncompounded exiftence; where he is not the people, neither are the people him. In this point of view, he ftands high above every creature in heaven, on earth, and under the earth; he is *there* fairer than the fons of men, and the perpetual object of their worfhip.

But in his office-capacity, as he reprefented, and perfonated mankind; which he did in his birth, obedience, fufferings, death, refurrection, and afcenfion; and now doth in his everlafting life; he was the aggregate. He was in all *this*, the fum total of mankind; who were thus gathered into one body. But the aggregate, was subject to the simple. Hence it is, that the people, who are purified, and exalted in the aggregate; pay eternal homage to the simple; falling before his feet, and forever singing, Worthy is the Lamb, &c. And whilst they acknowledge him to be the Lord, to be the only holy, they confess that the simple is the head of the aggregate.

The apostle tells us, that the head of every man is *Christ*, and the head of *Christ* is God. From this, you may perceive, that we have no immediate *union* with God; much less an equality with him.

It is *Christ* only, in his simple existence; who is united to God: he only, is one with the Father: In him, the deity is immediate head to the human nature: which branch of human nature, in the man *Christ Jesus*, is immediately head over all things, to the aggregate; *i. e.* to his body the church.

By *Christ*, as the medium between God, and man; every good, and perfect gift cometh. He is the immediate receiver of all good, from God. He is the exalted, he is the anointed, he is the crowned King of kings, and Lord of lords: whilst we, without envy, without repining, rejoice in his glory; and are joyfully subject to him.

Should it be granted, that the hand, the foot, or the more uncomely parts of the body; have a right to claim an equality with the head, (which is not an unexceptionable rule) yet this right, in every member, must be limited to its own head. With what propriety then

then can we claim an equality with God, who is the head of *Chrift*, and not our immediate head?

We certainly can claim no more, than to be as our own head; nor is that claim afcertained any farther, than as he is confidered the aggregate: for in his fimple, and individual exiftence, he is anointed with the oil of gladnefs above his fellows. He is *there* the object of our worfhip, love, praife, delight, and eternal admiration.

From all which, I conclude, that the propofition of our being equal with God, is meer rant; and more than bordering upon blafphemy. It is productive of many hurtful and pernicious errors: it infpires mankind with luciferian pride; though in comparifon of the Almighty, they are lighter than vanity, they are lefs than nothing. It difhonours our Creator, by making him fuch a one as ourfelves. It deftroys the medium between God and man; which is *Chrift Jefus* the Lord. It denies the *pre-eminence* of our Saviour, as head over all things to his body the church.

But as Mr. *Richard Coppin*, in his writings, does not gather with *Chrift*; as he denies the body, and perfon of the Lord *Jefus:* it will be objected probably, that my arguments do not comprehend the grounds of his propofition. I believe I am as well aware of his meaning, as his admirers are; excepting none of them. But I confefs, there is fome difficulty, in framing arguments againft things which will *fcarcely* bear any: as is the cafe here. He fays that "Man is be-
" come one with God, in all that God was above
" man."

" man." But it is neither true in divinity, nor philosophy. Is man become one with God in his eternity, wisdom, power, purity, &c. &c.? the proposition is odious, and blasphemous.

Had he said of *Christ*, according to the properties of his *human nature*; that he is become one with God, in all that God was above him; he had erred against the truth. But, as he denies the person of *Christ*; he must by *man*, whom he says is one with God, mean the creature, himself, his brethren, &c. And does it appear, either to men, or angels; that man, a worm, subject to passions, and compassed about with infirmities, is one with God; in all the tremendous height of his glory and majesty? Nay, as the heavens are above the earth, so are his ways, and his thoughts above ours.

Again, as he denies the personality of *Christ*— as he treats all the scripture-account of things allegorically.—as he says, that the believer, and unbeliever, are, in every man, &c. He acts consistent with himself, in making out that salvation, [which our Saviour taking upon him the seed of *Abraham* by his obedience, sufferings, death and resurrection, wrought out for us in his own person:] to consist in a work, or operation, wrought within us.

" God (saith he) reveals all his secrets
" within, and all the works that he doth in
" this new creation, he doth within us: And
" therefore, let all those that desire to be
" made partakers of this new creation, look
" for it within them; for there will God
" work it." *Advancement of all things in Christ*, &c. pag. 24.

God,

God, who at sundry times, and in divers manners, spake unto our fathers by the prophets, said, *Be ye glad, and rejoice in that which I create.* But if this new creation is wrought in us; it follows that we are to rejoice in ourselves. But the apostle tells us, that *Christ* is made of God unto us wisdom, righteousness, sanctification, and redemption; that whosoever glorieth, should glory in the Lord. *Christ* says, *Look unto me all ye ends of the earth, and be ye saved:* but *Coppin* says, we must look unto ourselves for it. The apostle says, We *are God's workmanship created anew in Christ Jesus,* &c. But *Coppin* says, we are created anew in ourselves. The promise, which God made, of creating all things anew; *Coppin* says he fulfills, by working it within us. But *Christ* told the apostle *John,* that this promise was fulfilled in his person; *It is done, saith he, I am the Alpha, and Omega, the beginning and the end.* The prophet speaking of mankind, (not excepting Mr. *Coppin*) says, *The best of them is as a briar, the most upright is sharper than a thorn hedge,* &c. &c. *therefore will I look unto the Lord,* &c. The apostle speaks of the sentence of condemnation in ourselves, that we should not trust in ourselves, but in the living God.

If we try it by experience, reason, and common sense, this new creation is not discernable in man. There has no physical change passed over him; his body is the same, subject to pain, sickness, and death; and compassed about with manifold infirmities. Nor is there any inward change, answerable to a new creation: where old things are done away, and all things are become

become new. Those who pretend to the highest refinements, and spirituality, are men subject to like passions with others; as is very obvious in the author himself, who could not bear the least opposition from his antagonists. Their censures, and reflections, wounded his vanity, and self-importance, in such sort that he could not contain himself; but resolving not to be behind hand with them, he gave them as good as they sent; yea, I think rather exceeded them in the article of judgment and censure. But this I suppose he thought he had a right to do, as being more spiritual than his opponents. And I have sufficient reason to conclude, that the case is still the same, with some of his admirers.

And if men are censorious, proud, vain, and selfish, with what propriety, or justice, can they look for this new creation in themselves? and wherein doth it consist? If its a truth, that they love God, it is an invisible one. But it is a truth visible enough that they love the present world; and yet the apostle saith, *If the love of the world is in any man, the love of the Father is not in him.* They may tell us that they love their brethren, but it is a matter that we are no further sure of, then as we take their bare word for it; but this, we are very sure of, that they love themselves; that being notorious enough. And yet to be lovers of their own selves, is ranked by the apostle among the reprobate characters.

In fact, where men differ nothing from others; (except in partiallity to themselves) opinion, sentiment, or theory, is not sufficient to
prove

prove them fpiritual men, or that the new creation is within them.

Pray, is not this enthufiaftic conceit, this vain-glorious imagination, or the good principle in man; the beaft, *that was, and is not?* that it is full of the names of blafphemy, I think is plain enough: for, it arrogates the perfonal characters, names, works, fufferings, death, refurrection, afcenfion and glory; of our only Lord and God, *Jefus Chrift*; ufurps his crown, and throne; and exalts itfelf againft all that is called God, and that is to be worfhipped.

This is the beaft that all the world worfhippeth, and goeth after. Pagans, Mahometans, Jews, Chriftians of all denominations, and of every fect, worfhip this beaft; going after him perpetually, in their admiration, defires, and efteem.

This beaft, bears different names, according to the different languages of men: The Heathen call him virtue. The Jews, and Mahometans, call him obedience: only the one refpect *Mofes*, (as their prophet and legiflator) and the other, *Mahomet*. Amongft Chriftians, this beaft bears divers names, according to their various divifions; and every diftinct name, by which it is called, may be confidered as the fhibboleth of the fect, making ufe of it. By fome he is called grace, and the falvation of man, very cordially imputed to him; to the difhonour of the Son of God.

By others, he is called inward holinefs, fanctification, imparted righteoufnefs, inherent righteoufnefs, &c. Whilft others, call him the inward light, the Spirit, &c: and make him infallible in reproof, inftruction, and doctrine.

And again, there are others, as *Coppin, &c.* who call him *Christ*, the elect, the believer, yea, God himself.

Now I say, that the different names, and epithets, made use of amongst all these; (notwithstanding their various attachment to men and things) makes no difference at all, with respect to their object of admiration, and worship, or to their hope of salvation: for the terms, virtue, obedience, grace, holiness, light, or *Christ* as supposed to be naturally in man, are all congenial: and characteristics of the beast *that was, and is not:* And this beast is always manifest, from its being opposed to the person of *Jesus Christ* our Lord: and to that free, and gracious salvation which he has wrought out for mankind, without works of righteousness; as done by them.

As to the *origin* of this supposed good in man, its admirers are not perfectly agreed about it: there are some, such as *Coppin, &c.* who consider it as the seed of God, sown in man at his first creation; which was not totally lost, or extinguished by the fall; but buried only, as it were, under a heap of rubbish: from whence, not being quite dead, it sends forth, some weak breathings by way of conviction, repentance, desire, *&c.* until it hear the voice of God, and come forth out of its grave. But others reject this, as unscriptural, unwarrantable, and enthusiastic; and tell us, that this good is only to be attained by study, by industry, by observing and copying good examples, *&c.* Others, tell us, that it proceeds from the impressions which the belief of particular doctrines makes upon the mind.

mind. And others, that it is the free gift of God to them, without any confideration whatever. Thofe divers opinions, caufe difputes, and bickerings, even amongft fuch who are otherwife perfectly agreed in patronizing the fame matter.

But in the general, it is enough; to be orthodox in this particular. To profefs it, to make pretenfions (at leaft) of being poffeffed of it, to converfe much of it, to declaim in its favour, to paint out its beauties, &c. *this*, in general, I fay, is thought fufficient to denominate a man virtuous and good. But if he add to this, an appearance of care and diligence, in cultivating it; by practifing fome aufterities, relative to meats, drinks, reft, fleep, and things of that nature; if his apparel, gefture, fpeech, and manner, bear any, even the leaft correfpondence with his pretenfion, it is then enough *indeed:* it makes no difference, whether he believes in God, and in *Chrift*, or not: and though he may have many lufts, and vices predominant in him; fuch as pride, incontinence, covetoufnefs, deceitfulnefs, cruelty, fuperftition, &c. yet thefe, if known, are in the eftimation of mankind, abundantly over-ballanced by the fuppofed good which is in them: though the latter, in reality, can only be in *appearance*, whereas the former is *manifeft*.

Upon this principle it is, that numbers among the Chriftians, both antient and modern, have thought it right to compliment the Heathen, fuch as *Socrates, Cicero, Seneca,* and others, with the favour and falvation of their God: and that not becaufe they were human creatures,

creatures, or the offspring of *Adam*; but because they were great men! good men! wise men! they said a great many wise and good things. Their admirers among the Christians, in order to make them speak some knowledge of the true God, and of *Christ*; stretch their sayings upon the tenter-hooks of their enthusiastic fancy, in such sort, that they break their connection, and render their fine things quite unmeaning.

Thus the relator of *Anson*'s voyage, &c. tells us, how that a jesuit, (in favour of Mr. *Anson*) explained that article of the Romish church, which denies the salvation of heretics; in a lax and hypothetical sense: Wherefore? why truly, on the account of some supposed goodness in him: he did not ravish their women; nor kill and eat their men; that fell into his power: though it was not their persons, but their gold, that he was in search of: In the taking of which from them; neither his modesty, as a philosopher, nor his self-denial, as a christian, was so very conspicuous, as to encourage them to canonize him. But constitution, or accident, (befriending him in some other particulars) gained him the reputation of a saint (in those parts) it seems.

But

It is said of the grand vizior *Cuprogli*, that when dying; some of the last words that he spake, fixing his eyes upon the Alcoran, were these: "Prophet, I shall soon see whe-
" ther thy words are true; but be they true or false, I am
" sure of being happy, if virtue be the best of all reli-
" gions" He was certainly a person of much sagacity; courageous, and faithful to his master: But if this is virtue,

it

But a perfect, uniform practice, is not at all necessary to the formation of this character; to be a zealous theorist is sufficient: with some specious appearances of virtue; however irregular, or tarnished with pride, self-seeking, &c. Thus a person of this character, shall be judged to have a sure title to happiness: whether he believe in God, in *Christ*, in *Moses*, or in *Mahomet*; or indeed if he believe in neither. Diametrically opposite to truth, as resting upon reason and experience: and in the most glaring contradiction to divine revelation: it is asserted upon this principle, that every truly happy man, is wholly the son of his own actions: without being under the least obligation to the grace, mercy, and love of his God and Redeemer.

Mankind in the general, make this their fundamental, whilst matters of faith, are considered, rather as a science to be studied: or as somewhat calculated for men to employ their wits about. Thus, whatever they profess to believe; in every time of danger, their corpse of reserve is their own goodness.

I call

---

it is not impossible to find a virtuous dog. This man, so virtuous in his own eyes, was, to all appearance, a stranger to humanity, to the universal love of mankind, and to that self-denial, &c. which constitute true virtue. He was proud, cunning, and cruel; but assiduous in his office: and an instrument perfectly qualified to raise the pride and pomp of a tyrant, in the destruction of thousands of his fellow-creatures. And yet this is the person, who, in the article of death (when he can do no more mischief) sings a requiem to his soul, because virtue is the best of all religions,

I call this the beast, because I think it answers to the character of that beast spoken of in the book of the Revelations, whom all the world goeth after: the character is there drawn up very brief; *i. e.* WHICH WAS, AND IS NOT. By which, I suppose, we may understand; that there was once, before the fall of *Adam*, some truth, in what man now vainly, and falsly pretends to. Therefore, that which *was, is not:* it hath now, none other existence in man, than what it has in pride and ignorance.

Upon this beast, rides the great whore, or the false church, composed as I have shewn, of all nations, kindreds and tongues; and of all professions.

And yet, notwithstanding there is such an admiring multitude, such a cloud of witnesses daily chaunting forth the praises of this beast: The most curious searcher, can never find out, by reason and scripture, (nor by reason alone, consistent with its ideas of the divine perfections) this boasted good, this divine stamina in man: nor can the most intelligible speaker describe it, as existing in the creature, in any degree of consistency, with what is notorious, demonstrable and certain in him.

Nay, God himself, (whose eyes are as flames of fire, and whose eyelids try the heart of the children of men) cannot find out this good in man: he says, that he *looked down from heaven upon the children of men, to see if there were any that did understand, that did seek God: every one of them is gone back; they are altogether become filthy; there is none that doth good, no not one,*

Pf. liii. 2, 3. and xiv. 2, 3. God, upon examining the human heart, tells us, that every imagination of the thoughts of man's heart, is evil and that continually; and that the heart, is desperately wicked and deceitful above all things. And again, that the good man is perished out of the earth; there is none upright amongst men: the best of them is as a briar; and the most upright, is sharper than a thorn hedge. Our Saviour and his apostles, testify that this good is not in man. Our blessed Lord, though holy, harmless, undefiled, would not suffer them to give *him* the epithet of good, whilst they saw him only as man, saying, Why callest thou me good? *there is none good but one, even God.* And the apostles saith, if any man hath whereof he may glory in the flesh, I more. Yet he counts it all but loss, for the excellency of the knowledge of *Christ Jesus* his Lord; yea, but dung, that he might win *Christ*, and be found in him. How vain and frivolous then, are all the pretensions of men, to this new creation, salvation, or holiness as wrought in them.

Again, Mr. *Coppin* says, with a great degree of boldness, and certainty; that all mankind shall be saved, No. 1. ch. 6. Hence, I can account for the attachments of particular people, to his writings: for had he been a professed Infidel, with respect to faith in *Christ*, this very opinion, of universal salvation, would sufficiently recommend him to those who have nothing besides to comfort their minds with; which, it is to be feared, is the case with too many of such who make a point of it.

But

But in this, the author is strangely inconsistent: for his hypothesis is, that salvation, the *new creation*, &c. is wrought in the creature; and that every man is to look for it in himself. But it remains to be proved, that this new creation, this salvation, is wrought in every man: And yet, except it be thus wrought within them, they cannot be saved, according to him: But the apostle says, All men have not faith. And as the terms faith, *Christ*, salvation, &c. are synonimous with Mr. *Coppin*; either he, or the apostle, are in the wrong, if he say, that this salvation is in every man: For my own part, I shall, for some weighty reasons, always give the preference to the apostle.

Had he asserted the salvation of all mankind, upon the principle of *Christ*; through what he has done, and suffered for them in his own person; it would at least have had a more plausible, and consistent appearance: but to assert it upon the following principles, which are his: "Let all those who desire to be made "partakers of this new creation, look for it "within them, for there God will work it." And again, "Not to look for the rising of a "fleshly body, but a spiritual body within, "for the truth of all things is within." I say, to assert universal salvation upon those principles, so very repugnant to the scriptures, and to common sense, was a most unadvised conceit. If every man is to judge of his future and eternal state, by those inward and divine appearances; and not according to the love of God, manifest through the sufferings, death,

and

and resurrection of the Lord *Jesus:* there are but few, nay there are none, who will have a just and clear title to it.

But alas, we are only upon the surface as yet, we have not sounded the depths of this author.—In the first chapter of this book, intitled, *The advancement of all things in Christ;* he tells us, that he had observed amongst professors, people of opposite sentiments; the one part holding, that all mankind should be saved; and the other asserting, that a part only should be saved: Upon which Mr. *Coppin* says, " There is a mistake in both these parties, nei- " ther of them understanding the mind of God, " nor the mystery of his will, as laid down in " a dead letter.*" A most surprizing declaration

---

* It is a very pernicious error, to call the scripture a dead letter: for our Saviour saith, *The words that I speak unto you, they are spirit and they are life.* By which words, he means, those which the evangelists penn'd from his mouth: As also those which he, in the Spirit of truth, put into the mouths of his apostles. Again, to consider the scriptures as a dead letter, is to deny them as a rule for the trial of spirits: which is to give all private spirits an opportunity to assert their being of God: however inconsistent and contrary to each other. Again, If the writings of the apostles be a dead letter: then, every man supposing himself to be led by the Spirit, is at liberty, not only to put what construction he pleases upon their doctrines; but also to correct them, and contradict them, where they do not suit him. Hence, may be easily discerned, what disorder and confusion must necessarily follow the proposition that the scriptures are a dead letter. It is not of the scriptures, that the apostle speaks where he says *the letter killeth.* Nor is it of that spirit, by which any man professes to be led, and instructed, in a manner independent of the scriptures: that he speaks, where he says *the Spirit giveth life.* It is the meer coinage

ration indeed! neither the whole of mankind, nor a part of them are to be saved! I should have thought, that the most simple, and unbiassed mind upon earth, would have readily concluded, that the one or the other was in the right: that where there was a salvation of mankind, either the whole, or a part of them would be saved, though they might not determine

---

coinage of an antichristian brain to call the scriptures a dead letter: and as foreign from the design of the apostle, as light is from darkness. The apostle, by the letter understands the law of commandments contained in ordinances; which, by reason of their darkness and contrariety unto us, are a dead and killing letter. And by the Spirit, he intends the Lord Jesus, the substance, and fulness of all grace, signified by the ordinances; who having abolished them in himself, as being the end of the law, is called the Spirit which giveth life. The law consists of precepts, requisites and threatnings: and the depravity of human nature, being such; that mankind are utterly incapable of fulfilling the precept, of producing the requisite, or of enduring the punishment, they are, in point of consolation, dependance, and hope from themselves condemned and slain by the law: therefore it is called, a killing letter. The life-giving Spirit, is the gospel, or that infinite love, and dispensation of grace: where the commandment is fulfilled in Christ: where all requisites, as repentance, faith, love, &c. are produced in him, and the punishment as perfectly adequate to our offences sustained by him. This, is Spirit, as being the alone work of the Spirit, wrought in Christ; and perfectly free from the spot of human righteousness. This being the quickening Spirit, it is said to give life, because it gives the perfect salvation of Jesus, freely unto such who are dead by the law. And thus it is, that the letter killeth, but the Spirit giveth life. With what propriety then, can any man call the written word of God wherein those things are contained, a dead letter? or wherefore must the person who believes, what he reads in the scriptures, be accounted of as a mistaken man?

mine which, but rather have waited for the day of decision.

But as the knowledge, and enjoyments, which are yet future, with respect to such as me; were present to this author, (if you will believe him) and are so now to his disciples—he immediately determines the matter, by affirming, that neither a part, nor the whole, of mankind shall be saved. He declares that the persons of mankind are neither saved nor damned, that they are neither hated, nor loved of God: but, that it is the good and evil which is in them, that God loves, and hates, which he saves and damns.

" God, saith he, hates no man's person,
" but the evil in the person: neither doth he
" love any man's person, any further than as
" they shew forth something of himself; as
" they were created by him: and in this sense
" he loves all creatures." I look upon this first chapter of his *Advancement of all things in Christ*, to be a compleat compendium of his whole system. All the fruit of his labours, the produce of his wisdom and knowledge, stands here delineated, and may without prejudice, or critical narrowness, be summed up, and perfectly comprehended in the following proposition.

God at first, put forth mankind, and all creatures, as an outward image, or form of himself, and sowed the seed of eternity, or planted *Christ* the good principle in them: but evil taking place in time, they had two opposite qualities, or principles in them: and these two principles, constitute the different characters, which are applied to the persons of men, as believer, and unbeliever, &c. they also constitute the characters of *Christ*, and *Belial*, &c. After the will of God is accomplished upon them, man dies: and in the article of death, *Christ*, or the good principle, or quality, returns to God, and is absorpt in him, whilst the evil principle is destroyed in his wrath. As for the person of man, that being only erected as a stage, for those principles to combat each other upon for a season, (for whose diversion, I cannot pretend to say) it is thrown down in death, and being there annihilated, it perishes eternally as a beast.

This is a perfect anatomy of his body of divinity, not something meerly deducible from his writings; but what he in sundry parts of his works, has positively affirmed for truth: This he hath cloathed with consequent propositions, such as denying the personality of *Christ*, the resurrection of the body, and the salvation of man's person.

He saith, that the person of man, is no more than a beast, and hath no pre-eminence above a beast. From hence it follows, that there is nothing lost, nor saved, but the good and evil qualities in man. As these qualities are no part of man, but are, by him, distinguished from the persons of men, it follows, that the persons of men are not at all interested in the fate of either: Nay, he says, that the persons of men, hath only the portion of a beast, to die and be no more.

As we must necessarily lose all intelligence, and consciousness of existence, in the loss of our persons, it remains to be asked, for what
purpose

purpose were we created? wherefore was man distinguished from the brute, by being possessed of the powers of thinking, reasoning, reflecting, hoping, fearing, &c.? Wherefore the desire of immortality, and the perfect aversion to annihilation, which we feel within us? To what purpose did *Coppin* himself write; and what was his hope under the persecutions, which he reports to have met with in the world?

Is this, the salvation that he hath promised to all mankind? Truly they are not much obliged to him: I believe, that the generality of those who think, will not thank him for the tidings he brings to their ears, nor once bid him God speed. But such inconsistent, and horrible whims, are ever the consequence of men's forsaking their own mercies, to follow lying vanities.

And yet there are those, whose attachment, to the opinion of universal salvation, is such, that rather than part with it, they will be content, that some very minute part of them only, shall be saved: Or, with *Coppin*, that only some principle of good, in them, shall be saved, whilst their persons shall perish everlastingly: Yea, they would rather that the whole race of *Adam*, should be annihilated, than that all should not be saved.

The cause of which, is easily discovered: They are a people, whose conscience reproaches their conduct, and will not suffer them to have any hope from themselves. They are also destitute of that faith in *Christ*, which as the evidence of things unseen, and the substance of things hoped for; gives assurance of personal interest in the salvation of Jesus.—Thus, that they might not be left as persons without hope; necessity compels them to have recourse to the opinion of universal salvation.

I do not mean that this is the case with all, who are of this opinion: there may be some, who though well persuaded of their own personal interest, in the salvation of *Christ*; are yet touched with sympathy, and compassion for their fellow-creatures: and seeing nothing in themselves better than others, perceive no reason why others should not be benefited by *Christ* as well as themselves. They may also reason from the riches of divine love, from the all-sufficiency of redemption by the blood of *Jesus*, &c. But after all, this opinion is not essential to their happiness; they do not make a point of it; nor would they in the least respect, sacrifice the glory and honour of our Saviour to it: They may desire, hope, and think, but they are not positive. It would be uncharitable, and cruel, to censure such as those, whose *hearts* seem to be right with the Lord.

It is therefore rather to the serious consideration of the former, than to the latter, that I would recommend the following objections to their darling opinion: as they consist with the scriptures, and with reason.

I will begin with a question once proposed to our Saviour upon this head: *Lord, are there few, that be saved?* Luke xiii. 24. It is certain that the person who asked the question, had drawn such conclusions from the doctrines, which he had heard *Christ* preach. Remark the Lord's answer: *Strive to enter in at the strait gate: for many, I say*

say unto you, will seek to enter in, and shall not be able. Doth not our Saviour seem to approve of this person's ideas, and to confirm them rather, by his answer? or what are we to understand by the strait gate; through which but few comparatively enter?

Again, *But if our gospel be hid, it is hid to them that are lost,* 2 Cor. iv. 3. That all men do not believe the gospel, or that it is hidden from some, is so very notorious, that it requires no proof from me. It remains for us then, only to enquire into the meaning of the term *lost,* as it is applied in the text. First, it cannot intend our being lost in *Adam,* for that would be to make the apostle say, if our gospel be hid, it is hid to them who are lost in *Adam:* But all mankind are lost in *Adam;* and yet the gospel is not hidden from all mankind: as appears from the distinction made in the text. Doth not the term *lost,* in the text, relate to the present and future misery of such, who believe not the glorious gospel of the son of God? if not, what does it then relate to?

Again, our Saviour saith, *If ye believe not that I am, ye shall die in your sins.* And again, *Whither I go, ye cannot come,* John viii. 24, 21. As it is needless for me to attempt proving, that all mankind do not believe in *Jesus:* we have only to consider the meaning of those words: *Ye shall die in your sins. Whither I go, ye cannot come.* What does a person's being in his sins intend? does it not imply a guilty conscience, unwashed, impure, and miserable: a conscience not believing, not apprehending the great salvation: and therefore as unhappy through ignorance, and unbelief, as if the Saviour had not died, and risen again? Is not living and dying in this state; what is meant by dying in their sins? and if they die in their sins, wherefore should it be supposed, that their state is changed in the article of death? Is not this ascribing the glory, and honour of our Saviour, to death; which is an enemy? If a man was to die a thousand times, he will not be the happier for that. True happiness consists in beholding the glory of God, in the face of *Jesus Christ*. It is not by death, that we believe the gospel, but by faith, which is the gift of God, and which cometh by hearing. It is not death, that purifies the heart, and purgeth the conscience from dead works: but the blood of our Lord *Jesus Christ*. It is not by death, that we are changed, but it is by beholding the glory of the son of God.

Thus death, cannot in any sense, be said to be our Saviour. If death infallibly cured all ills, and rendered every soul happy that passed through it; it would be adviseable for all the miserable to fly to it with speed: as they would find in death a sure refuge from all distress*.

How

---

* To be, or not be: that is the question;
Whether 'tis nobler in the mind to suffer
The slings and arrows of outrageous fortune,
Or to take arms against a sea of troubles,
And by opposing end them. To die, to sleep——
To sleep perchance to dream: ay, there's the rub;
For in that sleep of death what dreams may come,
When we have shuffled off this mortal coil,
Must give us pause: there's the respect
That makes calamity of so long life.

For

How shall we understand those words: *Whither I go, ye cannot come?* do it not suppose, that there are some, who at death, cannot enter into that glorious bliss, where Jesus is gone? If this, is not the meaning of the words, I would gladly know what the true meaning is.

Again, Our Saviour saith, *Marvel not at this, for the hour is coming, in which all that are in the graves shall hear his voice, and shall come forth, they that have done good, unto the resurrection of life; and they that have done evil, unto the resurrection of damnation,* John v. 28, 29. Doth not this intend the future resurrection of the body? As to what *Coppin* says upon these words, I pay no attention at all to it, because it is unscriptural, and irrational. If it is objected that the grave in scripture, signifies hell. I answer, it doth not intend it here, for two reasons. First it is in the plural number; *i. e. graves,* which it never is, where it intends hell. Secondly, we read here of good and bad, coming out of their *graves;* which cannot be applied

---

For who would bear the whips and scorns of time,
Th' oppressors wrong, the proud man's contumely,
The pangs of despis'd love, the law's delay,
The insolence of office, and the spurns
That patient merit of the unworthy takes,
When he himself might his *quietus* make
With a bare bodkin? Who would fardels bear,
To groan and sweat under a weary life,
But that the dread of something after death,
(That undiscovered country, from whose bourn
No traveller returns) puzzles the will,
And makes us rather bear those ills we have,
Than fly to others that we know not of?
      SHAKESPEAR.

ed to hell: because it is not supposed, that such who have done good, are in hell: and therefore cannot come forth thence.

It will be objected possibly, that the term *graves*, is figurative; and implies that darkness, and ignorance, wherein we are dead and buried by nature: and from which, we are brought forth in the person, and salvation of *Jesus*. I answer, sometimes the term *graves*, as used in the scriptures, may be understood thus: as in the 37th of *Ezekiel*, &c. But this doth not appear to be its meaning in the text before us, for two reasons. First, here are two distinct characters, raised out of their graves: they that have done good, and they who have done evil: which cannot be applied to that, which is raised in the person, and salvation of *Jesus*; because those only were raised by him, who were dead in trespasses and sins. Secondly, It is spoken of as a future matter, *the hour is coming*, &c. whereas our salvation in him, was not future, but present as well: And respecting the purpose, execution, and manifestation thereof; it may be said, to be that which *was*, which *is*, and which is to come. Thus speaks our Lord, ver. 25. *Verily, verily I say unto you, the hour is coming, and now is, when the dead shall hear the voice of the son of God: and they that hear shall live.* There is a very manifest difference, between saying the hour is coming, and *now is:* and that of saying only, the hour is coming. The former intends the present, as well as the future; but the latter intends the future only; the former, by proposing, that what now *is*, is yet coming, bears witness of a divine progression; in quickning mankind to the knowledge of the truth: But the latter, speaking in the future tense *only*, relates wholly to the resurrection of the body.

If it should be objected, upon *Coppin*'s principles, that those terms, they that have done good, and they that have done evil, do not relate to the persons of mankind: but to the principles of good and evil, which are naturally in every man; and which are raised, the one to salvation, and the other to damnation.

I answer, it must first be proved that the evil principle was dead, and buried in man, before it can be said to be raised: And here lies a great difficulty, because there are so many witnesses to prove, that the evil principle has been always alive in them, and therefore needed no resurrection; *when I would do good, evil is present with me*. Good and evil, being qualities only, or principles, as *Coppin* calls them; they bear no personal characters in the scripture: But the characters mentioned in the text, are personal; and therefore cannot intend the qualities of good, and evil. Would it be sense, to say of the principle of good, they shall arise to the resurrection of life? or of the principle of evil, they shall arise to the resurrection of damnation? Good and evil, as qualities, or principles in man, have none other mode of existence, than by the actions, words, thoughts, inclinations, desires, &c. of the person in whom they are: seperate them from the persons, and they lose their mode of existence, and become names without meaning. Good, and evil, as applied to man, have the persons, faculties, and fruits of mankind, for their substantives:

and

and it is eafily feen, that the ufe, meaning, and exiftence of the adjective, depends upon the fubftantive: So do the terms, good, and evil, when applied to man, depend upon their perfons and conduct.

How extravagantly filly, muft it then be, to talk of raifing, faving, or damning, the meer principles, or properties of good, and evil: diftinct, and feparate from the perfons of mankind! To talk in that manner, is indeed fo to fight, as one that beateth the air.

Laying afide all partiality, and prejudice, doth it not appear that the text under confideration, hath this meaning? There is a day approaching, when the Almighty *Jefus*, by the fame all-powerful word, which in the beginning, fpake the things which are, out of nothing, into materiality: fhall call the dead to life again. That they fhall all arife, refpecting good, or evil; or that ftate of confcience wherein they died, in the fame ftate they were in, when they laid down the body*: And that their

---

* I would not be mifunderftood, as if I meant that the foul dies, or fleeps with the body until the refurrection. No: God forbid! as a chriftian I am affured from the fcriptures, and as a man, I am perfuaded from reafon; of the contrary. But, where I fay, that the dead will arife, refpecting the confcience, in the fame ftate wherein they died: I mean, that it is the blood of our Lord *Jefus Chrift* (and not death) that is the fountain opened for fin, and for uncleannefs. To fuppofe that mankind are faved in the article of death, whether they have believed on the Lord *Jefus* or not: is to make death a purgatory; through which, whoever paffeth is made meet for the kingdom of God: or otherwife it fuppofeth, that all iniquity, and oppofition to God,

is

their expectations will be according. Some, as conscious of salvation; arise in full expectation of a glorious immortality: whilst others, conscious only of their sins, arise in woeful expectation of damnation! I say, doth not this appear to be the simple, genuine meaning of the text? As to the characters, they that have done good, and they that have done evil; that spirit who gathers with *Christ*, can easily account for these: They who have done good, are those, who believing on the son of God, and properly apprehending him; appropriate his obedience,

---

is of the body; and consequently dies with it: or else, it is to imagine, that God, not only reverses his decree; but also for their sakes, inverts the order of things; by making them happy without believing on his Son: by feeding them with bread which they have not eaten, or by warming them with a garment which they have not put on: but the minors are false, as contrary to scripture and reason; and therefore the major is not true. Mankind are naturally miserable, and if they do not all feel it, it is owing to such things in life, as divert their thoughts and attentions from it: as ambition, honour, power, riches, pleasure, diversions, &c. But in death, all these are cut off from man; and he is left to miserable reflections, and feelings. This must be the case with all who die in their sins; *i. e.* without the faith, and knowledge, of their sins being done away, by the blood of *Jesus*: Their ignorance and unbelief is hell; and as such it will be felt, when there remains nothing to divert the attention from it. And as we know of no dispensation, for their delivery, between death, and the restitution of all things; therefore was it, that I said: They would rise, respecting good, or evil, or their state of conscience; in the state they were in, when they laid down their body. If it should be asked, whether it is not possible, for such who were once believers in *Jesus*; to lie down in sorrow? and whether they will remain in that state of misery wherein they died? I answer, that, which from

obedience, and sufferings: and thus by union with him, are conscious of *his* good doings; in which consciousness, they live, and die, and rise again. They who have done evil are the contrary character; they believe not, they appropriate not; they are only conscious of their own works, &c. which being all evil, they are characterized accordingly.

I might quote many other passages of scripture, as objections to the opinion of universal salvation; but as they are all of like nature with those already mentioned, I shall mention no more of them here; but shall now, offer such

---

from the fears, terrors, and complaints of a dying person, may appear very dark to the survivors; may yet be cleared up to the afflicted, before they have left the body: and when they are incapable of giving standers-by, any account thereof. As in the mariner's compass, when the needle, which is touched by the loadstone; is set upon the pivot, it naturally points towards the north; nor will it stand to any other point, without a force put upon it: So the real christian, is a person whose heart the Lord hath touched, and *Christ* is the pole to which it points. If it is left to the bias which is given it by the divine contact, it will not bear to any other point: Therefore, whenever we find the heart thus touched, varying from its pole, we conclude; that it is held by some malignant power, contrary to its spiritual bias: Should this continue until death, which may be the case with some; the power which restrained the heart, is then broken; and it gladly returns to *Christ* the center of all its joys. Thus, though the enemy may for a time, make the christian heart vary from its pole; by working upon their bodily infirmities: such as nervous disorders, melancholy, lunacy, phrensy, idiotism, deliriums in fevers, &c. Yet death frees the soul from all these; and administers an entrance for it into the fulness of that bliss, which, at any time it had tasted, in the knowledge of the son of God. This, is the difference in death, between the christian, and the infidel.

such objections, as reason and common sense suggests, to this opinion. Doth not the opinion of universal salvation, suppose; that the irreligious, and unbelieving part of mankind; hath greatly the advantage of others? The Psalmist saith of the former, *They are not in trouble as other men: neither are they plagued like other men.* If all, who die, go immediately to glory; then the state of that person, who passeth through life, without thought, without conviction, without fear, without temptation, without reproach, without persecution, &c. which is the state of an unthinking infidel, of the man of pleasure, the worshipper of the God of this world: I say, the state of such a person, must be vastly preferable, to that of the religious man, i, e. of the true believer. The apostle saith of the latter, We *were troubled on every side: without fightings; within fears.* They are troubled with the plague of a corrupt heart; (of which others are not convinced) they are troubled with the temptations of *Satan*; (whereas in others, the strong man armed keeping his palace, all his goods are in peace) they are troubled from without; hated, despised, and persecuted in life. But, if unbelievers, and despisers, are equally advantaged with them in death; then instead of gaining by the faith of the son of God, we suffer loss: which God forbid!

This argument, will be answered, with saying: That where troubles abound, as in the true christian, consolations much more abound: and that the happiness, which a believer feels, through the faith of the son of God, much more

more than compensates for all the afflictions, which he has sustained more than other men. That there are unspeakable consolations in the knowledge of the son of God, I readily confess: and, that there is something in the religion of *Jesus*, so delightful, and satisfactory to the mind; that such who know it, cannot chuse but think, and say, that if there was nothing farther than the grave, it is preferable to all that this world can afford. But this is not always the case; let it be remembered here, that the religion of *Jesus* proposes a future state; and such a state is believed, by those who make their confession as above. Besides, every christian hath not equal consolations: There are some, who are children of affliction all their days; subject to bondage, and to the fear of death; and are yet dependant on *Jesus*, under a particular dispensation. Again, the generality of those who talk much of their happiness, are but proud boasters; they have taken up christianity, as a system; they know nothing of themselves, and, not having *Christ* revealed in them, by the Spirit, there is no opposition from the enemy: they are not plagued as other men; but being of chearful, joyous dispositions, they think themselves perfectly assured, of matters which they know nothing at all of. Such as these cannot say with the apostle, *If we had only hope in this life, we should be of all men most miserable.* Neither the prophets, nor apostles, ever proposed, that the enjoyments which we have, of divine matters, over balances the distresses, which every real christian meets with in life; but quite the reverse. Hence it is, that we are directed

directed to that, far more exceeding and eternal weight of glory, which remains for us; in comparison of which, our present afflictions indeed are but light; but they would be heavy enough, if we had no *future* expectations.

Again, if according, to the opinion of universal salvation; all mankind went immediately through death, to glory: the scriptures are of no use, they have been continued unto us, to no purpose; and the preaching of the gospel is vain. If all are equally saved, unto what purpose do we read, and study the scriptures; beseeching our Saviour, to give us a true understanding of them? possibly it will be answered, they might as well be let alone; every man might spare himself the pains of reading and studying them; since when they come to die, they would be equally as well off as *Paul*, or *Peter*, or any other of the apostles who wrote them.—Is not this a true state of the case, if the abovementioned opinion be true. But least any one, should, through the stupor of this opinion, neglect the great salvation; and find themselves most miserably deceived when they come to die. Let us treat the matter seriously, as being of some importance.

We must acknowledge, that, through a series of divine providence, the holy scriptures have been continued to us even to this day: And that, though they have passed through the hands, not only of such, who believe not the true gospel, but even through the hands of such who are enemies to christianity in general; yet they have not been lost. This is the Lord's doing, and its marvelous in our eyes. Our
Saviour

Saviour bids us search them, for they testify of him. But to what purpose were they continued unto us, and wherefore did the Lord bid us study them; if they were not designed to be our guide, and directory, and to make us wise unto salvation? But, if all, are saved at death, the scriptures are of no use; and our Saviour's advice to read them, to search them, is altogether unimportant.

Again, if the opinion of every man's entering into glory when they die, be true; would it not be truly politic, to imbibe the popular sentiment, though it should be with the denial of Christ? By that means we should avoid, the censure, calumny, reproach, hatred, and condemnation of the world; which otherwise falls upon us, for our sentiments, and manners. From what such who call themselves christians, have imbibed from heathen philosophers; I may expect this objection. A christian, without having any view to future matters, loves truth, and makes choice of it for its own sake; when at the same time he knows he should be altogether as happy after death, if he despised it, and poured the utmost contempt upon it. To this argument, there are two very material objections. The one from the nature of man, and the other from the nature of God. First, I think the compliment a great deal to high, which is paid to human nature: in making it capable of loving virtue for its own sake. (Excepting that man who laid down his life for his enemies) I may challenge proof, that any one individual of *Adam*'s race, in any one action of life, were perfectly detached from self. The
apostle

apostle tells us, that *Moses*, when he forsook *Pharaoh*'s court, to suffer affliction with the people of God; had *respect unto the recompence of the reward*. There is not one action of our lives, however disinterested, and generous it may seem; but what we promise some advantage, some consolation or pleasure to ourselves by it. Hence I affirm, that the profession, of loving truth, or virtue, meerly for its own sake, is theory, only; altogether without practice.

Again, should it be granted, that mankind may act from their love to truth; for its own sake: as this would be obedience in the superlative degree; shall we not suppose that the divine Being, holy, righteous, and equitable as he is, would distinguish such a spirit; and in some sense manifest his approbation of it? But this is not done in life, according to the testimony of experience, and of the scriptures: Since the same events happen to the one, as to the other; and if all are equally happy when they die, it is not done then: which would be to suppose that good, and evil, are alike to God. A proposition, blasphemous in itself, and highly dishonourable to the divine Being.

Again, if this opinion be true, wherefore did our Saviour send forth his disciples, into all the world, to preach the gospel to every creature? and wherefore did the apostles, martyrs, and confessors of *Jesus*, suffer the most cruel torments, and even *death* for his name sake? If all, were to be equally happy in death, the apostles certainly preached in vain: for mankind had all been saved, had they been silent.

It had been more genuine mercy, not to have disturbed the world, with the animosities, and bloody persecutions, which took place upon preaching the gospel; nor to have distressed individuals, by interrupting their peace, and repose, with convictions, and manifold troubles. Wherefore did the apostles, under innumerable hardships, labour incessantly, to bring souls to the knowledge of the truth, since if they had left them alone, they had been equally happy?

If the latter be the case, the apostles, confessors, and martyrs of *Jesus*; were guilty of the most egregious folly, in subjecting themselves to such hardships as they did; in giving their bodies to be stoned, to be beheaded, burned, crucified, &c. for a testimony, the belief of which, gave them no advantage above any one of the human race: A testimony, which, if they had recanted, and denied, it could not have prevented their happiness.

Again, it makes void, and totally destroys all divine retaliations*. With what reason, or from

---

* It may not be unnecessary to distinguish here, between grace; and providence: according to the former, God having concluded all under sin; the free gift is upon all men, unto justification of life. But even here, a man cannot fill his belly with the east wind: he cannot have any personal happiness, until believing in the son of God, he knows his personal interest in the great salvation. When this is apprehended, whether the person was a bloody persecutor, a rapacious publican, an avowed enemy of God, of Christ; of mankind, &c. before; or not: it makes no difference, because, it is seen here, that all manner of sin and blasphemy is forgiven unto men. He who owes but fifty pence, is not

more

from what revelation, can we suppose, that the mocking infidel, the bloody persecutor, the barbarous, the cruel, the avowed enemy of God, of *Christ*, and of mankind, shall when they die, though they die in the same state wherein they lived; be equally happy with *Paul, Peter, John,* &c.? I would ask the christian, can any man be happy by *Jesus Christ*, without believing on him? And let me also ask the Infidel, can any man be happy on the principles of human goodness, without being possessed of that goodness? Thou forgavest them

---

more frankly forgiven, than him who owed five hundred pence. *Paul* speaking of himself, says—who was before a blasphemer, and a persecutor, and injurious; but I obtained mercy because I did it ignorantly in unbelief, 1 *Tim.* i. 13. The mercy which he obtained, exempted him from guilt, and condemnation; but not from the retaliations of providence: for he, who with a merciless and unrelenting eye had beheld the torments of his fellow-creatures; and had even been an abettor, and assistant, in stoning the martyr *Stephen*: was stoned himself at *Lystra*, and drawn out of the city for dead—He who had pursued the disciples of *Jesus* with the fury of the destroyer, even unto cities remote from *Jerusalem*; was pursued, himself; by the *Jewish* nation, in the elders of the people, in *Ananias* the high-priest, and in *Tertullus* the orator, even unto *Cesarea:* where they accused him before *Felix,* as a blasphemer, &c. a man worthy of death. He, who was used to make havock of the church, haling men, and women to prison: was in process of time, upon the very same principles, cast into prison himself. When *David* sinned heinously against the laws of society; in defiling the wife of a faithful servant; and then, to cover his shame, murdering the innocent worthy husband; by the hand of the children of *Ammon:* even then the prophet pronounced his iniquity forgiven: but gave him to understand that the sword should not depart from his house: which probably occasioned this saying; Thou wast a God that forgavest them, though thou tookest vengeance of their inventions, Ps. xcix. 8. Nor

them (faith the Pfalmift) but thou tookeft vengeance on their inventions. But we do not always fee thofe characters retaliated in this life; on the contrary, they flourifh as a green bay tree: but it is unreafonable to fuppofe, that when they die, they fhall be equally happy with *Noah, Daniel,* and *Job.*

Again, hath not this opinion a bad effect upon the minds of mankind? doth it not make them loofe, frothy, and carelefs? doth it not teach them to laugh at ferioufnefs, to defpife, and make a jeft of divine matters? do they not

from

---

was it long before *Tamar* the daughter of *David*, was deflowered by her brother *Amnon*—and when this grief began a little to fubfide; behold *Amnon* is murdered by *Abfalom*, and the murderer becomes an exile. When time had in a meafure erafed the memory of this evil, and partly affwaged the grief of the king; lo *Abfalom* was permitted to return. Soon after he raifed a rebellion againft his father; chafed him from his royal palace, and from his beloved capital; and then entring into his father's houfe, he fpread a tent upon the top thereof, and lay with his wives before all *Ifrael*: Nor, did *David*'s troubles ceafe, when *Abfalom* was dead. From thefe, and many more inftances which I might mention from the fcriptures; we may obferve that there is a diftinction to be made between grace, and providence. The former pardons all, as fin againft God; but the latter, one time or other, retaliates refpecting our behaviour towards our brethren, or fellow-creatures. And if faith in Chrift, the knowledge of the forgivenefs of fins, doth not exempt perfons from fuch a retaliation; as appears from *David, Paul, &c.* what muft be the end of fuch who believe not the gofpel, but are rather enemies to it all their days? We do not fee that they always meet with retaliations in this life. The pfalmift fays, that they are not plagued as other men: but to fuppofe, that thofe who live, and die in fuch a ftate, fhall enter into glory, without meeting any retaliation at all, is to impeach divine juftice and equity, and to make God a refpecter of perfons; which God forbid, that any man fhould think.

from hence, neglect the scriptures; and preferring their own opinions, despise the gospel of our Lord *Jesus Christ?* In brief, do they not by means of this opinion, lose what they had attained unto; and sink into infidelity, or what is as bad, dwindle into an unthinking, stupid, careless state: and all from the opinion of universal salvation? Doth it not encourage the use of unlawful means, as suicide, *&c.* to escape present trouble; by entring into that bliss, unto which it pretends to entitle all mankind?

Again, it destroys the nature, properties, and use of faith: by deriving all hope, and certainty of future bliss, from false reasoning.—Having first laid down this proposition, All mankind shall be saved: what follows, but this conclusion; if every man is saved, I shall be saved? But the major is not proved; therefore the hope, and comfort, which is drawn from the minor, is precarious, and unsatisfactory. But faith is of a divine original, it is not something acquired; it is the gift of God: it consists of light, persuasion, and power: its properties are to make manifest, to persuade, and to evidence the truth of unseen things; to repel opposition; to lean, trust, hope, and depend on manifested truth; and to assure the mind of future bliss, from the veracity of the divine record. As light, it manifests *Jesus Christ* in the heart; according to the scripture report of him as our Redeemer and Saviour: it persuades us of the truth, of what we discover, it repels our fears, and false reasonings, and gives us joy and peace in believing. This is not of ourselves,

selves, but of the free gift and operation of God our Saviour.

But to conclude, that we shall be saved, upon the supposition that all shall be saved; hath no faith at all in it: but it is a low reasoning, a reasoning from very great uncertainties; from an opinion that hath no foundation in revelation. Therefore I said, it made void faith; which indeed it does, and also the preaching of the gospel; and the hearing of the word, by which faith comes; as I have already shewn.

These are a few of the many objections, occurring to my mind; against the opinion of universal salvation. And these, I submit to the serious consideration of those, who are attached to that opinion.

I think I have now done with *Coppin*'s works; except a few remarks, which I shall make upon the preface, to his book intitled, *The advancement of all things in Christ*, &c.

Mr. *Cayley*, the author of this preface, in order to recommend the book, more effectually, tells us, that it was written above an hundred years ago. Pray what dependance hath truth upon antiquity, or wherein consists the necessary connection? Is it necessary to our happiness that we should be antiquarians in divinity; or was that book written in an ÆRA of time, when men were infallible? Mr. *Cayley* pretends, that the design of his writing the preface, (was for the sake of weak brethren) to remove their prejudices, &c. And here I cannot but observe; that he must have a high opinion of himself, even beyond all rules of proportion; to suppose, that his very name would frighten

the

the adverfary, and remove the prejudices of the weak brethren: befides which, we have nothing but his bare word, for the glorious truth contained in this book. Mr. *Cayley* tells the reader, that, if he is a father in *Chrift*, the unction of God, in him, will witnefs to the truth, without any other argument. What a prodigious thing, felf-importance is! We are fathers in *Chrift*, if we think as Mr. *Cayley* does; if we rejoice with him, to fee fo glorious a teftimony; if the unction within us witnefs to the truth of it, without any other argument. I would gladly know, whether the unction in Mr. *Cayley* witneffed to the truth of it, without his reading it; for, needing not his confeffion, I am well perfuaded, that he did not attend to any argument, neither from reafon, nor fcripture, when he fet about recommending it.

Either Mr. *Cayley* perufed this book before he prefaced it, or he did not: If he did read it, he either underftood it, or he did not underftand it: If he did not underftand it, with what face of honefty could he recommend it? If he did underftand it, and recommend it, he muft be fuppofed to be of the fame principles with thofe which I have expofed; and I hope confuted. But if he recommended it with fo much warmth, without reading and confidering it, which I almoft fufpect, from his pretending, that fathers in *Chrift* (of which he is no fmall one in his own conceit) know the truth of books, without attending to argument. I fay, if he did this, I cannot but confider him as an enthufiaft, if not fomething worfe.

But

But what if we cannot palate, cannot digest this precious morsel? Why then according to Mr. *Cayley*, we are babes, meer little-ones, who as yet feed on milk, and know not how to digest strong meat; not having as yet, our spiritual senses exercised, to discern between the mystery of good and evil. The apostle saith, *Not a novice, least being lifted up with pride, he fall into the condemnation of the devil.* Was I called upon to give my opinion of the novice character, I would do it thus: A novice, is a person of but small experience in the knowledge of God, or of himself. Hence he arrogates characters, and authorities, disallowed of by God and man: he expects that you should implicitly receive his sayings, or what he recommends for truth: he would persuade mankind, that he is possessed of an unerring unction: by which, without attending to argument, or making any use thereof, he knows, writes, and speaks the truth infallibly. Hence it follows, that whoso receives not his sayings, are absolutely babes, have no knowledge of spiritual things, &c. I need not say that this is a being lifted up with pride; and with such pride, as is very nearly related to the devil's pride; a spiritual pride, productive of opposition, to the person of the son of God. Mr. *Cayley* charges the babes, the little-ones, to beware of judging, or censuring what they understand not; which by the way, is to tell them that do not approve of it, that the fault lies altogether in *their* understanding, for that the book is faultless. As to his cautions, advice, &c. I think them sufficiently impertinent, as applied to the reading

ing of human compositions; for I know of no faith, or credit, which we owe them; any farther than they consist with the word of truth; and with the argument of reason: and where the latter is not the case, we are at liberty to reject them as error, or nonsense, whoever the writer be. He charges us, to be so reasonable, as to embrace what we can comprehend; and what is out of our reach, to leave it to God, and judge it not: perhaps what is dark to-day, may be light to-morrow. What a person is convinced of, comprehends, and believes to be true, that he naturally embraces: advice upon this head, is therefore needless. As to our not judging what is out of our reach, but leaving it to God; I would observe, that what is out of the reach, of our experience, may not be out of the reach of our understanding: therefore we are at liberty to judge of the truth of a proposition, from its rationality, consistency, &c. without having recourse to our experience; *i. e.* to such operations and effects, produced in our minds, as are perfectly correspondent with such a proposition. Every reasonable man, has a right to judge of the truth of what he reads, in the former sense, though he may be a stranger to the latter. Therefore, though what Mr. *Coppin* and Mr. *Cayley* says, may be out of our reach; respecting the experience of it; it cannot be out of the reach of any reasonable man; respecting its rationality, consistency, and consonancy with scripture; according to these he hath a right to judge of it.

As to his saying, what is dark to-day, may be light to-morrow; I see not how it relates to
truth

truth and error, for they are always the same. *Jesus Christ* is not yea and nay; he is the same yesterday, to-day, and forever: but that which opposeth him, is darkness to-day, and to-morrow also. Beware, saith he, of pinning thy faith on any man's sleeve; (a poor unmeaning saying!) Learn to see the Sun of righteousness (saith he) with thine own eyes, and not through another man's spectacles, which may deceive thee. A saying of the same nature with the former, but intended as a caution to us, against thinking; or seeing things in a different light from Mr. *Cayley*.

I would desire thee, O reader! (saith he) to take notice, that the spirit, which breathes in the following treatise, is nothing but *glory to God on high, and on earth, peace and good will towards men:* which is the true mark of a gospel-spirit.

I must confess, that I had once a better opinion of Mr. *Cayley*'s judgment. I could not have thought, that he would with so much confident warmth, have recommended a book so very repugnant to the scriptures: and even to common sense. But there is one thing to be said indeed on his behalf: that he does not attend to argument; or to what the book says, so much, as he does to the breathings of the spirit in it. But whether the book, or the spirit that breathes in it, has deserved the character given it by Mr. *Cayley*, I have already shewn in the course of my remarks upon it. If denying the body of *Christ*, the person of *Christ*, the resurrection, and ascension of Christ, the salvation of Christ; the resurrection of *our* bodies, the salvation of *our* persons. I say, if these glorify God in the highest,

&c.

&c. then Mr. *Coppin* has done it; and Mr. *Cayley* is not a false witness; otherwise, the contrary is manifest. But whether these doctrines, and this spirit, breathes glory to God on high, peace upon earth, and good-will towards men; or not, judge all ye people. Here (saith he) is no encouragement to sin, but great encouragement to sinners, *to behold the Lamb of God, who taketh away the sin of the world*. In short, in this book, (saith he) there is contained a *feast of fat things*, furnished with what is suitable both to men and babes. Is it possible, that Mr. *Cayley* should be so greatly charmed; and that he should have such a prodigious relish for things which he did not understand: Nay, let us rather in a judgment of charity suppose, that he did perfectly understand it; and that when he read it, he not only found it to be savoury, but to be the most delicious food to his soul. Such a supposition, and none but such, will excuse that fervent zeal, with which he recommends it. Let us also imagine, that it is from hence, he declares, that there is no encouragement to sin in it.

What encouragement it may be to sin, in telling a man that his body shall not rise again, that God neither hates, nor loves his person; that his person is neither the object of salvation, nor damnation; that every man hath in him, the principles of good and evil; and that the good principle shall be saved, and the evil one lost: I say, what encouragement these may be to sin, I shall leave to others to determine. But I am very well assured, that there is no encouragement given to sinners: to look to the
Lamb

Lamb of God who taketh away the sin of the world, as he insinuates; because first, in denying the personality of the Lamb of God, and that salvation from sin, which is by his sacrifice upon the cross; he *destroys* him, and sets up in his stead, a creature of his own fancy; a meer calf, gilded with the supposition of a good principle in man. Mr. *Cayley* will call this the Lamb of God, if he pleases, but it is not the person whom *John the Baptist*, called the Lamb of God, that is certain: nor does looking to the Lamb of God, in Mr. *Cayley*'s sense, intend any thing more, than a man's looking to himself. But here, again, I am almost tempted to think, that he does not perfectly understand the system which he has adopted; for according to *Coppin*, man is no more a sinner than the beast that perishes. The person of man, is neither good nor evil; but only a theatre, a temporary convenience, whereon those jarring elements, those opposite principles, and powers, make war upon each other for a season; the person of man, being quite neutral, hath nothing to do in the affair.

Oh reader (saith he) do not fall out at table, and turn this feast into a battle, by rash judgings, and censurings, of what thou cannot yet understand.

I sincerely ask my friend *Cayley*'s pardon, if I appear as one, who falls out at table. It is because he hath invited me to a feast where there is nothing to eat: but what I (supposing myself possibly, as good a judge as himself) know to be unpalatable, and unwholesome: and this, to a person of appetite, is no small disap-

disappointment. I am not quarelling, but giving my reasons only, why I cannot partake of his feast; which I take to be a point of good manners, where I am with so much earnestness pressed to eat.

Possibly, the title page of the book, which Mr. *Cayley* prefaced, was not a small inducement to his doing it; where we are told that the book contains *some sparkles of that glory, and some beams of that light, which shines and dwells in Richard Coppin*. What an enthusiastic, and antichristian puff, this is! O *Paul!* you were but a babe, when compared with these apostles. I do not remember to have read any such language in your writings, as this: being some sparkles, of that glory, and some beams of that light, that shines and dwells in me *Paul*. Nay, but you taught, and yet teaches, that all the sparkles of glory, and beams of light, shines and dwells in *Jesus Christ:* who is the sun of righteousness, the bright, and the morning-star.

Thine, O great apostle, was the spirit of truth: Thou bearest not witness of thyself; though if any man had whereof he might glory in the flesh, thou hadst more: But thou glorifiedst *Jesus*, by receiving of the things which were his, and shewing them unto us: It was thy business to espouse mankind to one husband, as a chaste virgin to *Christ*.

But not so Mr. *Coppin*, who talks of sparkles of glory, and beams of light shining and dwelling in himself; he bears witness of himself, and his witness is not true.

If

If Mr. *Cayley*, or any of *Coppin*'s admirers, think that I have misrepresented them, let them not only impute it to my ignorance, but let them convince me of it. It lies particularly upon Mr. *Cayley* to do it; by giving us a proper comment upon *Coppin*; and in so doing, he will act up to his own memento, at the close of his preface; nor has he any just reason, to think of me otherwise, than as his sincere friend, and well-wisher.

F I N I S.

The Life of CHRIST:

The Perseverance of the CHRISTIAN.

A

SERMON

Preached at

COACHMAKERS-HALL,

On *Sunday* Morning, *Jan.* 30, 1762.

BY

JAMES RELLY.

For if by one Man's Offence, Death reigned by one; much more they which receive Abundance of Grace, and of the Gift of Righteousness, shall reign in Life by one, Jesus Christ. Rom. v. 17.

LONDON:
Printed in the YEAR MDCCLXII.

JOHN XIV. latter Part of the 19th Verse.

Because I live, ye shall live also.

THESE are the words of *Jesus Christ* our Lord, designed for the instruction and comfort of his disciples. And surely nothing can be more consolatory, than to be assured of the truth of this proposition, from the divine Wisdom himself: *Because I live, you shall live also.*

The words of the text, claim our attention, and credit, from the consideration of the person who spake them:

1. As he is the *messenger of the covenant*, Mal. iii. 1. the person ordained of old to reveal and make manifest the love of God to man.

2. As he is the covenant itself: *and give thee for a covenant of the people*, Isa. xlii. 6. Therefore in *him* the covenant itself speaks:

In *his* words you may hear the voice of love, life, and peace.

3. He is that prophet of whom *Moses* spake; concerning whom you read, *The Lord thy God will raise up unto thee a prophet, from the midst of thee, of thy brethren, like unto me; unto him ye shall hearken.* Deut. xviii. 15.

4. They claim our chearful and unwavering belief, because he who spake them hath *the words of eternal life—I am,* says he, *the way, the truth, and the life.* Therefore, that which is spoken by him, must be unquestionably true: the lip of truth cannot err; not all the united powers of earth, and hell, can make that to be false which *he* hath declared to be true; and *this,* of all others, is a truth the most worthy of all acceptation: *Because I live, you shall live also.* The unspeakable goodness, and riches of divine Grace, which they contain and exhibit to mankind, renders them *apples of gold in pictures of silver.* They are not only words of truth, which they might be, and yet not of that *real* concern, and *infinite* importance to mankind; but they are words of eternal life: words of *weight,* of *consequence;* yea, of the very *last* importance to the children of men: Skin for skin,

but

but *all that a man hath, will he give for his life:* they extend not to our *present* life *only*, but they concern our *future*, and *everlasting* existence; as they are the words of eternal life.

Let this consideration, lead us to enquire into our Lord's primary and principal design, in speaking those words to his disciples: and what their use and signification is to us, in their true import and full extent.

Those words were not intended for his immediate disciples *only*; were not *only* spoken to the circumcised ear, to the understanding and believing heart; but designed as glad tidings unto all people: the voice and prophecy of love to those who are afar off, as well as to such who are near. The Lord commanded the prophet to speak to the dry bones, even to the bones which were *very* dry, and to say to them, *O ye dry bones, hear the word of the Lord!* Exek. xxxvii. 4. The dead shall hear the voice of the Son of God, and they that hear, shall live. In the words of the text his voice is heard speaking to the *living*, that *they* might rejoice; and to the *dead*, that *they* might hear and live.

Our Lord's principal design in the words, was, first, to point out the relation which he stood

stood in to the people; as the rock, upon which they were built: as the husband, and head of their body: as their surety, their substitute; yea, as containing their nature, persons, and condition in himself: in his life, death, resurrection, power and purity, and in eternal glory: hence this glorious promise, *Because I live, you shall live also.* His design was to lead his disciples from all sublunary and transient dependences, to himself; to have their hope and expectation of eternal life, founded wholly upon his success; where he undertook to lay down his life for their sins, to rise again for their justification, and to live for evermore for their final salvation: therefore is it he says, *Because I live, you shall live also.* The use of those words is instruction, and comfort, to all the followers of the Lamb: first, as it shews them their help laid upon one who is mighty; and that *his* life is the pledge and security of *theirs*.

The text contains *this* use of comfort also; it releases us from ourselves, from all jealousies, anxious cares, and fears, respecting perseverance, and eternal life: arising from the sense of the weakness, irresolution, and changeableness, of human nature. And thus

thus delivered from all fears, cares, hopes or expectations from *ourselves*; from the appearances of good, or evil, as in *us:* we are comforted and rejoice in God our Saviour, in his glorious unchangeable life; for *because he lives, we shall live also.*

That we all may suck at this breast of consolation, and be fed by the sincere milk of the word, I shall endeavour to shew:

1*st*, What life that is, which our Lord here intends.

2*dly*, How this life may be said to be dependent on *Christ*, so comprehended and included in *his* life, as not to be separated therefrom: these words, *because I live, ye shall live also,* naturally imply this.

Lastly, I shall consider the consequences, as manifest, 1. In the method of God's dealings with us: 2. In the joy, peace, and rest, of all those who believe.

To judge of the manner of life which our Saviour here speaks of, we need only consider the persons to whom they were spoken, and also the *time* when those words, so precious, so eminently distinguished for
their

their grace and truth, fell from his sacred lips.

They were spoken first to his Disciples, men indeed of low estate, but who had left their *all* to follow him. Men, who from their Master's doctrine, or example, had never had their expectations raised with the prospect of worldly advantages: nay, he had checked with awful severity; the very *first* motions of this nature in them: carefully stifling in the *birth* the offspring of their ambition. Hence it is plain, he intended not that life which consists in the enjoyment of things present.

To *live:* with the *sensualist*, is the continual gratification of all his appetites—with the *vain* and *ambitious*, it is grandeur, honour, power, &c. whilst with the more abject, to *live*, is meerly to *be*—with the pietist, to live, is to be found constantly in all the round of religious duties; and as the living out of the world, to be yet subject to ordinances: But *to live*; with *Jesus*, and with his disciples, consists in what is eternal and unseen: and not in what is present and seen; for his kingdom is not of this world: nor is it of works of righteousness done by us.

Our

Our Saviour having warned his difciples, of his leaving them; they were under many uneafy apprehenfions, on the account thereof. Though they had forfaken all to follow him, yet hitherto they had lacked nothing: nor did they fee any caufe to be fearful of want, oppreffion, ficknefs or death, whilft he continued with them; for in their prefence he had fed five thoufand fouls with five loaves, and a few fmall fifhes : on the conclufion of which feaft, the gathered fragments; were more than the real fubftance, at the beginning. How could they then fear the want of food, when they faw their Mafter had power to create it ? When called upon to pay tribute to *Cæfar*, though they had neither inheritance, nor trade, nor did they toil or fpin : yet fuch was the authority of their Mafter, that at his command, even an inhabitant of the deep, fupplied them with the neceffary coin. They were witneffes of his healing the fick, and of his raifing the dead, and of his ftopping the mouth of the moft fkilful and inveterate gainfayers; yea they had heard the very devils confefs their fubjection to him. Who then could fear under the conduct of fuch a leader ? But to have him taken away, to be deprived

prived of him; this was what filled them with fear. They were confcious of *their* being ignorant, and illiterate, and therefore unable to put their adverfaries to filence. They knew creation was not at *their* command, and therefore they might poffibly want food; money to pay their tribute, &c. They faw in their apprehenfions, ficknefs, and difeafe awaiting *them*, whilft their phyfician of value, was taken from their head. The dread of being left orphans, terrified them, and their heart was troubled. But in the words of the text, our Saviour fhews them, that he fhould not ceafe to be careful of their intereft; and that the removal of his bodily prefence, fhould make no difference in this particular: but, that their prefervation, in *time*, and in *eternity*, depended upon his life: and therefore he faid to them; *Becaufe I live, you fhall live alfo.* They might alfo be fearful on the account of religion; as if they had faid, How fhall we be fupported in the fpiritual life? It may be we fhall be fo befet by our enemies, as to render us unable to preferve our integrity, when you are abfent from us. And though we have fet our hands to the plough, we fhall peradventure look back, when our *Mafter* is departed

from

from us. This was a point they seemed to be doubtful of; and therefore to remove their fears in this particular, their Lord assures them: *because I live, you shall live also—Let not your heart be troubled,* says he, *you believe in God, believe also in me:* i. e. be not discouraged on account of your own weakness, and insufficiency: though you are conscious of imperfections, and feel the imbecillity of your nature, yet be not cast down, and dejected, for my grace is sufficient for you: *Because I live, you shall live also.*

The disciples had indeed a very great veneration for the *person* of their Lord, and therefore appeared as unable to sustain the loss of his presence: But alas, in those days they were mere novices in the faith, they had not properly understood, nor attended to the *mystery* of his person, nor to the end and design of his coming into the world: *for as yet they knew not the scripture that he must rise again from the dead.* John xx. 9. *Lord,* says Thomas, we know not whither thou goest, and how can we know the way? John xiii. 5. Their ignorance, and unbelief, more than supposes them at *that* time, uncertain, and doubtful of their eternal happiness: Therefore the words of the text was designed for their instruction, and

comfort

comfort in *this* particuliar; by assuring them of future everlasting blifs: Hence the life here spoken of, intends eternal life. Eternal life, is not only an eternity of existence, but an eternity of all possible, (and to us at present) inconceivable happiness: Because I know not that the scriptures has any where, made mere immortality, a contradiction to misery. Eternal life in scripture phrase, is, what can only be conceived of; by considering the properties of the divine Being: Eternal purity, love, joy, peace, adoration, thanksgiving, and glory: all perfect, unchangeable, eternal. This is eternal life: and though whilst in the body, knowing but in part, seeing but in part, we cannot comprehend the glories thereof: yet such who are blessed with the enjoyment of fellowship, and communion, with the Father, and with his Son *Jesus Christ*, in *this* life; have the undoubted prelibation, or foretaste of *eternal* life: there God is all in all, and the whole is subjected to him: There our life, which is hid with *Christ* in God, is manifested in all its fulness; in all its unspeakable variety of happiness. To conceive or to speak, with a just propriety; of the inexplicable glories of *that* state, is impossible: Let it therefore

therefore suffice, that it is to be, ever, ever with God, and with the Lamb: To behold *his* glory, to rejoice in *his* person, in the obedience that he learned through the things which he suffered: In his victories, and triumphs, over sin, death, hell, and over him that had the power of death, even the devil. Briefly, *Jesus* is our eternal life: and to *have* eternal life, is to have *him*: to be as *he* is: to be so truly one with *him*, and he with *us*, as to have *our* life, and happiness, dependent on *his*: according to his blessed word, *Because I live, you shall live also*.

Having considered the life, intended by our Saviour in the words before us: I hasten now to shew how this life may be said to be dependent on the life of *Christ*: according to the implication of his own words.

1. *Our* life depends on *his*, as the life of the *child* does upon that of the *parent*: who feeds it, cloaths it, guides it: continually preventing with careful love, those needs and distresses, which would otherwise soon accomplish its ruin.

2. As the life of the *sheep* depends on the life of the *shepherd*: their safety is wholly owing to *his* watchfulness, courage and skill:

they having neither *principle* nor *difpofition* of defence in themfelves: Therefore *he* as the good fhepherd, laying down his life for the fheep, and taking it up again; fays, Becaufe *I live, you fhall live alfo.* As their *high prieft* and *interceffor*, their life depends upon his. He ever liveth, to make interceffion for us. As he is our *furety*, and *fubftitute :* perfonating us in his life, death, refurrection and glory: *Our* eternal life, is dependent on *his*.

For if when we were finners, we were reconciled to God by the death of his Son, how much more being reconciled, fhall we be faved by *his* life. *Our* life is built upon *his* as he is the Redeemer: Our bodies, fouls, peace, and happinefs, he redeemed with his own: therefore are we faid to be bought with a price. He bare our fins in his own body upon the crofs, and put them away by the facrifice of himfelf. He fuftained our guilt, when the pains of hell gat hold upon him; but his foul was not left in hell, nor did the Holy One fee corruption. *He*, from the Father's choice, from his own confent, and defire; from the right of redemption pertaining to him as the neareft kinfman; ftood charged with all our debts: and having paid them all,

he

he cancelled, and blotted out the hand-writing which was againſt us. His reſurrection is our legal diſcharge. He aroſe for our juſtification, thus is *our* life dependent on *his*. He gave himſelf for us. He put himſelf into our condition, and was accepted as a law-fulfiller; and as a puniſhed ſinner, in lieu of the people. The people were to be treated according to his ſucceſs: Had he failed to pay their debts, to expiate their guilt, to ſubdue their enemies; there would have remained nothing for them, but the eternal pains of the ſecond death. But if he ſucceeded in his undertakings, if he aroſe from the dead, unto everlaſting life; they were to live alſo. The equity, reaſon, and baſis of this; is the union ſubſiſting between *Chriſt* and his church; which the apoſtle thus deſcribes; *As the body is one, and hath many members, and all the members of that one body, being many, are one body; ſo alſo is Chriſt.* 1 Cor. xii. 12.

The inſtruction of which is evidently this: *Chriſt* being one, hath *many* people, children, diſciples, or members; and all thoſe being many, make one *Chriſt*.

The union ſubſiſting between the man *Chriſt Jeſus*, and the church, hath for its foundation

dation and reality, 1. The brotherhood: they having originally one Father; thus testifies the apostle: *Both he that sanctifieth, and they who are sanctified, are all of one: for which cause he is not ashamed to call them brethren.* Heb. ii. 11.

The Lord *Jesus* when triumphant over sin, death, hell, and the grave, declared the same truth: saying, *Go to my brethren, and say unto them, I ascend unto my Father, and your Father, and to my God, and your God.* John xx. 17; and that this kindred relation, or brotherhood, was antecedent to his birth at Bethlehem; and did not consist *in*, or commence *upon* his taking flesh of the virgin; is manifest from the argument of those words: *Forasmuch then as the children are partakers of flesh and blood; he also himself likewise took part of the same.* Heb. ii. 14.

That they were *children*, and consequently his *brethren*, before he took part of the same flesh and blood with them, is very conspicuous in the words: and is there rendered as a *reason* of his taking part of their flesh and blood.

That *Jesus* had (according to those properties which constitute him *The head of every man,*

man, The *one Mediator between God and man,*) an existence with the Father before the world was, appears from his prayer: *John* xvii. 5. *And now, O Father, glorify thou me with thine own self, with the glory which I had with thee before the world was.* And he tells us afterwards, that this glory was given him: given by the *Father* to *him*, and by *him* to his disciples: A plain proof that he speaks of himself according to his human nature: which in the glorious person of *Immanuel*, receives honour, glory, and power, from the divine nature: and according to which, tho' rich he became poor for our sakes, &c.

And again, it is in this nature, that the head of every man is *Christ*, and the head of *Christ* is God: And that he is called the beginning of the creation of God: the firstborn of every creature, &c. And as we are thus taught to conceive of *Christ*, as existing with the Father before worlds: so are we taught in the scriptures also, that the *church* existed in *Christ* before worlds. We were in him to the *eye* of the Father, to the *love* of the Father, to the *choice* of the Father, always present: *Blessed be the God and Father of our Lord Jesus Christ, who hath blessed us with all spiritual*

spiritual blessings in heavenly places in Christ: According as he hath chosen us in him, before the foundation of the world. Eph. i. 3. 4. *Who hath saved us, and called us with an holy calling, not according to our works, but according to his own purpose and grace, which was given us in Christ Jesus, before the world began.* 2 Tim. i. 9. Our Saviour, under the character of Wisdom, speaks thus: *I was daily his delight, rejoicing always before him: Rejoicing in the habitable part of his earth, and my delights were with the sons of men.* Prov. viii. 30, 31. Hence it appears, that as *Christ* existed with the Father before worlds, so the sons of men existed *in* and *by* him. They inhabited him: and his delights were with them. They, as comprehended in *him,* as *his* fulness, as the dew of his youth, were begotten and born in *him:* in the beauties of holiness, from the womb of the morning. *They* were comprehended in *his* sonship, hence they are said to have the adoption of sons by *him. They* were included in that love, wherewith the Father loved *him:* Therefore is it, he says *Thou hast loved them, as thou hast loved me:* and again, *For thou lovedst me, before the foundation of the world.* Thus *his* election, *his* sonship,

sonship, *his* love, *his* purity, *his* eternal life, *his* union to the Father, was the purpose and grace which was given *us* in *him* before the world began. O the love of God! how amazing! how stupendous! whilst we confess his priority, and pre-eminence, as the first-born of many brethren, and the head over all things to his body the church: we yet conceive of *his* being in *us* as *our* representative, as *our* reality of existence, and the truth of *our* state and condition with God. And of *our* being in *him*, as *his* fulness, and the dew of his youth from eternity; as God is truth: begotten in his eternal love, and purpose, and born from the womb of the morning. Hence the ordinance, so much insisted on in the law of *Moses*, that the *first*, or that which openeth the matrix, shall be the Lord's. Thus it appears, that the *sanctifier* and the *sanctified* are both of one: and that the *former* is not ashamed to call the *latter* brethren.

When the appointed time of the Father was come, that the children, (i. e. the younger brethren, respecting priority) should be partakers of flesh and blood, they were exhibited in an earthly image: they were put forth in the man who was of the earth, earthy:

earthy: this image in its most perfect state, was not the very substance of the purposed grace; nor the *real* purity, and dignity of human nature: The apostle tells us, that the first *Adam* was but a figure of him who was to come. Rom. v. 14. The children as partakers of flesh and blood, held the reins but a very short time. The fable says that *Phaeton* attempting the chariot of the sun, could not guide it for one day. But with much more propriety is it said, that *man being in honour abideth* not. His capacity for government, was quickly lost: his power, and skill, was no more: Rebellion immediately ensued: all his passions rebelled, his judgment was lost, his innocence was slain, concupiscence, guilt, and fear, grew riotous: whilst reflection on the past, the present, and to come, continually goaded him with pain.

But in the midst of all this, hear the voice of love enquiring after him: O! *Adam* where art thou? He was indeed fallen under the dominion and power of the serpent, whose existence was *wrath*; and originally designed as a contrast to *love*, for the production of everlasting harmony: The deliverance of the children, from the corroding slavery

slavery of the *first*, and their eternal rest in the *latter*, was promised them in those words of threatning, to the serpent: *it* (i. e. the seed of the woman) *shall bruise thy head*; that is his power and dominion: to effect this, because the children were partakers of flesh and blood, he also himself partook of the same. He married them: Like the patriarchs of old marrying into their own families; and those of their nearest kindred. How the union of *Christ* and his church, is the substance, truth, and reality of the *husband* and *wife*, the *vine* and *branches*, the *head* and the *body*, the *foundation* and *building*, I shall not attempt explaining here: But shall refer you for that, and for what remains to be said on the nature of union, to my treatise called Union.

But from what *has* been said, I think this truth is manifest: that our eternal life is dependent on the life of *Christ*: and that *his* life, is the certain pledge, and security of *ours*. And thus, would I explain his meaning in the words of the text: *Because I live you shall live also*.

When withdrawing our attention from the judgment of commentators, when laying aside fide tradition and partiality in opinions; we attend to the *letter* fenfe, reafon, and argument of the words, we muft conclude from them; that the life of *Chrift* is the *caufe*, prefervation, and final fecurity of our life. If our life is thus wholly dependent on the life of *Jefus Chrift* our Lord, it does not depend on ourfelves: not any improvements we can make, not on any difpofition, obedience, or conftancy of *ours:* nay not on the degrees, or ftedfaftnefs of our *faith*, refpecting our abiding in him. It has not any dependence on man, or on the things of man, but is altogether dependent on the life of him, who is the *fame, yefterday, to-day, and forever.*

It is a matter of the higheft importance to us, to know that *Jefus* who was dead, is alive, and lives for evermore: and hence it is, that this truth is fo often propofed in the fcripture, as the foundation of our life, and the fole caufe and affurance of our *prefent* comfort, and *future* happinefs. An inftance of which, we have in our Lord's appearing to *John*, in the ifle called *Patmos:* To give *prefent* comfort to his afflicted heart, and to fuftain his foul in life, his Saviour fpeaks to him in the following words: *Fear not; I am the*

the first and the last: I am he that liveth, and was dead, and behold I am alive for evermore; Amen: and have the keys of hell and of death. Rev. i. 17, 18.

When our Saviour arose from the dead, he was particularly careful to set the reality of of his resurrection beyond all dispute: and to confirm the faith of his disciples in that important point. He appeared in the midst of them, when assembled together; saluting them; with, *Peace be unto you:* But as they yet remained doubtful, and were terrified; supposing they saw a spirit: with infinite condescension he offered them the utmost demonstration of his resurrection: yea the resurrection of his *real* body: by proposing that they should *handle* and *feel* him: and by being convinced that he had flesh and bones, be assured that he was no phantom. And, that (whilst they were assured of his having a *real substantial* body) they might not doubt its identity; he exhibited such undeniable proof, of his being the very same man that was crucified, by shewing them his pierced hands, and feet, that they had no more doubtfulness in this particular to combat: but what arose from the inundation of joy which brake in upon on them. And in order to calm, and smooth their surface; so disturbed, and ruffled with surprize, wonder, and joy; and to familiarize them to his presence, as risen from the dead: he asked them as he was wont, *Children, have ye any meat?* and when they gave him broiled fish, and honey-comb, he eat it before them.

The argument of which condescension is this: My disciples, I would have you, and all my followers, be so fully convinced that I am indeed risen from the dead, in that *same body* wherein I was crucified, and which was laid in *Joseph's* sepulchre, that you may become certain, and infallible witnesses thereof: and that it may be handed down with that unquestionable credibility, and assurance, which a truth of this nature and importance deserves. For this fact, is intended to be the reason, and ground, of christian triumph over sin, death, hell, and him who had the power of death, even the devil: and to be considered as the *cause, support,* and *security,* of their eternal life. The proofs which I have given you, may convince you of what consequence it is to the sons of men, to know that I am risen; and am alive for evermore: and how

how it relates to thofe words of comfort, which I fpake unto you whilft I was yet with you, when I faid, unto you; and to all who have an ear to hear: *Becaufe I live you fhall live alfo.*

It was upon this fact, alone, without the confideration of any thing relative to the faith or obedience of man, that the apoftle founded his challenge; when rejoicing in fpirit, he faid, *Who is he that condemneth? it is Chrift that died, yea rather that is rifen again.* He exults in the life of *Chrift,* as all-fufficient to preferve us, body, and foul, to everlafting life: and through the faithful *view,* and *perfuafion* thereof, to fuftain, and comfort our hearts, all the days of our appointed time upon earth.

If *Chrift* be our life, than in that life, *we* are as *he* is: all the members rejoice in the honour of the exalted head. The head does not live without the body; nor the body without the head: the fame life, the fame condition, and circumftances, are alike applicable to the head: and members: (the pre-eminence excepted, which *Chrift* the head, has over all things to his body the church) it is impoffible the *one* fhould be honourable, and the *other* difho-

dishonourable: It is impossible that the *head* should be pure, and the *body* impure: *For if the first fruit be holy, the lump is also holy: and if the root be holy; so are the branches.* Rom. xi. 16.

God the judge of all men, ever beholds us in the life of *Christ:* therefore are we always holy and unblameable in his sight: he hath presented us in himself, a glorious church; without spot, or wrinkle, or any such thing. We are entitled to the peace of his life. Before he died, he bequeathed it unto us; saying, *My peace I give unto you*: and after his resurrection, he confirmed it: saying, *Peace be unto you.* His life is our peace with God: beholding us in that life, he hath sworn *that he will not be angry with us, nor rebuke us for ever.* In that life, we have also peace with God; because *there* we have the answer of a good conscience towards him: in *this* life, our hearts condemn us not; therefore have we confidence towards him. In his life, the gift of God to man is manifest: that eternal life which he hath given us in his son: and of which he speaks, when he says, *Because I live you shall live also.*

Consider the beauty, excellence, and glory of this life: the righteousness, holiness, triumphs,

triumphs, unchangeableness, and eternity thereof: and having considered the unsearchable riches, learn to rejoice in them with joy unspeakable; as *your own* durable riches, and righteousness.

In this life, let all who are troubled, rest with us: *For if when we were enemies, we were reconciled to God by the death of his Son: much more being reconciled, we shall be saved by his life.* Rom. v. 10. What then can ever move him to cast us away? can we at any time sink into a *lower* character, or into one *more* opposite to the divine nature, than that of *enemies?* And in *that* he found us when he reconciled us by the death of his son; there remains then no ground for the fear of our being rejected: but that being reconciled by his death, we shall *much* more be saved by *his* life. Moreover, if his *death*, shameful, ignominious, and accursed, was efficacious to our reconciliation: shall not his *life*, all glorious, victorious, triumphant, holy, and powerful; *much* more, save us with an everlasting salvation: for which in his *life* he stands engaged; as he did in his *death* for our reconciliation: it certainly will, for we hear him say, *Because I live, you shall live also.*

Great is the buftle, which is made in the world, about what is called the perfeverance of the faints; fome there are, who affert that after they have been juftified, and fanctified, they may yet fall finally away: and that as God loves them no longer than they are faithful, and obedient, they may after *all* their attainments, perifh eternally. Whilft their antagonifts maintain the contrary: i. e. that their inherent grace, and goodnefs, can never be totally extinct: though they may fall fo foully, that their graces do not appear: And that God being fovereign, and unchangeable in his love, will reftore them again.

This controverfy concerns not us, nor fhall we take any part therein; becaufe we judge that God has fhewn us a more excellent way. He has taught us that our *perfeverance* and prefervation to eternal life, depends upon the life of *Jefus Chrift* alone: *who died for us, that whether we wake, or fleep, we fhould live together with him.* 1 Theff. v. 10. Therefore inftead of looking to our own faithfulnefs, our own obedience, or grace; or once expecting that God fhould be a refpecter of perfons on *our* account, we look to *him* only, and to *his* life who fays, *Becaufe I live, you fhall live alfo.* O! how balmy are thofe precious words! they

are

are full of grace and truth: They were intended to make us perfect in love, by casting out all fear. When under the deepest sensations of our natural misery, poverty, blindness, and nakedness; and when the painful fears, of your coming short of eternal life at last, presses hard upon you: In the divinity of *those* words, you have deliverance from all: they repel, and cast out your fears, and sap all their foundations: and whilst you feel the sentence of condemnation in yourselves, they raise you to a sure trust in the living God: *Because I live, you shall live also.* O precious *Christ!* O glorious grace! What! wilt not thou live without us O Lord? Is thy blessed life our security? and may we indeed depend upon what thou sayest? And is there no other cause, or condition, of our eternal life, but that thou livest? Glory, honour, thanksgiving, and praise, be thine for ever; our God, our Saviour: over whom death hath no more dominion, who liveth for evermore.

Through all the vicissitudes of life, under all pains, and sicknesses of the body, when heart and flesh faileth, these words are a rich cordial in the hand of the great Physician, held out to you: *Because I live, you shall live also.* In the hour of temptation, which comes upon

upon all the world; to try them that dwell therein: When men rife up againſt you with implacable hatred; for the truth's fake; yea, when hated of all men for *his* name's fake: when they endeavour by all means to diſtreſs you, and would even think they did God ſervice in killing you, remember the word of the Lord: it is a preſent help in the day of trouble, and a ſufficient reaſon wherefore you ſhould not fear ſuch as can *only* kill the body: *Becauſe I live, you ſhall live alſo.*

At the approach of the king of terrors, when the keepers of the houſe tremble, when the ſtrong men bow themſelves, when the grinders ceaſe becauſe they are few, and thoſe that look out of the windows be darkened; when the doors are ſhut in the ſtreets, when the ſound of the grinding is low, when he riſes at the voice of the bird, and when all the daughters of muſic are brought low: when there is fear in the way, and the very graſshopper is a burden, and deſire fails; when the ſilver cord is looſed, when the golden bowl, the pitcher at the fountain, and wheel at the ciſtern, are broken: when the duſt is about to return to the earth, as it was, and the ſpirit to God who gave it: How expreſſive, how glorious are the words of our beloved Lord! *Be-cauſe*

cause I live, you shall live also. This is life in the midst of death: and his strength perfected in our weakness.

When *Christ* who is our life, shall appear, then shall we also appear with him in glory. Then shall our life, which at *present* is hid with *Christ* in God, be made manifest. It shall *then* be known, that *he* is our life: that *he* lives *us:* lives in our nature, names, and persons: that the life of his human nature, as hid in the eternity, power, and glory of his Godhead, was the hiding of *our* life. Then shall the full meaning, and substance of these words, *Because I live, you shall live also*, be manifest in perfection to all. Until *he* comes, to be glorified in his saints, and to be admired in all them that believe: This alone is our consolation, that he who was dead, is now alive, and lives for evermore. His life are we to consider, as our own: *ours* by the gift of God, *ours* by the love of *Jesus*; who gives us the glory that the Father hath given him: *Ours* by union to our living head: the head, and members, in one body; have but one life. Unto *his* life let *us* aspire: to the victories, triumphs, purity, peace, joy and eternity thereof: Married unto him who is risen from the dead, and so truly one with the

ever-

everlasting *Jesus*, we come up to *his* life, and live with him in the same: The joy, peace, and purity of the conscience therein; is without the consideration of any other matter whatsoever; yea, that triumphant boldness, and perfection, which we have pertaining to the conscience, is in the life of *Christ* alone: and that under all the difficulties, trials, and temptations, which we meet with in life: and is a proof that we walk in newness of life: and that the life of *Jesus* is manifest in our mortal flesh.

Our Saviour saith, that whoso gathereth not with him, scattereth. To gather with him, is to know nothing by ourselves, to have no hope or expectation from ourselves, not from any thing *we have* done, or *may* do: where we have been wholly, or in part, active: But to conclude of *our* state, and condition with God, from *his* as received into glory: Yea to gather all our purity, peace, joy, and eternal rest, by him; by the mystery of *his* person, by the labours of *his* life, by the sorrows of *his* death, by the power and triumph of *his* resurrection. And to gather all our hopes of eternal glory by *his* life, who says, *Because I live, you shall live also.*

F I N I S.

www.ingramcontent.com/pod-product-compliance
Lightning Source LLC
Chambersburg PA
CBHW030552300426
44111CB00009B/949